Jennifer Howell

TEACHING WITH

ICT

Digital Pedagogies for Collaboration and Creativity

OXFORD
UNIVERSITY PRESS
AUSTRALIA & NEW ZEALAND

OXFORD
UNIVERSITY PRESS

Oxford University Press is a department of the University of Oxford.

It furthers the University's objective of excellence in research, scholarship, and education by publishing worldwide. Oxford is a registered trademark of Oxford University Press in the UK and in certain other countries.

Published in Australia by Oxford University Press
253 Normanby Road, South Melbourne, Victoria 3205, Australia

© Jennifer Howell 2012

The moral rights of the author have been asserted.

First published 2012

National Library of Australia Cataloguing-in-Publication data

Author: Howell, Jennifer.

Publication Title: Teaching with ICT : digital pedagogies for collaboration & creativity / Jennifer Howell.

ISBN: 9780195578430 (pbk.)

Notes: Includes bibliographical references and index.

Subjects: Educational technology—Study and teaching.
Information technology—Study and teaching.
Teachers—Training of.

Dewey Number: 371.33

Reproduction and communication for educational purposes
The Australian *Copyright Act 1968* (the Act) allows a maximum of one chapter or 10% of the pages of this work, whichever is the greater, to be reproduced and/or communicated by any educational institution for its educational purposes provided that the educational institution (or the body that administers it) has given a remuneration notice to Copyright Agency Limited (CAL) under the Act.

For details of the CAL licence for educational institutions contact:

Copyright Agency Limited
Level 15, 233 Castlereagh Street
Sydney NSW 2000
Telephone: (02) 9394 7600
Facsimile: (02) 9394 7601
Email: info@copyright.com.au

Edited by Valina Rainer
Cover design by Canvas
Text design by Canvas
Typeset by diacriTech, Chennai, India
Proofread by Amanda Morgan
Indexed by Russell Brooks
Printed by Sheck Wah Tong Printing Press Ltd

Links to third party websites are provided by Oxford in good faith and for information only. Oxford disclaims any responsibility for the materials contained in any third party website referenced in this work.

ACARA neither endorses nor verifies the accuracy of the information provided and accepts no responsibility for incomplete or inaccurate information. In particular, ACARA does not endorse or verify that:

- *The content descriptions are solely for a particular year or subject;*

- *All the content descriptiins for that year and subject have been used; and*

- *The author's material aligns with the Australian Curriculum content descriptions for the relevant year and subject.*

You can find the unaltered and most up to date version of this material at http://www.australiancurriculum.edu.au/

This material is reproduced with the permission of ACARA.

TEACHING WITH
ICT

Digital Pedagogies for Collaboration and Creativity

*To R and K Howell. You continue
to inspire me every day, thank you.*

Contents

List of Figures and Tables

Preface

Technology has become an increasingly pervasive force in the modern world. Most aspects of our lives have undergone a 'technologising' in recent years and the speed of change has been remarkable. In the 1980s, research began to emerge about the use of computers in education. Many working in the education profession were polarised into two distinct viewpoints: those who thought the addition of computers in the classroom were an exciting development, and those who feared their impact on teaching and learning. As a field, we have moved forward, much research has been conducted to show the impact technology has on teaching, learning and student engagement. Technology itself has moved forward from the large desktop computers of the 1980s, to exciting mobile tablet PCs that enable movement, collaboration and dynamic learning activities. Classrooms in Australia have undergone a dramatic change; in the past, technology might have been a shared movie projector or overhead transparency machine. Now, it is common to see classrooms equipped with interactive whiteboards, PCs and data projectors. Some schools have a laptop program, so that every student in your class is sitting at a desk with a laptop in front of them, ready to learn. This increase in the amount of technology present in our classrooms has meant that teachers have needed to equip themselves with the necessary skills to teach in a digital age.

The need to have a digital pedagogy is more important now than ever before. The need to have a suite of skills and experiences that will ensure teaching and learning activities are rich with technologies is vital. Students are habitually using technology in their personal lives at a far greater level than previous generations. They are experienced in a range of digital technologies such as: smartphones, web browsing, platform games (ie X-box), online gaming, Web 2.0 (ie Facebook) and popular 'apps'. They expect their future professional lives to be rich with technology and they expect their education to be likewise. A digital pedagogy should not to be mistaken as a form of digital fluency, the ability to use a wide range of different technologies. It is in fact the ability to select technologies that will enhance teaching and learning. We could all very easily use more technology in our teaching, but will they ensure learning outcomes are met? Have they supported the teaching? Have they enhanced the learning experiences of our students? An effective digital pedagogy will equip teachers with the abilities to achieve all of these goals.

This book offers in-service and pre-service teachers a digital pedagogy specifically designed for the different phases of learning they are practitioners in; early, primary or secondary. These three digital pedagogies have been customised to meet the needs of both teachers and learners within these different phases of schooling. The digital pedagogies are grounded in theoretical underpinnings, some of which will be familiar to teachers and some which are specific to educational technologies. They offer a framework for teachers to implement the use of technology in each phase of learning, provide detailed examples of different technologies and tie their use to the learning outcomes associated with each phase.

The journey towards becoming a teacher who uses digital technologies in their teaching and learning is a complex one. It requires a commitment and energy to explore how current and emerging technologies may assist in teaching and learning. It is reliant upon teachers possessing an inquiring mind, a fearless attitude and being a creative practitioner. These are skills that should be present in all educators, across all phases of learning. This book has been designed to provide you with the necessary information to develop your own digital pedagogy, aligned to the needs of your students in the phase of learning within which you are working.

Outline of the book

Chapter 1 introduces the idea of a digital pedagogy and explores why teachers need to equip themselves with such a set of skills and practices—it explores the changing nature of today's students and the assumptions we have made about their levels of digital fluency. Finally, it explores the drivers behind the need for a digital pedagogy.

Chapter 2 explores the theoretical underpinnings of educational technology. It examines eleven different theoretical approaches that are associated with the use of technology in learning. Some are more traditional theories that have been adapted as digital technologies have become more prevalent, others have emerged as a result of the digital world we occupy.

Chapter 3 examines the policy trends currently impacting on schooling in Australia. It explores a number of different policy documents from Australia and from four other countries (New Zealand, United Kingdom, USA, and Singapore) in order to situate Australia within the wider context of educational reform and change. It also introduces some of the key research organisations concerned with the use of educational technologies.

Chapter 4 brings together the ideas presented in Chapters 1 through to 3 and introduces the idea of digital expectations. It explores the drivers of these expectations: students, parents, teachers, government and employers. Finally, it examines how digital expectancy will change teaching and learning.

Chapter 5 introduces the section 'Creative technologies and learning' and begins with an examination of the role digital technologies may play in emerging literacy and numeracy. This includes a closer examination of literacy and numeracy, and the way different types of technologies may assist in development.

Chapter 6 begins with an examination of 'creative technology' and how it may be used in play. This chapter is concerned with the use of technology in the early and primary phases of learning and explores nine different technologies, their characteristics, lesson ideas and how they could be used creatively.

Chapter 7 concludes the section on creative technologies and learning by presenting the characteristics of a digital pedagogy suited for creative technologies. It explores the characteristics of digital fluency in early and primary phase learners and presents the Technology and Play Framework as a tool to assist teachers in the development of a digital pedagogy suited for these phases of learning.

Chapter 8 introduces the section 'Creative, purposeful and experimental learning with technology' and begins with an exploration of the role of technology in the primary, and early secondary classrooms. It examines the typical skills of learners in these phases of schooling and different ways teachers can engage learners with technology via three types of learning activities: creative, experimental and purposeful.

Chapter 9 presents a mixture of technologies aimed at building skills and expanding learners' digital experiences. Twelve technologies are examined, lesson ideas are presented and how each of these technologies enables students to become digital content creators, technology innovators and digitally fluent is examined.

Chapter 10 concludes the section on creative, purposeful and experimental learning with technology, and examines how to structure a digital pedagogy aimed at developing skills in digital fluency, digital content creation and technology innovation in learners within the primary and early secondary phases of learning.

Chapter 11 introduces the final section of the book, 'Digital technologies for all subject areas'. Primarily, this last section is concerned with the senior secondary phase of learning and, due to the nature of secondary schooling and the impact of learning within different subject areas; development in the use of technology has been examined in three stages.

Chapter 12 explores the various discipline-specific technologies used in secondary schooling and focuses on the refining of proficiency in these learners. Ten technologies are explored, lesson ideas are presented and, finally, each technology is examined for specific learning outcomes.

Chapter 13 concludes the section by presenting how to develop a digital pedagogy for digitally fluent learners in the senior secondary phase of schooling. Finally, it re-examines the different pedagogies needed for each of the three phases of schooling; early, primary and secondary, and shows how each set of skills within each of these different pedagogies builds on each other and the skills of the students.

Jennifer Howell

Acknowledgments

I would like to acknowledge the many students, pre-service teachers and teachers who have enriched my understanding of the use and, more importantly, the value of technology in education. This journey began many years ago as a classroom teacher struggling to incorporate the exciting new technologies that were emerging at the time. The enthusiasm of my students when we used computers, surfed the internet and made use of other now seemingly archaic technologies, inspired me to keep going. What I realised very quickly back then was that my students could teach me more about emerging technologies than I could hope to learn from other means. Finding tools that excited my students and re-engaged them with learning was a light bulb moment for me, and that spark of interest when new technologies are used remains today in the students I now teach in pre-service teacher education programs. We work in a dynamic profession, change is continuous, but the fastest change is the types of technologies we use. How we are currently teaching will not be the way we will be teaching in five years time. This simple idea drives me to equip pre-service teachers with a digital pedagogy that will help them to become the teachers they want to be and more importantly, need to be.

I would like to acknowledge my colleagues, friends and family, who were extremely tolerant and patient during the preparation of this book. I would like to thank the anonymous reviewers for their constructive feedback and the work of the helpful staff at Oxford University Press.

Finally, I would like to make a particular mention of the students who have passed through my units and graciously allowed me to try new ways of delivering content. Your feedback and patience have been greatly appreciated.

PART 1

Digital Pedagogy

CHAPTER 1

What is a digital
pedagogy and why
do we need one?

Learner Outcomes

After reading this chapter, you should be able to:

- understand the concept digital pedagogy
- describe the need for developing a digital pedagogy of your own
- know some of the imperatives that drive change in educational practices
- list the reasons that require education to become more digitalised.

Key Terms

- digital pedagogy
- digital native
- digital Immigrant
- digital fluency

What is a digital pedagogy?

During your studies you will have encountered the term *pedagogy* and be familiar with what it refers to. It is the basis of our profession and many of us would have an idea in our mind of what an effective pedagogy would be for the phase of learning or subject area we are planning to specialise in. For purposes of clarity, let's define it as the study of being a teacher and the process of teaching. There has been much research and speculation about the use of computers in the classroom, and technology has often been viewed as a *tool* to assist both teachers and students. But is that all? Research has shown that we learn differently and engage in different types of knowledge creation when we use technology. Research on the use of technology in teaching and learning has informed developments in learning theories such as constructionism, distributed constructionism and connectivism. Technology has also changed the way we view teachers. No longer is the traditional paradigm of the all-knowing, all-powerful teacher at the front of the class distilling knowledge into the empty minds of the students relevant. While this paradigm was at its peak in popularity during the 1960s to 1970s, it does still remain in some traditional classrooms across Australia. Technology was first viewed with great excitement by some educators as its potential was being explored. There was a lot of predictive comment made about the computer replacing the teacher, which led to some negative backlash regarding incorporating technology into classrooms. As this initial flurry of reactive commentary started to settle down, educators started to examine the potential of new technologies in teaching and learning. Technology has furthered the shift towards more independent, student-led inquiry modes of learning. Teachers now assume the role of co-collaborator or eModerator. So technology appears to be more than a mere tool in the classroom: it changes how and what we learn.

Throwing a computer into a classroom doesn't make the learning effective: teachers need to understand how to use technology effectively, understand the learning theories behind the practice and know how to select the right technology for the learning outcomes they seek. Teachers need a **digital pedagogy**. In simple terms, a digital pedagogy is the study of how to teach using digital technologies. This chapter explores why teachers need to develop a digital pedagogy. It examines the changing nature of students and the context in which we teach. It argues why we need to develop our skills in digital technologies and outlines the learning outcomes we can expect. Students and their parents expect that children will learn and be taught via digital technologies. It's a strong imperative: we either up-skill and embrace digital technologies or we get left behind by our students. The rewards for including technology in the classroom are numerous. This text guides you in detail through some of the ways of teaching with technology.

Why do we need a digital pedagogy?

Today's students use technology (IM, Facebook, Flickr, Skype) to be constantly connected—to friends, family, information and entertainment. Technology allows them to connect with more people, in more ways, more often... The current generation seamlessly transition between their 'real' and digital lives (BECTA 2008, p. 12).

Educators face the constant challenge of refining teaching and learning techniques to keep up with the increasing demands and expectations of students, whom we describe as *digitally expectant*. Students expect that the teaching and learning they will experience across their years of formal schooling will be rich in digital technologies. It is an expectation grounded in students' personal and recreational pursuits. The non-schooling part of their lives is rich in digital technologies: they watch digital TV; listen to digital radio; use smartphones; are fluent in Web 2.0, social networking, digital images and editing, mashups, Wii, Xbox, NintendoDS, iPad, electronic text ... the list is endless. As new technologies enter the market they are enthusiastically taken up. The current generation has been eagerly labelled as 'Gen C', 'Gen I', 'Net Gen', 'Gen Y', 'Gen Z', 'Internet Generation', '**digital natives**', and so on. But are they really digitally fluent across all spheres of their life? An increasing number of educators and researchers think that these students are digitally fluent in their lives outside school, but markedly less fluent within the educational context.

The characteristics and behaviours of these students are distinctly different from those of their teachers. Teachers in the majority resemble Prensky's (2001) **digital immigrants**—they range along a continuum of those who have attempted to use information and communication technology (ICT) to those who have not embraced the use of ICT in the instructional process. Most teachers tend to be self-taught or peer-taught. Their technology skills tend to be limited to what is in their home and work environment. Most teachers are using technology every day, but the types of technology they use might not be as up to date as their students, nor even their teaching requirements, need them to be. Technological skills are not the defining factor for an effective digital pedagogy. This chapter does not argue that we all need to become expert programmers or web page builders. Digital pedagogy is more about an attitude towards and aptitude with digital technologies. It is more about a willingness to use them in the classroom effectively and to understand how and why they should be used.

It is not only the expectations of students that need to be considered. Increasingly, parents, employers and the wider community expect the education system to produce technologically fluent students—students who can use a wide variety of digital technologies, and who have the behaviours and knowledge that will enable them to use emerging technologies.

Let's have a closer look at these expectations. Parents are aware of the increasingly digital world within which their children live. It would be normal for parents to assume that the teaching and learning their children engage in includes digital technologies. Schools are increasingly asked to bridge the gap between what the parents can afford to have in their homes for their children to use, and the types of technologies they would like their children to experience or be fluent in. Employers are digitally expectant of employees. Whether employees are secondary students in part-time jobs or students exiting from the education system, employers expect them to be able to use digital technologies. These expectations include fluency in basic programs commonly used, but some expectations might be subject-specific depending upon the types of subjects the students studied and the field they are entering. Finally, there are the expectations from the wider community. It would be a commonly held belief that schools are using a wide variety of digital technologies in their teaching and learning. The media often report on schools that are doing a particular project using digital technologies, people see students using digital tools and there are government initiatives such as the laptop program that create in the minds of the wider community a sense that schooling is increasingly digital.

Figure 1.1: Factors that drive a digital pedagogy

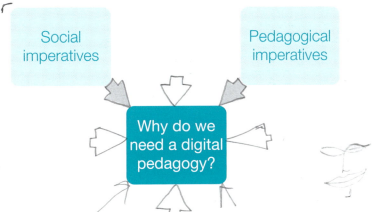

So far, we have explored some of the reasons that drive the need for a digital pedagogy. Largely, they are all concerned with a sense of expectancy and they are all social, they involve *people*. The social imperatives outlined so far include students, parents, employers and the wider community. But what about teachers? Do they feel digitally expectant? For teachers, the sense of expectancy might be different. There is certainly a sense of digital pressure. New programs such as the laptop roll out, new classroom technologies such as interactive whiteboards or digital projectors certainly add to feelings of digital pressure. Teachers want to be able to use new technologies effectively and they want to know ways that will result in positive learning outcomes. This is where a digital pedagogy comes in. It provides teachers with the ability to meet new digital technologies and be able to use them effectively in their classrooms.

Social imperatives are not the only drivers for a digital pedagogy, as shown in Figure 1.1. There are also pedagogical imperatives. As mentioned earlier, there have been new developments in learning theories and educational research that has shown that technology has great potential in teaching and learning. These theoretical underpinnings are explored in further detail in Chapter 2.

Critical Reflection
How 'digitally native' are you?

In 2001 Marc Prensky published his article 'Digital Natives, Digital Immigrants' and it has received both acclaim and criticism. When it was published in 2001 there was a climate of exploring how technology was changing life, people, how we communicate and how we learn. It was an exciting time with lots of speculative ideas and thoughts being shared. The concept of a digital native was exciting; it was going to transform education, transform how we teach, how we perceive our students. It was also frightening to some educators. Panic ensued; how were they going to cater for these digital natives and their learning needs?

In the settling down of this climate of excitement and debate, a few concepts remain in our vernacular—digital natives and digital immigrants are two such examples. Here is how Prensky (2001) described digital natives:

"Digital Natives are used to receiving information really fast. They like to parallel process and multi-task. They prefer their graphics before their text rather than the opposite. They prefer random access (like hypertext). They function best when networked. They thrive on instant gratification and frequent rewards. They prefer games to 'serious' work. (Does any of this sound familiar?)"

- Do you think Prensky's description of digital natives is accurate? Or are there sections of this you agree or disagree with?
- How 'digitally native' are you?
- What response would you have had as an educator after reading Prensky's article?

Personal Reflection

What are your drivers for developing a digital pedagogy?

As you see in Figure 1.2, two types of imperatives have been identified as drivers for a digital pedagogy. But are the imperatives limited to these two categories? Or can you think of some other drivers that perhaps have motivated you to develop a digital pedagogy?

Figure 1.2: Drivers for a digital pedagogy

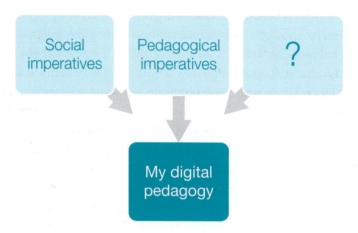

How do we develop a digital pedagogy?

We have established the case for a digital pedagogy and hopefully you are starting to realise the importance of adopting such a strategy. But how do we develop a digital pedagogy? Do digital pedagogies come via coursework? The simple answer to this question is no. It would be lovely to think that we could complete a unit at university entitled 'Digital Pedagogy' and that would be it. *"A digital pedagogy* is many things, but most importantly it is an attitude and aptitude. This sounds" nebulous, but think about the nature of digital technologies. They are fast-changing and evolving quickly, particularly web-based applications. Think back over the past couple of years: new Web 2.0 tools have emerged rapidly, we have moved from text SMS messaging and emailing to Twitter and Facebook as a means of communicating with friends and family. What will be next? This constant evolution means that we can't rely upon a single unit or professional development workshop to provide us with a digital pedagogy. Rather, we need to develop an attitude and aptitude that leads us to engage with new technologies as they emerge and look for their educational applications. It sounds easy. You are probably sitting there thinking, 'Well, I am open to new technologies', but we need a breadth of theoretical knowledge and understandings to help us to take a new digital technology and embed it meaningfully into an educational context. Not so easy now is it? It is almost as if we need to be technologically fearless. Think about how your students jump in and try new technologies. Adopt the same behaviour. Ask your students or your peers what they use; learn from them; be guided by them. There is a sense that we are all in this together.

One of the hardest transitions for teachers is the move from being the expert in the class to being the co-collaborator, and digital technologies often force us to adopt this position whether we want to or not! For example, you might have decided on a particular program for the students to produce their work with, but a student in your class might suggest a different way or a different program, something you might not be familiar with. The technologically fearless teacher would stop, listen and explore that suggestion with their class. The traditional 'expert' teacher might resist that suggestion and stick with the idea they had with the technology they know. See the difference? But this is all about attitude, and hopefully by engaging with the material in this text you will see why that is so important.

Now what about aptitude? A digital aptitude is grounded in theoretical understandings. It involves understanding the learning theories that are attached to digital pedagogy, the types of learning opportunities it affords and the learning outcomes that are expected. It is a meshing of our pedagogical expertise with digital technologies. While this is examined in greater detail in Chapter 2, a brief look at the impact digital technology has made on learning theories is warranted here. As pedagogues, we are aware of constructivism, its meaning and role in learning. What happens to constructivism when technology is added? This was a question Seymour Papert (1993) explored that led to the term constructionism in his book, The Children's Machine: Rethinking school in the age of the computer. It is inspired by the constructivist theory that individual learners construct mental models to understand the world around them. However, constructionism suggests that learning can happen most effectively when people are also active in making tangible objects in the real world—in a sense, learning by doing. The key to the difference between constructivism and constructionism is that constructionists perceive learning to be most effective when part of an activity the learner experiences is constructing a *meaningful product*—more specifically that the meaningful product is created using *technology*. Papert's early work was based on using the computer programming language, Logo, to teach mathematics.

Constructionism has evolved since Papert's work and it has often been defined as active learning with the added element of technology. Learning with computers or learning with technology resulted in a new learning theory emerging in the field. This was revolutionary. The addition of technology *changed* how children learnt. It opened up new learning opportunities; a new learning theory in education had not been seen since the mid-1970s. This has been just a short examination of how educational theory has evolved since the rise of technology in classrooms; it is explored further in Chapter 2. What we can take from this short synopsis is that digital technologies have had a huge impact on teaching and learning, not just in the form of the types of technological tools available for use, but also in the way we understand how learning occurs. An effective digital pedagogue understands these elements and they form the scaffold upon which teachers construct their lessons.

CASE STUDY

Read the following scenario and answer the questions that follow:

After two years working as a supply teacher and completing a couple of term-long contracts, I had secured my first full-time teaching position. I was absolutely thrilled and raring to go. About the same time the school received a large grant for technologising the school, it was decided that a computer lab would be created that could be used by different subjects. The idea was that all the technology was to be in one room and timetabling would share the room out across teachers. Now, the potential here for very little access to this room was high—we had 74 teachers on staff. But as it turned out, very few teachers wanted to use the room. The percentage of digital immigrants on staff was low. It wasn't that they were not prepared to try, but a whole room of technology was overwhelming and fearfulness was a typical reaction.

As a relatively young teacher, I thought the computer lab was irresistible, so I enthusiastically arranged for all my different classes to have some time scheduled in there. As the term progressed, I found my students were happy and excited when their computer lab lesson came round; it was a great motivator for them to get through the harder content and then engage in some inquiry-based learning in the lab.

As the term progressed, I found that I was starting to be on the receiving end of some very negative comments from my colleagues. They felt I was slacking off and not working, that my class would be falling behind, that I wasn't covering the content. It reached a point where I was asked to see my HoD and explain what I was doing and how I was covering the content. Essentially, I was asked to justify the time I spent in the computer lab with my classes. I had to produce evidence that the students were actually learning something. As you can imagine, this was all very confronting and disillusioning for a new teacher. When I think back on that now I get so angry. The students were engaged, motivated, enjoying the content and, most importantly, they were *learning*. Yet, according to my peers, I was negligent and not teaching.

1. How do you justify the place of technology in the classroom?
2. Do you think it is still perceived to be an easy, lazy option for teachers?
3. Do you think that teachers need to do very little when they take a class to a computer lab or similar? Is it just a matter of 'crowd control' and keeping them on task?
4. What are your perceptions of lessons that are technology-based?

Critical Reflection

An often quoted statement by Marc Prensky (2001) is:

"*Today's students are no longer the people our educational system was designed to teach.* "

- Do you agree?
- Think back to your schooling, are the students you encounter now different to your schooling days?
- In what way are they different?
- Is the difference solely due to technology?

Why bother? I know how to use a computer!

"Many teachers would be of the opinion that they are already digitally fluent. They can use a computer to generate great worksheets, use an Excel spreadsheet to record grades, Google for information, send a text message on their phone, email and play Wii at home. Yes, they are certainly fluent in the technologies of their choice, but could they justify why they are better to use? What type of learning results from their use? What other types of learning do students acquire working with technology, apart from new knowledge or content knowledge? Do they understand the types of learning styles technologies favour or enhance? Could they justify their use in the classroom to parents? There are pedagogical reasons that justify the use of particular technologies in the classroom."As professional educators we have acquired pedagogical expertise via our pre-service programs and through our experience as teachers. We understand the value of various approaches, how to cater for particular learning preferences or styles, how to meet the needs of all the learners in our classroom. Let's turn to the wider field of educational research to see if it can answer the question of why we should bother.

Reason 1:
We are situated in a global information society

"*Traditional notions of education are no longer sufficient to prepare a workforce for a contingent and dynamic world. Currently, we live in an era driven by information, global competition and new technologies that are changing the way we think, live and work. The Industrial Revolution was built on machinery, skills and labour; however, the information and knowledge-based revolution of the 21st Century is being built on investment in intellect and creativity. New jobs are emerging which require a different set of knowledge, skills and attitudes (Pillay, Boulton-Lewis & Wilss 2004, p. 17).* "

The phrase *global information society* is much used; it can be taken that we are living in a highly interconnected world. "Information and communication are no longer limited to our local environment; they are not restricted by boundaries. The types of skills required in traditional professions have changed due to technology and the machines we use across a range of industries and professions, and because the way we conduct business has changed."New professions are constantly emerging due to the increase in technologies. The students in our classrooms will be entering this new digitalised workforce and "schools bear some responsibility in preparing them for that. While much debate exists on 'whose job it is'—schools' or universities'—there needs to be an acknowledgement by all sectors of education that society and our working life are increasingly digital. Preparing students to be successful, contributing members of that society is a shared responsibility.

Reason 2:
The Australian workforce needs to be digitally prepared

> As the world becomes more interconnected and global markets for skills and innovation develop even further, it will be crucial for Australia to have enough highly skilled people able to adapt to the uncertainties of a rapidly changing future. Higher education will clearly be a major contributor to the development of a skilled workforce (The Bradley Review of Higher Education 2008, p. 11).

Increasingly, educationalists believe that our information-based society requires a rethinking of the skills and knowledge traditionally disseminated by schooling. Digital competence, the confident and critical use of ICT for employment, learning, self-development and participation in society is an expected attribute of a skilled workforce. This movement parallels developments in teaching and learning, which have seen the embedding of ICTs in classrooms, as online learning, and the use of digital tools and learning platforms across phases of education.

Reason 3:
Not everyone is a digital native

The prevalence of digital technologies in our lives has meant that "students have different needs, goals and skill requirements from those of previous generations, hence the need for new disciplinary methodologies to provide students with the skills required to contribute meaningfully to society. "This implies redefining the parameters of traditional schooling. There has been much commentary on the current students' cohorts, having been labelled 'digital natives' (Prensky 2001) or the 'Net generation' (Tapscott 1996). However, the reality is far from what has been prophesied. While the use of digital technologies has been widespread, it has been most commonly a recreational not scholastic pursuit. Students have lower levels of skills than would have been expected. Given that the modern workplace requires ICT-literate knowledge workers, it is imperative that students attain the skills required to succeed.

Reason 4:
Using digital technologies in the classroom is engaging and motivating

Imagine you are in a traditional classroom where the favoured strategy is the didactic model of instruction. One day your teacher arrives and announces that the class is being moved to the computer lab and that you will be engaging in an inquiry task using the internet. Your first reaction—excitement? How about your level of motivation? Or would you feel bored at the thought of such a lesson? The answer is obvious. But often we overlook the excitement new approaches can have in the classroom. It is by no means limited to technology—a new approach, a different strategy, the use of visuals, artifacts, guest presenters; all would result in increased engagement and motivation.

However, as classrooms are increasingly technology-rich learning environments, and students are engaging in digital technologies outside schooling, it would foolish to ignore their appeal. Here is a teaching and learning strategy that comes with a predisposition in the users; students like technology, they enjoy using technology and they find learning tasks that involve technology are more engaging and motivating.

Is technology more suited to a particular phase of learning? In a word, no. The range of technologies available to teachers means that their applicability is across the phases of learning. As you will see from this text, there is a section dedicated to the use of digital technologies in the early years, primary and secondary. Due to the combination of their experiences outside school with technology and a sense of techno-fearlessness, students have the potential to engage with technologies across all phases of schooling.

Reason 5:
Life-long learning

'Life-long learning' is phrase that has become increasingly visible in educational policy documents, curriculum documents and syllabus documents. Educational outcomes are no longer restricted to the years of formal schooling; we are now concerned with developing the skills and aptitudes in our students that will ensure they engage with learning across their lifetime. This does not mean that they enroll in university or formal courses; what is being imagined here is the use of digital technologies as a tool to engage in life-long learning. Imagine you are post-formal schooling, but have access to the internet. Your learning never ceases; you Google information, read various websites, perhaps subscribe to RSS feeds, share your thoughts in a blog or read other people's blogs. You are constantly exposed to, engage with and create information digitally. You are *learning*, you are expanding your knowledge and understanding. You need to have been shown how to use, or to have experienced these technologies in order to carry them over into your post-schooling life. So we need to incorporate digital technologies, develop digital literacy in our students and help them critically evaluate the technologies during formal schooling. Effective learning in school that is rich in digital technologies will ensure learning longer through life.

We have seen five reasons why we should 'bother' to acquire a digital pedagogy. Are these the only reasons? Absolutely not, but they are the main drivers in our current educational landscape. We are all members of the global information society. Initially its impact was limited to how we accessed and exchanged information or how we communicated. Now it is impacting on our curriculum and students' learning outcomes. We are rethinking the end result of our education system. After the exciting speculation at the start of 2000 on the impact of technology upon learning, we are starting to realise that not all people are digitally fluent or are digital natives, and that the much hypothesised **digital fluency** appears to be restricted to recreational pursuits, not educational. Educationalists are seeing a need to up-skill students in digital technologies during their schooling. The educational benefits appear to be powerful reasons to adopt a digital pedagogy—who would not want a more engaged or motivated class? Finally, apart from the policy imperatives that we develop in students the skills needed to be life-long learners, there is also the motivation to ensure that inquiry and learning never stops. The benefits to the individual and wider society are limitless. So are you convinced yet? The need for a digital pedagogy that works alongside or with your current pedagogy is clear.

Critical Reflection   FR

In his book _Grown Up Digital (2009)_ Donald Tapscott describes the characteristics and behaviours of people he refers to as the 'Net Generation'. These are people who were born after 1990 and who have grown up in a technology-rich world. Tapscott believes that this particular generational cohort has different needs and behaviours from previous generations. How they will engage in the workforce will be different from previous generations' workforce engagement, how they spend their recreational time is different; how they seek information, shop and interact with their friends is unique to this generational grouping. Tapscott extends this difference to education and builds on Prensky's suggestion that the current educational system is not suited to our current students. He calls for changes and suggests seven ways for educators to tap the Net Gen potential:

1. Don't throw technology into the classroom and hope for good things.
2. Cut back on lecturing.
3. Empower students to collaborate.
4. Focus on life-long learning, not teaching to the text.
5. Use technology to get to know each student.
6. Design educational programs according to the eight norms (choice, customisation, transparency, integrity, collaboration, fun, speed and innovation in learning experiences).
7. Reinvent yourself as a teacher or educator.

- Do you think the characteristics of your generation influence the type of teacher you are? Do you think there are particular teaching strategies you favour because of your generational grouping?
- Do you agree with this list?
- Are you a Net Gen yourself? When you read the list above, did you think that these summarised your generation's preferences and strengths?
- Think about the students you have taught—are they indicative of the Net Gen or do you think that this might not be true of all students?
- Is there anything you would add to this list?

These are interesting questions to ponder and will probably lead to some absorbing discussions with your peers. It would be interesting to see if the types of teachers we become are largely influenced by the generational grouping we are a part of. Do you think it is possible to unlearn your generation's preferences? Perhaps this is what Prensky was suggesting with his term 'digital immigrant'—those from previous generational groupings who have not grown up in a technology-rich environment but who now find themselves teaching in one. Maybe it's a case of jump in or be left behind?

Summary

The case for developing a digital pedagogy in a teacher's repertoire is persuasive. The prevalence of digital technologies in our lives has been steadily increasing in recent years and our understanding of how we should be teaching and how students learn best has been constantly evolving. It would be logical to predict that these two elements would at some stage collide. There has been a growing body of research since the early 1980s on the impact technology has in the classroom. It has been seen as a transformative technology: it has transformed how students learn and it has transformed how we teach. The simple act of introducing technology into the classroom is not enough. Teachers must understand how technologies will affect learning, what the outcomes are likely to be and the teaching strategies that need to be used. Teachers must also be able to use the technologies themselves.

It has been shown above that the need for a digital pedagogy is driven by two imperatives: social imperatives, such as the expectation that learning will be digital; and pedagogical imperatives, such as the effect technology has upon learning. But these are perhaps not the only drivers. Our society has changed due to the impact of technology. Society is no longer constrained as being local or even national; we are all members of a global information society. The way we communicate and acquire information has become digital. The workforce that our students will eventually enter is affected by technology. Professions and industries have been undergoing a digital revolution of their own; the types of technology used across professions now are increasingly digital. One of the aims of the schooling system is to prepare students to enter the workforce; hence there is a need to include digital technologies in the curriculum. A further reason for the need for a digital pedagogy is that people are not all equal in their digital fluency; not everyone is a digital native and schools are often required to bridge the gap between those who can access digital technologies and those who cannot.

Perhaps one of the strongest reasons a digital pedagogy is needed is the impact digital technologies have on student engagement and motivation. Learning is viewed more positively and hence learning outcomes are often easier to achieve due to the added element of digital technologies. It is a simple idea: students enjoy using digital technologies in their lives outside of school and so come to school with a predisposition towards digital technologies. Lesson or learning experiences that include such tools are viewed more positively.

Last, there has been a change in the outcomes of education as expressed in policy documents, curriculum and syllabus documents. No longer is schooling focused upon learning outcomes achieved over a certain number of years; the skills we are endeavouring to develop in our students are supposed to ensure that they become life-long learners. This paradigm shift in the minds of educators and policy makers is interesting to note and also perhaps made possible by digital technologies. Prior to the internet, was schooling concerned with what students did after formal schooling? Possibly not, but because we are increasingly reliant upon digital sources of information and because we now see the potential for learning to carry on outside of the classroom, there has been a shift in focus. Schooling and the skills we impart during formal schooling are now to be carried on and used post-school. As these skills and post-school education are largely digitally based, the importance of teaching these skills well and of teaching the associated skills of critical inquiry and digital literacy should be embedded in our lessons.

FURTHER READING

DEEWR (2008). *Review of Australian Higher Education. Final Report.* [Online] From http://www.deewr.gov.au/HigherEducation/Review/Pages/Review ofAustralianHigherEducationReport.aspx.

Dye, J. (2007). *Meet Generation C: Creatively Connecting through Content.* [Online] From http://www.econtentmag.com.

Goldberger, P. (2003). *Disconnected Urbanism.* [Online] From A. Lenhart, M. Madden, A. Ranking Macgill & A. Smith (2007). *Teens and Social Media. Pew Internet and American Life Project.* [Online] From http://www.pewinternet.org/ pdfs/PIP_Teens_Social_Media_Final.pdf.

Lessig, L. (2002). *The Future of Ideas.* New York: Vintage Books.

Lorenzo, G., Oblinger, D. & Dziuban, C. (2006). *How Choice, Co-creation, and Culture are Changing What it Means to be Net Savvy.* [Online] From http:// connect.educause.edu/Library/EDUCAUSE+Quarterly/HowChoiceCo CreationandCul/40008.

McNeely, B. (2005). *Using Technology as a Learning Tool, Not Just the Cool New Thing. Educating the Net Generation.* EDUCAUSE E-book. [Online] From http:// www.educause.edu/UsingTechnologyasaLearningTool,NotJusttheCoolNew Thing/6060.

Oblinger, D. G., & Oblinger, J. L. (2005). *Educating the Net Generation.* [Online] From http://www.educause.edu/educatingthenetgen.

Papert, S. (1993). *The Children's Machine: Rethinking School in the Age of the Computer.* New York: BasicBooks.

Pillay, H., Boulton-Lewis, G., & Wilss, L. (2004). Changing workplace environments: Implications for higher education. *Educational Research Journal*, 19(1), 17–42.

Prensky, M. (2001, October). Digital natives, digital immigrants. *On the Horizon.* Vol. 9, No. 5: NCB University Press. [Online] From http://www.marcprensky.com/ writing/.

Tapscott, D. (2009). *Grown Up Digital.* New York: McGraw Hill.

Taylor, M. (2006). *Generation NeXt Comes to College: Today's Postmodern Student.* [Online] From http://globalcscc.edu/tirc/blog/files/Gen%20NeXt%20 handout%2006%20oln.pdf.

Trendwatching. (2004). *Generation C.* [Online] From http://www.trend watching.com/trends/GENERATION_C.htm.

Windham, C. (2007). *Father Google and Mother IM: Confessions of a Net Gen Learner.* Presented at ELI Annual Meeting, January 23, 2007. [Online] From http://connect.educause.edu/library/abstract/FatherGoogleandMothe/39228.

WEBSITES

http://www.marcprensky.com/

While Prensky is not an educator, you could describe him as a social commentator. His articles are noteworthy, as he coined the terms 'digital native' and 'digital immigrant', so it's worthwhile having a look at his ideas.

http://www.papert.org/articles/const_inst/const_inst1.html

This is a transcript of a speech Seymour Papert delivered in Japan in the early 1980s, just at the start of his work with Logo programming and the development of constructionism. It's an interesting speech as it explores the differences between constructionism and instructionism.

http://trendwatching.com/

The name pretty much explains what this website is about. It's an interesting source of current trends and predictions about future trends.

http://dontapscott.com/

An interesting website of yet another social commentator. It provides some nice reviews of his books, which give you a better idea of the types of speculative offerings he makes. His work should be noted and, interestingly, his books are based upon his own children and what he has observed as they have grown up (a little like Piaget and his work observing his daughter!).

http://www.metropolismag.com/cda/

An online magazine that tends towards articles on worldwide trends, the impact of technology and how society is changing.

CHAPTER 2

Theoretical
underpinnings

Learner Outcomes

After reading this chapter, you should be able to:

- understand the different theoretical underpinnings that explain the relationship between learning and technology
- know how theory impacts on educational practices
- understand the interconnectedness of learning theories pertaining to technology.

Key Terms

- constructivism
- social constructivism
- distributed cognition
- constructionism
- distributed constructionism
- social constructionism
- connectivism
- computer-supported collaborative learning (CSCL)
- technological pedagogical and content knowledge (TPACK)
- community of practice (CoP)
- online community of practice (OCoP)

Introduction

As a pre-service teacher you will be aware of the learning theories that inform our practice. During your studies you will have developed deep understandings of the work of leading figures such as Jean Piaget, Jerome Bruner and Lev Vygotsky. Learning theories are important as they inform our practices in many ways but, more importantly, they equip us with insights and understandings on how learners create new knowledge, build on existing knowledge and apply knowledge to new contexts. For much of the early research concerning learning, the debate was focused on determining how we learn best. Was it an individual pursuit or a social activity? Much of the research was polarised between these two approaches. However, as educational research has advanced, we know that learning is not a case of either or, but one of *both*; we learn in many different ways simultaneously, dependent upon the content and context.

When computers first emerged there was too much speculation about their impact on teaching and learning. Initially, teachers and practitioners largely dismissed their potential use; however, educational researchers persisted with examining how technology might affect the way we teach and how we learn. Early theoretical work explored the impact of technology on existing theoretical approaches to learning, and from this early work, new theories began to emerge. This chapter discusses a number of theoretical approaches underpinning the use of technology in learning: some of them predate but have proved suited to technology-based learning; others are new. See Figure 2.1 for an overview.

Figure 2.1: Overview of theoretical underpinnings of educational technology

Considering our increasingly digital world, it is safe to assume that theory is still evolving. New theories will continue to emerge was we change how we communicate, search for information and becoming more digital in our daily lives.

Constructivism

Constructivism is a theory of knowledge or *epistemology* that states that individuals generate knowledge and meaning from the interaction between their experiences and their ideas. Jean Piaget's theory of constructivist learning has had a wide-ranging impact on learning theories and teaching methods in education. Piaget described and set out the stages by which knowledge is internalised by learners.

Sensorimotor stage: From birth to age two, infants build an understanding of themselves and reality (and how things work) through interactions with the environment. They are able to differentiate between themselves and other objects. Learning takes place via assimilation (the organisation of information and absorbing it into existing schema) and accommodation (when an object cannot be assimilated and the schemata have to be modified to include the object).

Preoperational stage: From ages two to seven, children are not yet able to conceptualise abstractly and need concrete physical situations. Objects are classified in simple ways, especially by important features.

Concrete operational stage: From ages seven to eleven, as physical experience accumulates, accommodation is increased. Children begin to think abstractly and conceptualise, creating logical structures that explain their physical experiences.

Formal operational stage: From ages eleven to sixteen, cognition reaches its final form. By this stage, children no longer require concrete objects to make rational judgments. They are capable of deductive and hypothetical reasoning. Their capacity for abstract thinking is very similar to that of adults.

Piaget suggested that, through processes of accommodation and assimilation, individuals construct new knowledge from their experiences. When individuals assimilate, they incorporate the new experience into an already existing framework without changing that framework. This may occur when individuals' experiences are aligned with their internal representations of the world, but may also occur as a failure to change a faulty understanding; for example, they may not notice events, may misunderstand input from others, or may decide that an event is a fluke and is therefore unimportant as information about the world. In contrast, when individuals' experiences conflict with their internal representations, they may reframe their mental representation of the external world to fit the new experiences. Accommodation can be understood as the mechanism by which failure leads to learning: when we act on the expectation that the world operates in one way and it violates our expectations, we often fail, but by accommodating this new experience and reframing our model of the way the world works, we learn from the experience of failure, or others' failure.

It is important to note that constructivism is not a particular pedagogy. In fact, constructivism is a theory describing how learning happens, regardless of whether learners are using their experiences to understand a lecture or following the instructions for building a model airplane. In both cases, the theory of constructivism suggests that learners construct knowledge out of their experiences.

However, constructivism is often associated with pedagogic approaches that promote active learning, or learning by doing.

Personal Reflection
Constructivism meets technology

The summary above provides a brief overview of the key aspects of constructivism. You probably have a deeper understanding of this learning theory. Your task:

1. Draft a lesson plan—this should be tailored to the phase of learning you intend to teach in and can be on a topic of your choice.
2. The lesson should be constructivist in its approach.
3. Now re-examine that lesson and add technology to it—perhaps you might need to change how you were going to teach the lesson, but make sure the learning and teaching are now technology based.

You could now exchange your draft with a fellow student, or complete the next stage yourself. Answer the following questions:

4. Does technology fit a constructivist approach to teaching and learning?
5. How effective is technology in this type of lesson?
6. Are there any difficulties with including technology in constructivist learning?

This reflection task is aimed at helping you see the connections between technology and constructivist approaches to learning.

Social constructivism

Social constructivism has been a popularly adopted approach to learning by teachers and educational researchers. As we saw earlier, constructivism is one of the major theories (behaviourism, social learning, constructivism and social constructivism) of child development, and is based on Jean Piaget's theory of cognitive development. Piaget's stage theory (describing four successive stages of development) also became known as constructivism because he believed children needed to construct an understanding of the world for themselves. Social constructivism extends constructivism by incorporating the role of other actors and culture in development.

Social constructivism posits that social interactions precede the development of knowledge and understandings, which are in fact the end product of socialisation and social interactions. It is based on the work of Russian psychologist, Lev Vygotsky. There are three major aspects to social constructivism:

1. Social interaction plays a key role in the development of knowledge.
2. The 'more knowledgeable other' (MKO)—an individual who has a better understanding or high level of knowledge than the learner, for example a teacher—is important to learning.
3. All learning occurs within the 'zone of proximal development' (ZPD), which is the distance between a learner's ability to perform a task under adult supervision, or when working with peers and their ability to perform the task independently.

Critical Reflection

Applying the Zone of Proximal Development to educational technology?

Figure 2.2 illustrates the concept of the ZPD within which all learning occurs. Let's apply this idea to the use of educational technology in the classroom.

Figure 2.2: The zone of proximal development (ZPD)

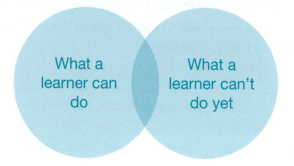

1. Select a particular grade or if you are a secondary teacher, a subject and grade.
2. Now list all of the different types of technology skills and experiences you hope that your students might have during the year. Some examples:
   - basic computer skills—saving, printing, installing and deleting programs, transferring files and performing basic tasks
   - proficiently using word processing, spreadsheets and presentation software
   - using efficient internet search techniques, Boolean operators and truncation
   - critically evaluating sources of information
   - creating animations using a variety of different media
   - producing digital videos and editing software
   - taking digital images and basic editing of images
   - recording and uploading a podcast
   - using blogs, wikis, online communities and common Web 2.0 applications such as Twitter, Facebook and Tumblr
   - proficiently using publishing software
   - understanding and having basic skills in web design, html coding and software programs such Dreamweaver
   - expertly using digital communication (for example, eBooks)
   - using creative technologies such as robotics and gaming.
3. Now allocate where you would anticipate each of these technology skills or experiences currently to be for your selected class or grade.
   - KW—already known
   - NKW—not known
4. Examine the list and try to brainstorm how you would, as the class teacher, move the technology skills or experience from NKW (not known) to KW (known).

Distributed cognition

Distributed cognition is a branch of cognitive science that proposes that human knowledge and cognition are not confined to the individual. Instead, they are distributed by placing memories, facts or knowledge in our environment. Distributed cognition is a useful approach for understanding the social aspects of cognition by putting the emphasis on individuals and their environment. Distributed cognition views a system as a set of representations, and models the interchange of information between these representations. These representations can be either in the mental space of the participants or external representations available in the environment. If we apply this system to networks and electronic connections, acts of communication and exchanges of knowledge between individuals via the internet, distributed cognition has some resonance.

Constructionism

Constructionist learning is inspired by the constructivist theory that individual learners construct mental models to understand the world around them. However, **constructionism** holds that learning can happen most effectively when people are also active in making tangible objects in the real world. In this sense, constructionism is connected with experiential learning, and builds on Jean Piaget's epistemological theory of constructivism.

Idit Harel and Seymour Papert defined constructionism in a proposal to the National Science Foundation entitled *Constructionism: A New Opportunity for Elementary Science Education* as follows:

> *The word constructionism is a mnemonic for two aspects of the theory of science education underlying this project. From constructivist theories of psychology we take a view of learning as a reconstruction rather than as a transmission of knowledge. Then we extend the idea of manipulative materials to the idea that learning is most effective when part of an activity the learner experiences as constructing a meaningful product (Sabelli 2008, p. 196).*

Papert's ideas became well known through the publication of his seminal book *Mindstorms: Children, Computers, and Powerful Ideas* (1980). Papert described children creating programs in the Logo language. Papert has been a huge proponent of bringing IT to classrooms, as in his early uses of the Logo language to teach mathematics to children. Constructionist learning involves students drawing their own conclusions through creative experimentation and the making of social objects. The constructionist teacher takes on a mediational role rather than adopting an instructionist position. Teaching 'at' students is replaced by assisting them to understand—and help one another to understand—problems in a hands-on way.

Critical Reflection
Applying constructionism to other learning contexts

As stated above, constructionism is concerned with the creation of authentic artefacts collaboratively with peers. Early work by Harel and Papert was with the Logo language and programming a turtle to move around based upon mathematical understandings. This work was then extended with LEGO Robotics, with the development of Mindstorms and NXT. The creation of a working, moving robot that can be programmed using a software program illustrates the idea of constructionism—learning occurs when we create real, authentic artefacts. If we think about this type of learning, it not only draws on social constructivism, but also pedagogical strategies such as cooperative learning, collaboration, discovery learning and inquiry learning, and blends these ideas into a theoretical approach.

Constructionism has been commonly associated with the use of technology, largely due to the early work with Logo and LEGO. However, if we examine the definition above, it is not *limited* to technology. It can be used across all learning contexts and content areas.

Task:

Consider the following content areas—they are very broad content areas, so, regardless of specialisation, you should be able to complete this task.

Brainstorm a lesson idea for each of these content areas that is based upon constructionism. They should not include any educational technology.

Content area	Lesson idea based upon constructionism
English or Literacy	
Mathematics	
Science	
History	
Health & PE	

Now let's revisit those ideas and 'technologise' them. Brainstorm some lesson ideas that use technology.

Content area	Lesson idea based upon constructionism that uses technology
English or Literacy	
Mathematics	
Science	
History	
Health & PE	

Now answer the following questions:

- What do you think are the strengths and weaknesses of this approach?
- Do you think this approach favours the use of technology?
- Could you adopt this approach for all of your teaching? Why?
- Have you had any experiences of this approach, either as a student or teacher?

Distributed constructionism

Mitch Resnick (1996) coined the term **distributed constructionism** to explain how computer networks could be used to support the shared construction of knowledge, particularly where students work together on design and construction activities. The theory argued for an alternative 'vision' of the use of computer networks in teaching and learning, with the salient difference being that:

> *This vision puts construction (not information) at the center ... It views computer networks not as a channel for information distribution, but primarily as a new medium for construction, providing new ways for students to learn through construction activities by embedding the activities within a community. (para. 5)*

Distributed constructionism (Resnick 1996a, 1996b) views computer networks as the medium for construction with the networks providing the space for learners to engage in collaborative construction activities. It gives a label and theoretical frame to the understanding that knowledge—as a 'spiral of knowing'—is constructed through reflection and mental engagement with people, problems and artefacts (Wells 2002, pp. 200–2).

Social constructionism

A major focus of **social constructionism** is to uncover the ways in which individuals and groups participate in the construction of their perceived social reality. It involves looking at the ways social phenomena are created, institutionalised, known and made into tradition by humans. The social construction of reality is an ongoing, dynamic process that is (and must be) reproduced by people acting on their interpretations and their knowledge of it. A social construction (also called a social construct) is a concept or practice that is the construct (or artefact) of a particular group. When we say that something is socially constructed, we are focusing on its dependence on social variables.

Personal Reflection
isms-r-us?

This chapter is presenting a lot of different learning –isms and these are only a fraction of the ones you have probably already covered in your studies. Learning theory can feel overwhelming but there is also a sense that you can see the connections between all the different approaches. One builds on the work of another, or works in the opposite direction of another. You might be experiencing a sense of 'which do I use?' at present, and this is a good question, one I am asked often by pre-service teachers. You will encounter in the teaching profession ism-experts—individuals who subscribe to one particular learning theory, who hold that to be the way real teaching happens and who dismiss all other theories.

When I first started teaching I was working in a large, urban secondary school. As a new teacher I was still familiarising myself with my workplace and also the people who worked there. One afternoon after school I was in the staff common room reading the papers on the noticeboard. Out of the corner of my eye I saw a rather stern, officious looking lady come in. She came straight over to me and said, 'Ah, you're the new English teacher aren't you?'

I confirmed that I was and said hello, to which she replied, 'Yes, well tell me … what ism are you?' and looked very expectantly at me.

'What ism am I?' I thought, at which point my mind emptied of all learning theories or ideas and I think I might have mumbled something, but cannot really remember what.

'Hhmmm,' she replied, 'well I am a constructivist,' and with that, she spun on her heel and left the room.

I had experienced my first ism hit-and-run, and I can say it wasn't my last! Many practitioners identify with a particular approach to learning and as a young teacher I wasn't really prepared to state one particular approach. At this stage I was full of different ideas and learning theories, and was looking forward to trying them all. If I had my time over I often wish I could have replied to that lady differently. If I could, I would have said, 'I am an every-ism; I choose my approach based on the content, context and students.'

Some questions to think about
- Do you have a particular learning theory that you identify with more than others? Why?
- Have you observed particular learning theories or approaches 'in action'? Where you able to identify them?
- Do you feel as if you are developing a repertoire of theoretical expertise? That you have a wide selection of approaches that you could use?
- Generally, learning theories can be divided into two broad groupings: the social theories which believe knowledge creation is the result of social interaction; and individual theories, which see knowledge creation as the result of the individual interacting with their environment and assimilating knowledge and learnings internally. Which grouping do you align with?
- Are there any theories that you have dismissed? If so, why?

Connectivism

Connectivism was introduced as a theory of learning based on the premise that knowledge exists in the world rather than in the head of an individual. Connectivism proposes a perspective similar to the activity theory of Vygotsky, as it regards knowledge as existing within systems which are accessed through people participating in activities. One aspect of connectivism is the use of a network with nodes and connections as a central metaphor for learning. In this metaphor, a node is anything that can be connected to another node within a network, such as an organisation: information, data, feelings, images. Connectivism sees learning as the process of creating connections and developing a network. Not all connections are of equal strength in this metaphor; in fact, many connections may be quite weak. This network metaphor allows for a notion of 'know-where' (the understanding of where to find the knowledge when it is needed) to supplement to the ones of 'know-how' and 'know-what' that make the cornerstones of many theories of learning.

Principles of connectivism include:
- Learning and knowledge rests in diversity of opinions.
- Learning is a process of connecting specialised nodes or information sources.
- Learning may reside in non-human appliances.
- Capacity to know more is more critical than what is currently known.
- Nurturing and maintaining connections is needed to facilitate continual learning.
- Ability to see connections between fields, ideas and concepts is a core skill.
- Currency (accurate, up-to-date knowledge) is the intent of all connectivist learning activities.
- Decision-making is itself a learning process. Choosing what to learn and the meaning of incoming information is seen through the lens of a shifting reality. While there is a right answer now, it may be wrong tomorrow due to alterations in the information climate affecting the decision.

Critical Reflection

Knowledge as nodes on a network

Connectivism is an interesting theoretical approach, and when it first emerged it was dismissed as being purely speculative. The idea that we would no longer internalise knowledge, but keep it externally in digital repositories which we would access and use on demand appeared to be quite hard to accept. This might have been due to the fact that, up to this point, the development of knowledge and learning was an internal process— whether it was due to our social interactions with others or by our individual interactions with the world, the knowledge that was created was stored in our minds, it was personal, internal yet intangible. Knowledge wasn't something we could see or weigh, or measure. Yet connectivism and the knowledge that is created or accessed is tangible, it is stored electronically, we can see its size (that is, megabytes, kilobytes) and it is physical.

Connectivism is a theory that has finally reached its time—if we consider our current context, we are in an increasingly digital world that is storing its information electronically, information that we can access when we need and then dispose of. We are essentially nodes on a network! This type of theory has particular relevance when you consider the current trend towards cloud computing.

Some questions to consider:

1. What do you think of this theory? Do you agree with it?
2. How could you use this theory in your teaching?
3. Does this theory have any relevance to education or is really about our lives outside of formal learning?
4. One of the principles of connectivism is the *ability to see connections between fields, ideas, and concepts is a core skill*. How do we enable this ability in our students? What are some practical ideas?

Computer-supported collaborative learning (CSCL)

Computer-supported collaborative learning (CSCL) is a pedagogical approach wherein learning takes place via social interaction using a computer or through the internet. This kind of learning is characterised by the sharing and construction of knowledge among participants using technology as their primary means of communication or as a common resource. CSCL can be implemented in online and classroom learning environments, and can take place synchronously or asynchronously.

The roots of collaborative epistemology as related to CSCL can be found in Vygotsky's social learning theory. Of particular importance to CSCL is the theory's notion of internalisation or the idea that knowledge is developed by one's interaction with the surrounding culture and society. The second key element is what Vygotsky called the 'zone of proximal development' (ZPD). This refers to a range of tasks that can be too difficult for learners to master by themselves but mastery is made possible with the assistance of a more skilled individual or teacher. These ideas feed into a notion central to CSCL: knowledge-building is achieved through interaction with others.

Technological pedagogical and content knowledge (TPACK)

Technological pedagogical content knowledge (TPACK) is a framework to understand and describe the kinds of knowledge needed by a teacher for effective pedagogical practice in a technology enhanced learning environment. The idea of pedagogical content knowledge (PCK) was first described by Lee Shulman (Shulman 1986), and TPACK builds on those core ideas through the inclusion of technology. Punya Mishra and Matthew J Koehler extended on this work and constructed the TPACK framework (Koehler & Mishra 2008, Mishra & Koehler 2006).

The TPACK framework argues that effective technology integration for teaching specific content or subject matter requires understanding and negotiating the relationships between these three components: technology, pedagogy and content. A teacher capable of negotiating these relationships represents a form of expertise different from, and (perhaps) broader than, the knowledge of a disciplinary expert (say, a scientist or a musician or sociologist), a technology expert (a computer engineer) or an expert at teaching or pedagogy (an experienced educator).

TPACK consists of seven different knowledge areas:

1. content knowledge (CK),
2. pedagogical knowledge (PK)
3. technology knowledge (TK)
4. pedagogical content knowledge (PCK)
5. technological content knowledge (TCK)
6. technological pedagogical knowledge (TPK).

Technology knowledge

Technology knowledge (TK), within the context of technology integration in schools, appears to most often refer to digital technologies such as laptops, the internet, and software applications. Technology knowledge goes beyond digital literacy to having knowledge of how to change the purpose of existing technologies (for example, wikis) so that they can be used in a technology enhanced learning environment (Harris et al. 2009).

Content knowledge

Content knowledge (CK) may be defined as a command of a subject. It may also include knowledge of concepts, theories and conceptual frameworks, as well as knowledge about accepted ways of developing knowledge (Shulman 1986).

Pedagogical knowledge

Pedagogical knowledge (PK) includes generic knowledge about how students learn, teaching approaches, methods of assessment and knowledge of different theories about learning (Harris et al. 2009; Shulman 1986). This knowledge alone is necessary but insufficient for teaching purposes. In addition, a teacher requires content knowledge.

Figure 2.3: TPACK model (rights free)

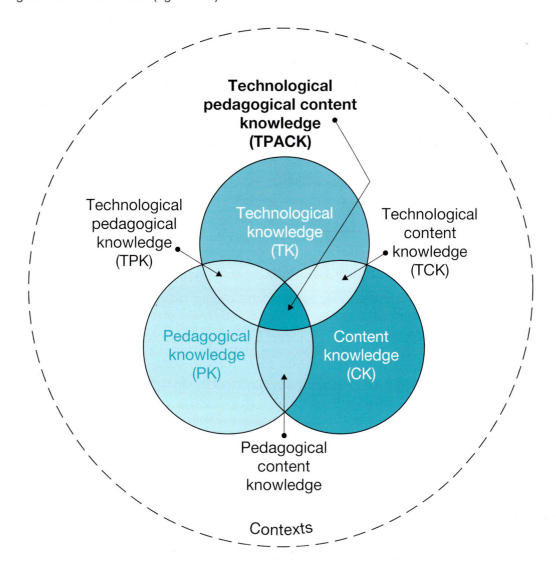

Pedagogical content knowledge

Pedagogical content knowledge (PCK) is knowledge about how to combine pedagogy and content effectively (Shulman 1986). This is knowledge about how to make a subject understandable to learners. Archambault and Crippen (2009) report that PCK includes knowledge of what makes a subject difficult or easy to learn, as well as knowledge of common misconceptions and likely preconceptions students bring with them to the classroom.

Technological content knowledge

Technological content knowledge (TCK) refers to knowledge about how technology may be used to provide new ways of teaching content. For example, digital animation makes it possible for students to conceptualise how electrons are shared between atoms when chemical compounds are formed.

Technological pedagogical knowledge

Technological pedagogical knowledge (TPK) refers to the affordances and constraints of technology as an enabler of different teaching approaches (Mishra & Koehler 2006). For example, online collaboration tools may facilitate social learning for geographically separated learners.

Technological pedagogical content knowledge

Technological pedagogical content knowledge (TPCK) refers to the knowledge and understanding of the interplay between CK, PK and TK when using technology for teaching and learning. It includes an understanding of the complexity of relationships between students, teachers, content, practices and technologies (Archambault & Crippen 2009).

Personal Reflection

Applying TPACK to your practice

The TPACK theory is an interesting approach that attempts to incorporate all of the different elements that inform pedagogical practice. For technology to be integrated effectively within a lesson, the teacher needs to understand the interrelationships between technology, pedagogy and content. This is quite logical if we break it down a little more to illustrate the point.

Technology—we need to know how to use the selected technology and how to teach students how to use it.

Pedagogy—which teaching strategy would be most effective, considering the anticipated learning outcomes, the technology, the content and the students?

Content—what content is to be covered?

By understanding each of these in a detailed manner, we can integrate technology successfully. Let's now practise this idea.

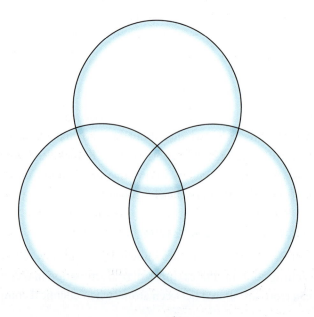

1. In the Venn diagram above, label each circle either 'technology', 'pedagogy' or 'content'.
2. Decide on a particular piece of content that you wish to teach; briefly write it down next to the circle marked 'content'.
3. Now write two or three learning outcomes you wish to achieve.
4. Decide on the technology and mark that down as above, then the pedagogical approach.
5. Critically examine what you have selected and answer the following questions:

   - Do these three choices 'fit' together? Do they support each other?
   - Do any of them need changing?
   - Will they achieve the anticipated learning outcomes?
   - What are the relationships between these elements in the shaded overlapping areas?

Community of practice

The term **community of practice (CoP)** was first used in 1991 by theorists Jean Lave and Etienne Wenger, who discussed the notion of legitimate peripheral participation. Communities of practice can be defined, in part, as a process of social learning that occurs when people who have a common interest in a subject or area collaborate over an extended period of time, sharing ideas and strategies, determining solutions and building innovations. Wenger gives a simple definition: 'Communities of practice are groups of people who share a concern or a passion for something they do and learn how to do it better as they interact regularly' (Wenger 2006, p. 1). Note that this allows for, but does not require intentionality. Learning can be, and often is, an incidental outcome that accompanies these social processes.

The group can evolve naturally because of the members' common interest in a particular domain or area, or it can be created specifically with the goal of gaining knowledge related to their field. It is through the process of sharing information and experiences with the group that the members learn from each other, and have an opportunity to develop themselves personally and professionally (Lave & Wenger 1991). CoPs can exist online, such as within discussion boards and newsgroups, or in real life, such as in a lunch room at work, in a field setting, on a factory floor or elsewhere in the environment.

Online community of practice

An **online community of practice (OCoP)**, also known as a 'virtual community of practice', is a community of practice that is developed on, and maintained using the internet. To qualify as an OCoP, the characteristics of a community of practice (CoP), as described by Lave and Wenger, must be met. To this end, an OCoP must include active members who are practitioners or 'experts' in the specific domain of interest. Members must participate in a process of collective learning within their domain. Additionally, social structures must be created within the community to assist in knowledge creation and sharing. Knowledge must be shared and meaning negotiated within an appropriate context. Community members must learn through both instruction-based learning and group discourse. Finally, multiple dimensions must facilitate the long-term management of support as well as enable immediate synchronous interactions.

Personal Reflection
Online communities of practice

An individual may be a member of a number of communities of practice at any one time (Lave & Wenger 1991), but they must undergo a process or transformation to become a full member. This can be more readily observed in online communities of practice, as newer members tend to sit ('lurk') around the edges of community discussions and contribute significantly less than more experienced members. Increasingly, we are joining online communities, but are we conscious of learning or that we are engaged in a formal process?

Think about an online community you are a member of, it might be a more formal community, such as a professional association with an email or discussion list, or it could be an informal community that you use in your personal life such as Twitter or Facebook. Answer the following questions:

1. When you first joined this community, what level of participation did you engage in? Could you have described yourself as a lurker?

2. Do you think over time your engagement in the online community has increased? Why?

3. What have you learnt from being a member of this community?

Summary

This chapter has presented eleven different theoretical approaches that are associated with the use of technology in learning. Some are more traditional theories that have been adapted as digital technologies have become more prevalent, others have emerged as result of the digital world we occupy. There are clear connections between the theories and its possible to see how they have emerged from the earlier work in the field.

The adoption of one approach or theory is not the aim of this chapter. An effective teacher selects the theory or teaching strategy that best suits the learning objectives, content, students, context and facilities that are available. These theories are of interest, as we are concerned with the use of technology in teaching and learning. Therefore it's important that we can see the theory that is behind the inclusion of technology in learning. Technology is not just a tool; it has an impact on the types of learning outcomes we can anticipate, it affects the types of learning we can engage in and it inspires new developments in understanding how we learn.

FURTHER READING

Archambault, L., & Crippen, K. (2009). Examining TPACK among K–12 online distance educators in the United States. *Contemporary Issues in Technology and Teacher Education*, 9(1), 71–88.

Harris, J., Mishra, P., & Koehler, M. (2009). Teachers' technological pedagogical content knowledge and learning activity types: Curriculum-based technology integration reframed. *Journal of Research on Technology in Education*, 41(4), 393–416.

Koehler, M. J., & Mishra, P. (2008). Introducing TPCK. In J. A. Colbert, K. E. Boyd, K. A. Clark, S. Guan, J. B. Harris, M. A. Kelly & A. D. Thompson (Eds), *Handbook of Technological Pedagogical Content Knowledge for Educators* (pp. 1–29). New York: Routledge.

Lave, J. & Wenger, E. (1991). *Situated Learning: Legitimate Peripheral Participation*. Cambridge: Cambridge University Press.

Mishra, P., & Koehler, M. J. (2006). Technological pedagogical content knowledge: A framework for teacher knowledge. *Teachers College Record*, 108(6), 1017–54.

Piaget, J. (1977). *The Essential Piaget*. Ed. by Howard E. Gruber and J. Jacques Vonèche. New York: Basic Books.

Papert, S. (1980). *Mindstorms: Children, Computers, and Powerful Ideas*.

Papert, S. (1991a). *Constructionism: A New Opportunity for Elementary Science Education*. Award Abstract #8751190. [Online] From http://nsf.gov/awardsearch/showAward.do?AwardNumber=8751190.

Papert, S. (1991b). Situating constructionism. In I. Harel, & S. Papert (Eds), *Constructionism* (pp. 1–12). Norwood, NJ: Ablex Publishing.

Resnick, M. (1996a). *Distributed Constructionism*. [Online] From http://llk.media.mit.edu/papers/Distrib-Construc.html.

Resnick, M. (1996b). Toward a practice of 'constructional design. In L. Schauble & R. Glaser (Eds), *Innovations in Learning: New Environments for Education* (pp. 161–74). Mahwah, NJ: Lawrence Erlbaum Associates.

Sabelli, N. (2008). *Constructionism: A New Opportunity for Elementary Science Education. DRL Division of Research on Learning in Formal and Informal Settings*, 193–206. [Online] From http://nsf.gov/awardsearch/showAward.do?AwardNumber=8751190.

Shulman, L. (1986). Those who understand: Knowledge growth in teaching. *Educational Researcher*, 15(1), 4–14.

Shulman, L. (1987). Knowledge and teaching: Foundations of the new reform. *Harvard Educational Review*, 57(1), 1–22.

Wells, G. (2002). Inquiry as an orientation for learning, teaching and teacher education. In G. Wells & G. Claxton (Eds), *Learning for Life in the 21st Century* (pp. 197–210). Oxford, UK: Blackwell.

Wenger, E. (2006). *Communities of Practice: A Brief Introduction*. [Online] From http://www.ewenger.com/theory/communities_of_practice_intro.htm.

Vygotsky, L. S. (1971). *The Psychology of Art*. Cambridge, MA: MIT Press.

Vygotsky, L. S. (1978). *Mind in Society. The Development of Higher Psychological Processes*. Cambridge, MA: Harvard University Press.

Vygotsky, L. S. (1989). *Thought and Language*. Cambridge, MA: MIT Press.

WEBSITES

Metropolis Magazine—Disconnected Urbanism by Paul Goldberger
http://www.metropolismag.com/story/20070222/disconnected-urbanism
This is a link to a specific article, *Disconnected Urbanism* by Paul Goldberger. It is an interesting social commentary on the impact of telecommunications on society. It has been included because of its links to connectivism.

eLearn Magazine
http://elearnmag.acm.org/index.cfm
A useful online magazine to keep bookmarked on your computer. All of the articles are written by practising teachers, so the tips and tricks are very practical.

Tech & Learning
http://www.techlearning.com
Another technology magazine, which is written by social commentators, journalists and researchers. It has few contributions by teachers, but still has some interesting observations.

Some interesting blogs:

EmergingEdTech
http://www.emergingedtech.com/
A semi-professional blog site with multiple contributors.

MusicTechNet
http://mustech.net/
An individual blog by Joseph Pisano—very interesting for music resources, commentaries and other links that might be useful for teachers.

TeachingWithTechnology
http://falconphysics.blogspot.com/
Steve Dickie is a secondary school teacher in America. Here he charts his thoughts, experiences and outcomes of trying to teach using different technologies.

CHAPTER 3

Policy and trends: Preparing life-long learners

Learner Outcomes

After reading this chapter, you should be able to:

- understand what are the key policy documents and programs that shape Australian education systems
- describe the aspects of the Australian Curriculum that concern technology
- know some of the policy documents from other countries that are concerned with technology and education
- become familiar with some of the professional associations and research organisations that work in the area of educational technologies.

Key Terms

- British Educational Communications and Technology Agency (BECTA)
- Joint Information Systems Committee (JISC)
- Education Services Australia (ESA)
- The Melbourne Declaration
- Digital Education Revolution (DER)
- The Australian Curriculum

Introduction

Educations systems are directed by the national policy directives of the countries within which they are situated. Policy is a dynamic entity, new revisions, new initiatives and reforms are constantly making an impact on education systems as a whole and, more specifically, on schools and teachers. Policy directs what we teach, when we teach it and what the desired learning outcomes are. This chapter explores a number of different policy documents, initially those from Australia, so that we can see the current situation and developments that shape schooling. Then it explores policy documents from four other countries: New Zealand (due to its proximity), the United Kingdom (due to its long history in the area of technology and education), the United States of America (as it is a large country with enormous influence) and Singapore (as it is geographically close, but has had one of the longest policy histories in the area of technology and education). Finally, the chapter examines key research reports by organisations such as the **British Educational Communications and Technology Agency (BECTA**, now disbanded), **Joint Information Systems Committee (JISC)** and **Education Services Australia (ESA)**. These have been included as they often herald calls for change and have produced research reports used by various departments of education around the world to implement curriculum reform. All of these provide you with a context within which you can situate the current state of technology use in Australian schools.

National

This section of the chapter explores the different policy documents from both a national and international perspective. While we might assume that national documents are the only ones of concern to us, much of the policy reform and renewal that occurs in Australia is based on reforms around the world. There is a general sense that all education systems, regardless of country or context, are reviewing the objectives and learning outcomes of their education programs in view of the increasing digitalisation of the world. This is driven by key changes:

- the shift towards a global knowledge-based society
- the changing nature of professions and workplaces (increasingly more electronic)
- the impact of eCommerce and how we now make money
- the digitalising of our personal lives and recreational pursuits.

There are different skills needed by graduates of education systems and these need to be accommodated by education programs.

Australia

Within Australia, each of the states has local technology plans, policy documents and strategies set out for its own education system. At a national level there are two policy documents of note. The first is *The Melbourne Declaration on Educational Goals for Young Australians* (2008) set out by the Ministerial Council on Education, Employment, Training and Youth Affairs (MCEETYA).

> *Rapid and continuing advances in information and communication technologies (ICT) are changing the ways people share, use, develop and process information and technology. In this digital age, young people need to be highly skilled in the use of ICT. While schools already employ these technologies in learning, there is a need to increase their effectiveness significantly over the next decade. (p. 5)*

The *Melbourne Declaration* is a national document that explicitly sets out the educational goals for Australian education systems. It is supported by a series of actions plans and covers 2009–2012. It includes representations from all phases of schooling (early childhood, primary and secondary), all states of Australia and all systems of schooling (government, Catholic, independent). This working party is convened to meet biennially to examine progress and share best practices.

Goals	
1. Australian schooling promotes equity and excellence	'ensure that socioeconomic disadvantage ceases to be a significant determinant of educational outcomes' (p. 7)
	'promote personalised learning that aims to fulfil the diverse capabilities of each young Australian' (p. 7)
2. All young Australians become:	
successful learners	'have the essential skills in literacy and numeracy and are creative and productive users of technology, especially ICT, as a foundation for success in all learning areas' (p. 8)
confident and creative individuals	'are enterprising, show initiative and use their creative abilities' (p. 9)
active and informed citizens	'are responsible global and local citizens' (p. 9)
Actions (explicitly related to technology)	
Promoting a world-class curriculum and assessment	'As a foundation for further learning and adult life the curriculum will include practical knowledge and skills development in areas such as ICT and design and technology, which are central to Australia's skilled economy and provide crucial pathways to post-school success' (p. 13)

The second National policy is the *Digital Education Revolution* (**DER**), which has the explicit aim of 'contributing sustainable and meaningful change to teaching and learning in Australian schools that will prepare students for further education, training and to live and work in a digital world' (p. 1). This policy has several key aims and actions:

- The effective integration of information and communication technology (ICT) in Australian schools is in line with the government's broader education initiatives.
- The National Broadband Network (NBN) will deliver high-speed broadband to schools, homes and workplaces.
- The National Secondary School Computer Fund will provide computers and other ICT equipment for grades 9–12 with the aim of achieving one computer per student by 2011.

- The ICT Innovation Fund will fund projects that will help teachers and school leaders to better use ICTs in the classroom.
- The Online Curriculum Resources and Digital Architecture is aimed at developing digital resources, tools and infrastructure to support schools.

The new **Australian Curriculum** has been drafted to reflect the intentions of the *Melbourne Declaration* described above. Of the general competencies stated for the Australian Curriculum, the one pertaining to technology states:

> *Students develop ICT competence as they learn to use ICT effectively and appropriately when investigating, creating and communicating ideas and information at school, at home, at work and in their communities. (ACARA 2009, p. 19)*

This general competency is interpreted by the different subjects in a number of different ways. The Australian Curriculum is being introduced into schools in phases, with particular subjects allocated to each phase:

Phase 1: English, Mathematics, Science and History
Phase 2: Geography, Languages and the Arts
Phase 3: Design and Technology, Health and PE, Economics, ICT, Business, Civics and Citizenship.

Table 3.1 shows the aspects of the Australian Curriculum pertaining to technology from phases 1 and 2, which are currently in draft form and available for public feedback. It is surprising to note the differences between each of the subjects as they interpret the general competency statement, quoted above, in their subject area.

Table 3.1: Technology in phases 1 and 2 subjects

The Australian Curriculum—statements pertaining to technology competency
English
6.4 The role of digital technologies
Australians conduct their routine daily activities through a wide and complex range of oral and written language and images. Our sense of belonging to local, institutional, national, and, increasingly, virtual communities, and our ability to contribute meaningfully to those communities, increasingly depends on how well we communicate.
Digital and online technologies continue to profoundly transform how members of Australian society work, meet, keep in touch, express themselves, share, build and store knowledge, and access material for pleasure and learning. Clearly, digital and online materials present the English curriculum with new teaching opportunities. Enhancing the access of all teachers and students to these resources is critical.
Mathematics
6.5 The role of digital technologies
6.5.1 An important consideration in the structuring of the curriculum is to embed digital technologies so that they are not seen as optional tools. Digital technologies allow new approaches to explaining and presenting mathematics, as well as assisting in connecting representations and thus deepening understanding. The continuing evolution of digital technologies has progressively changed the work of mathematicians and school mathematics (consider the use of logarithm tables and the slide rule), and the curriculum must continue to adapt.
6.5.2 Digital technologies are now more powerful, accessible and pervasive. For example, modern mathematical technologies (hand-held devices or computer software) support numerical, statistical, graphical, symbolic, geometric and text functionalities. These may be used separately or in combination. Thus, a student could readily explore various aspects of the behaviour of a function or relation numerically, graphically, geometrically and algebraically using such technologies. These approaches allow greater

(Continued)

Table 3.1: Technology in phases 1 and 2 subjects (*Continued*)

The Australian Curriculum—statements pertaining to technology competency
Mathematics (*Continued*)

attention to meaning, transfer, connections and applications. Digital technologies can make previously inaccessible mathematics accessible, and enhance the potential for teachers to make mathematics interesting to more students, including the use of realistic data and examples.

6.5.3 The curriculum and associated assessment will allow teachers to use appropriate technologies in the classroom that support learning and teaching mathematics. The curriculum will advise on standards and expectations for parts of mathematics which are better done mentally, and the need for students to make appropriate choices about when to use technology. To give just one instance, it is reasonable to expect that school leavers will choose mental calculation to multiply or divide by 10 or 100, or to calculate a 10 per cent tip, and that nearly all will be able to accurately estimate 15 per cent of a quantity. In the senior secondary years, current courses allow appropriate use of computer algebra systems and dynamic geometry, and an option for this will be preserved in the new national mathematics curriculum. |
| **Science**

6.5 The role of digital technologies

While the Australian science curriculum will not mandate particular technologies it will be important to recognise in the curriculum the possibilities that digital technologies provide for helping students understand science. Some of the technologies available include: internet-based inquiry resources, digital images, computer simulations, probeware tools for science investigations and online data for scientific analysis. Use of digital technologies can help to engage and maintain the interest of students provided that the context of their use is relevant and interesting. |
| **History**

6.4 Role of digital technologies

An important consideration in the structuring of the curriculum is to embed digital technologies so that they are not seen as optional tools. There should also be recognition that the digital technologies available to enhance learning are rapidly changing.

Students and teachers have access to a growing range of online information critical for historical analysis and understanding. These include digitised online materials such as historical documents, books, newspapers, images and items from museum collections, as well as other online resources including databases, reference works (such as dictionaries of biography), and indexes to library holdings.

A range of computer applications provide new and less linear ways of thinking about, interpreting and representing data. These include new ways for capturing oral history, such as digital audio visual recording, and tools for the creation of online timelines and graphic organisers. A range of other programs and applications for data collection and management enhance opportunities for gathering, interpreting and presenting historical material. ICT tools such as wikis and blogs have the potential to enhance students' analytical thinking capabilities in their study of history.
The new curriculum should use and build upon resources such as online learning objects to provide support in navigating the ever-increasing amount of online materials available for historical inquiry. |
| **Geography (draft only)**

19. Students develop ICT competence as they learn to use ICT effectively and appropriately when investigating, creating and communicating ideas and information at school, at home, at work and in their communities.

20. The geography curriculum will provide many opportunities to develop and use ICT skills. These include basic computing skills and the use of computer software to locate, manage, analyse and present geographical information. Geographical ICT skills include the use and application of geographical information systems (GIS) and global positioning systems (GPS) to create, manage, represent and analyse spatial data; the viewing and analysis of spatial data through remote sensing and 3D visualisations (such as Google Earth), and the management and representation of geographical data in graphical and other visual forms. The use of spatial technology is a rapidly growing area of ICT, with significant employment opportunities in the expanding spatial industry. The use of spatial technologies will be integrated into the curriculum from early primary school onwards to ensure the development of students' ICT skills matches their cognitive abilities, and the application of those skills in the topics being studied. The curriculum will also provide opportunities for students to explore the effects of these technologies on places, the location of economic activities and on people's lives, and to understand the changing spatial relationships enabled by ICT. |

The Australian Curriculum—statements pertaining to technology competency
Languages (draft only)
67. Information and communication technology skills: Learning languages is enhanced through the use of target language multi-media resources, digital environments and technologies that provide for both synchronous and asynchronous learning experiences.
Accessing live target language environments and texts via digital media contributes to the development of information technology capabilities. Accessing diverse real time contexts extends the boundaries of the classroom. In accessing information on the internet, students need to learn to synthesise ideas and information critically, to interpret information and to consider the reliability of information.
The Arts (draft only)
83. In the Arts, students will develop and use skills that lead to ICT competence through forming ideas, plans, processes and solutions to challenges or tasks. They may use ICT in learning a concept, completing an activity or responding to a need. It may be self-generated or requested to investigate questions and issues. They will also communicate ideas and information to others while considering purpose, audience and technology and applying appropriate social and ethical protocols and practices.

© Australian Curriculum, Assessment and Reporting Authority 2012

Critical Reflection

The place of technology across the subject areas

As you can see from the table above, technology is present as a competency in each of the subjects comprising the Australian Curriculum. The numbers have been left purposefully in the table and show where in the curriculum document the statement pertaining to technology is located. Some subjects have this statement quite high in their list of competencies and abilities, while some have relegated it to quite low down the list.

- What do you think this means?
- Does it translate to how you would expect this subject to use technology?

Task:

Go back over the above table and re-examine the wording and intent regarding the use of technology in each of the different subjects. Now write two or three key words or phrases you think summarise this intention. Write your ideas in the table provided.

	Key words or phrases that summarise the intention of the place technology has in this subject
English	
Mathematics	
Science	
History	
Geography	
Languages	
The Arts	

- Which subjects do you think value technology the most?
- Which subjects do you think value technology the least?
- Were any of these results surprising to you? Why?
- What do you think would be the learning outcomes pertaining to technology for students studying these subjects?

Rest of the world

New Zealand

A key document of interest is *The Digital Strategy 2.0* which resembles some aspects of Australia's Digital Education Revolution (DER). *The Digital Strategy 2.0* has the following aims:

- the national roll-out of high-speed broadband to homes, schools and workplaces
- the national education network, which will connect libraries, researchers and schools to collaborate and share content
- a commitment to developing digital literacy skills in all learners
- the development of digital technology guidelines for senior secondary classes to ensure that students leave schools with specialist digital technology skills that will assist them to work in the ICT field post-school.

The United Kingdom

The United Kingdom has undergone some interesting changes in recent years. It was a leader in the area of technology and education, with organisations such as BECTA and JISC established with the sole purpose of conducting research and releasing reports on the use of technology in educational settings, its impact on learning outcomes and its use as possible solutions for problems within schools. Many developed countries looked to the UK to see where reform was needed. However, with a change of government and successive economic crises, significant change has occurred. BECTA was disbanded, popular and well-used facilities such as Teacher TV were closed down, and technology is no longer a priority in policy documents or reform. Regardless, we should examine one influential document that has had an enormous impact around the world. This was the 2009 *Harnessing Technology: Transforming Learning and Children's Services*. It sets out actions for the schoolwide system and has the following key objectives, to:

- transform teaching, learning and child development
- engage hard-to-reach groups in new ways
- build an open and accessible system with more information and services online
- achieve a new level of efficiency and effectiveness in delivery.

In 2010 a new government white paper was released, *The Importance of Teaching*, which sets out a reform program for the schools system that places teachers at the heart of school improvement. With such an emphasis upon teachers being the most important element in education, it fails to make any statements regarding technology, its use in teaching and learning, or the digital fluency and skills students require. Currently, a review of the national curriculum is underway and it will be interesting to see if the presence of technology capabilities in each of the different subject areas remains.

USA

The key policy document in recent years in the USA has been the controversial and much criticised *No Child Left Behind (NCLB)*. It is interesting that, in the USA, policy documents are passed and ratified as Acts of law. This is a marked difference from the practice in other countries, where departments of education are responsible for the writing and implementation of national and state policy. The *No Child Left Behind (NCLB) Act, 2001* was the policy of the previous administration in the USA under President George W Bush. It was heralded as a blueprint for reform and had seven key areas of concern:

1. accountability and assessment
2. teacher quality
3. budget
4. choice and charter schools
5. flexibility
6. reading
7. supplemental education services.

It was a highly criticised program of reform that did not explicitly have a place for technology within its areas of concerns or goals. With the change of administration, a new education reform policy was proposed by President Barak Obama in 2011, entitled *Educate to Innovate*, which has been seen as a response to low results in both national and international standardised tests (for example, 2006 PISA comparison results showed that American students ranked 21st out of 30 in science literacy among developed countries). This new policy document has a strong Science, Technology, Engineering and Mathematics (STEM) focus. It aims to:

- increase STEM literacy so that all students can learn deeply and think critically in science, maths, engineering and technology
- move American students from the middle of the pack to the top in the next decade
- expand STEM education and career opportunities for under-represented groups, including women and girls.

While technology is a key component in this policy document, earlier in 2009 President Obama released the National Education Technology Plan, entitled *Transforming American Education: Learning Powered by Technology*, which called for applying the advanced technologies used in our daily personal and professional lives throughout the education system in order to improve student learning, accelerate and scale up the adoption of effective practices, and use data and information for continuous improvement. It has five explicit goals which address one of the five essential components of learning powered by technology:

1. Learning—engage and empower
2. Assessment—measure what matters
3. Teaching—prepare and connect
4. Infrastructure—access and enable
5. Productivity—redesign and transform.

Singapore

The Ministry of Education (MOE) in Singapore has been more pre-emptive than its neighbouring countries in SE Asia and has had several policy documents pertaining to ICT since 1997. The current masterplan for ICT in education has four goals:

1. strengthen competencies for self-directed learning,
2. tailor learning experiences according to the way that each student learns best,

3. encourage students to go deeper and advance their learning, and

4. enable students to learn anywhere.

To achieve these goals, the policy has four strategies:

1. bring ICT into the core of the education process

2. improve teachers' ICT skills

3. improve the sharing of best practices among educators

4. upgrade schools' ICT infrastructure to keep up with developments.

Critical Reflection
Linking international policy to Australia

You have now explored the different policy documents from four international examples: New Zealand, the United Kingdom, the USA and Singapore. It should be apparent that there are a lot of similarities between these countries and their policy documents with regard to the aims and intent of Australian policy relating to technology and education.

Your task:

Go back over the four international examples and jot down any similarities to or differences between their policy documents and the intent expressed in them, and the *Australian Curriculum* and the *Digital Education Revolution* (DER).

	Similarities to the Australian Curriculum and the Digital Education Revolution (DER)	Differences from the Australian Curriculum and the Digital Education Revolution (DER)
New Zealand		
UK		
USA		
Singapore		

What were your findings? Were the policy documents similar or were they quite different?

Research organisations and reports

The British Educational Communications Technology Agency (BECTA)

The British Educational Communications Technology Agency (BECTA) was the government agency leading the drive in the United Kingdom to ensure the effective and innovative use of technology throughout learning. It was a well-used resource for teachers and schools that provided research reports, brief updates on new technologies and tied them all to the context of teaching and schools. The 2009 *Harnessing Technology: Transforming Learning and Children's Services* report has been described above, so we will explore two reports that were published during the final year of BECTA.

Narrowing the Gap (2010)

This was a report that sought to explore the ways technology can support approaches to narrowing the gap for underachieving and low-achieving learners in secondary schools. The research addressed how technology could be used to meet the challenge of equipping young people with the skills to participate in learning throughout their lives. The specific focus was on low-achieving and underachieving learners, with the aim of identifying and analysing a range of effective pedagogical approaches that may help to narrow the gap for such students in secondary schools.

The Impact of Technology: Value-added Classroom Practice (2010)

This impact report looked at the ways in which digital technologies are supporting learning by looking in detail at the learning practices mediated by ICT in nine secondary schools in which ICT for learning was well embedded. The report presented an analysis of 85 lesson logs in which teachers recorded their use of space, digital technology, and student outcomes in relation to student engagement and learning. The teachers who filled in the logs were also interviewed. The report showed that:

- ICT makes possible new forms of classroom practice as a result of reconfigurations of space, new ways of orchestrating class activities and new possibilities of representation.
- ICT creates the possibility of a wide variety of learning practices such as exposition with multimedia facilities, independent research and construction with ICT tools.

CASE STUDY

Interactive whiteboards

The following is a brief description of how different schools use interactive whiteboards from BECTA. Read it carefully and then answer the questions at the end.

Interactive whiteboards and enhancing teacher efficiency

The use of interactive whiteboards cannot only extend and develop teaching styles, it can also enhance teacher efficiency by, for example, saving time by promoting the sharing of resources, making it easier to prepare lessons in advance, improving the flow of lessons and facilitating the keeping of records for continuity of learning.

Park View Community School is a comprehensive school in Chester-le-Street, County Durham. Staff in its maths department have been working collaboratively to produce individual lessons for use on their interactive whiteboards, and they report much greater efficiency in their planning and lesson delivery, as they share resources and exploit good practice. They have found that quite basic starters, such as target boards and matching activities, can quickly be altered to coordinate with the specific topic and ability of the class, saving the teacher a great amount of time. These activities immediately engage the pupils, thus allowing smooth, effortless starts to the lesson.

Cottenham Village College is a specialist maths and computing college for pupils aged 11 to 16, and staff have found that reliable access to an interactive whiteboard, and the knowledge that materials prepared on the teacher's laptop can always be used in class, have had a significant impact on ICT usage within the maths department. Teachers report that the overt presentation of links to software, slide shows or word-processed documents that will be used during the lesson has had a positive effect on pupils' attention and on the smooth movement from one activity to another. Pupils are aware of what is coming next and how far they have progressed through the lesson, which helps them stay on task and is especially beneficial to lower-ability sets.

Mark Towlson at the Sandwich Technology School, Kent, uses his interactive whiteboard as the platform for all his teaching, because it gives him the ability to record the work he presents on it. For example, he opened a Year 7 lesson with a couple of questions written on the board. As the children came into the room, they immediately began working on the challenges set in their own notebooks, and then wrote their answers directly onto the board to wrap the exercise up. This gave late-comers access to the work after the rest of the class had moved on.

For the main part of the lesson, pupils were presented with a 'spider chart' on the interactive whiteboard. Their initial timed task was to jot notes in their books about what they knew about angles. They then added their contribution directly to the board, which again recorded their contributions for later revisiting or for absent pupils. Mark's approach demonstrates the efficiency that interactive whiteboards can bring to classroom practice, and the ability they give to save and re-use all the spontaneous good practice that goes on as a matter of course in classrooms.

Questions for reflection

1. What strategies or tips can you can take away from these case studies? List them.
2. Do you agree that the use of IWBs can make teaching and planning more efficient?
3. Is there anything you would change in any of these examples? Something that could be done more effectively? Something you wouldn't do?

The Joint Information Systems Committee (JISC)

The acronym JISC stands for the Joint Information Systems Committee, and while this appears to be a dated label, this organisation has transformed itself over the years to become a leader in research and use of technology in higher educational settings both within the United Kingdom and internationally. However, this does not exclude its value to early, primary and secondary phases of schooling. Much of JISC's work is on emerging technologies and their practical use in education, which can be applied to all phases of learning. It has also focused a lot of research effort on the up-skilling of university graduates, including pre-service teachers, in digital technologies. As an example of this point, two have been selected for you below.

Getting started with Second Life (2009)

Second Life is a free 3-D multi-user virtual world developed by Linden Labs in 2003, and is inhabited by millions of residents across the world. It is used as a platform for education by many institutions, with over one hundred regions used for educational purposes. This guide is aimed at those who are wanting to use Second Life for teaching. It provides in-depth descriptions of all aspects of the immersive world both for direct use and facilitating others' use.

Effective Assessment in the Digital Age (2010)

Effective Assessment in a Digital Age draws on recent JISC reports and case studies depicting different contexts and modes of learning to explore the relationship between technology-enabled assessment and feedback practices and meaningful, well-supported learning experiences. It is proposed that technology, if used appropriately, can add value to any of the activities associated with assessment: from establishing a culture of good practice to the processes involved in submission, marking and return of assessed assignments; from the delivery of assessment to the generation of feedback by practitioners or peers.

Personal Reflection
Tips for planning

The following suggestions are based on a help sheet produced by BETCA.

How to plan an email project

Email is fast becoming a major medium of communication. A planned and monitored email project between two schools is an excellent way of increasing pupils' skills in this increasingly important area.

To begin, locate a partner school and establish good communication with the teachers there. Together you will have to decide on what your joint project will be, as well as clear aims for your pupils, using email. It's a good idea to meet face to face if you can.

Some of the decisions you have to make relate to:

- timing
- how to group learners
- introducing the work
- topics
- ensuring that communication is appropriate
- the mechanisms needed to deal with problems.

The students should understand:

- The language in emails should be appropriate for a general audience. Email is not a private medium and can be used for both 'one-to-one' and 'one-to-many' messages.
- Names or pen names must be included, and email should be addressed to a specific recipient, either an individual or a whole class.
- Any restrictions on the time when email can be written or sent should be explicit. Some schools may expect email to be written offline. Email may be checked at random or at set times.

- Email will be removed from the host server when accessed.
- Whether email (and any attachments) should be printed out or stored electronically will have to be decided.
- Rules and sanctions are in place to protect and support people in both schools.

Integrating email with classroom activity

All children should be involved in receiving, creating and sending email during the project. Groups or individuals will need time to collect email, reflect on it, create a response and send it. You will have to accommodate different speeds of working and different content. You will need to consider whether exchanges beyond the project can be exploited.

Task

- What grades could you use this activity with?
- Which content areas could such a project be tied to?
- Can you for see any difficulties?
- How do you think the students would respond to this type of project?

Education Services Australia (ESA)

Education Services Australia (ESA) was established in 2010, and is a merger of the Curriculum Corporation and Education.au. It is a national, not-for-profit company owned by all Australian Education ministers. It has an interesting set of priorities and was established to support the delivery of national priorities and initiatives in the schools, training and higher education sectors, in particular to:

1. advance key nationally agreed education initiatives, programs and projects by providing services such as:
   - researching, testing and developing effective and innovative technologies and communication systems for use in education;
   - devising, developing and delivering curriculum and assessment, professional development, career and information support services;
   - facilitating the pooling, sharing and distribution of knowledge, resources and services to support and promote e-learning; and
   - supporting national infrastructure to ensure access to quality assured systems and content and interoperability between individuals, entities and systems;

2. create, publish, disseminate and market curriculum and assessment materials, ICT-based solutions, products and services to support learning, teaching, leadership and administration; and

3. act, as required, as the legal company for the Ministerial Council for Education, Early Childhood Development and Youth Affairs (MCEECDYA).

There is one key technology program currently underway, due for completion in 2012, ICT in Everyday Learning—Teacher Online Toolkit, which aims to:

change classroom practice by increasing teachers' capacity to incorporate technologies into teaching and learning as they implement the Australian Curriculum. It will assist teachers to access online professional learning with local support to analyse, plan and implement changes to their teaching approaches and to access quality online resources. (ESA 2011)

Summary

This chapter explores the different policy documents, both nationally and internationally, concerned with the use of technology in education. Education systems are directed by the national policies of the countries within which they are situated. Policy is a dynamic entity; new revisions, new initiatives and reforms are constantly making an impact on education systems as a whole and, more specifically, on schools and teachers. Policy directs what we teach, when we teach it and what the desired learning outcomes are. Most of the countries presented in this chapter share a number of common intents regarding the use of technology in education.

It is an exciting time in Australia with the new Australian Curriculum and its clear prioritising of technology as a key competency. This chapter has provided a context for the ideas suggested in Chapter 1, specifically the changing nature of who our students are and their digital expectation of the education systems they are studying within. In Chapter 4, this concept, digital expectancy, will be explored more. Keeping in mind the intentions of the various policy documents we have just explored, digital expectancy will be situated within this educational climate of change.

FURTHER READING

ACARA (2009). *The Australian Curriculum. Phases 1, 2 and 3*. [Online] From http://www.acara.edu.au/curriculum.html.

BECTA (2009). *Harnessing Technology: Transforming Learning and Children's Services*. [Online] From http://webarchive.nationalarchives.gov. uk/20110130111510/http:/www.becta.org.uk.

BECTA (2010). *Narrowing the Gap*. [Online] From http://webarchive. nationalarchives.gov.uk/20110130111510/http:/www.becta.org.uk.

BECTA (2010). *The Impact of Technology: Value-added Classroom Practice*. [Online] From http://webarchive.nationalarchives.gov.uk/20110130111510/ http:/www.becta.org.uk.

DEEWR (2007). *Digital Education Revolution (DER)*. [Online] From http://www. deewr.gov.au/Schooling/DigitalEducationRevolution/Pages/default.aspx.

Department of Education (2010). *The Importance of Teaching*. [Online] From http:// www.education.gov.uk/.

MCEETYA (2008). *The Melbourne Declaration on Educational Goals for Young Australians* [Online] From http://www.mceetya.edu.au/mceecdya/melbourne_ declaration,25979.html.

JISC (2009). *Getting Started with Second Life*. [Online] From http://www.jisc. ac.uk/publications/generalpublications/2009/gettingstartedsecondlife.aspx.

JISC (2010). *Effective Assessment in the Digital Age*. [Online] From http://www.jisc.ac.uk/whatwedo/programmes/elearning/assessment/digiassess.aspx.

Ministry of Education (2008). *Masterplan for ICT in Education (Singapore)*. [Online] From http://www.moe.gov.sg/media/press/2008/08/moe-launches-third-masterplan.php.

Ministry of Economic Development (2008). *The Digital Strategy 2.0*. [Online] From http://www.med.govt.nz/templates/StandardSummary_____43904.aspx.

US Department of Education (2001). *No Child Left Behind (NCLB)*. [Online] From http://www.ed.gov/esea.

US Department of Education (2011). *Educate to Innovate*. [Online] From http://www.whitehouse.gov/issues/education/educate-innovate.

US Department of Education (2009). *National Education Technology Plan*. [Online] From http://www.ed.gov/technology/netp-2010.

WEBSITES

ACARA

http://www.acara.edu.au/curriculum.html

The Australian Curriculum, Assessment and Reporting Authority is the body responsible for the Australian Curriculum. This site has all of the new curriculum documents, plus the drafts open for public feedback. There are links to assessment and reporting programs, such as The National Assessment Program, NAPLAN and MySchool. The material is updated regularly and, with all the changes in this area within Australia, it is a site that should be bookmarked on your computer.

ESA

http://www.esa.edu.au/

Education Services Australia is an interesting organisation, which primarily enacts the reforms and policy of MCEECDYA. Along with this, there are several projects currently being conducted concerning technology. It is a body that will probably undergo some changes in the future.

JISC

http://www.jisc.ac.uk/

The Joint Information Systems Committee is a government organisation concerned with the use of technology in higher education. It has a number of research reports freely available for downloading, plus useful 'tips and tricks' sheets for teachers.

DEEWR

http://www.deewr.gov.au/Schooling/DigitalEducationRevolution/Pages/default.aspx

The Department of Education, Employment and Workplace Relations, is the national education authority in Australia. Of particular note on this site is the *Digital Education Revolution*.

CHAPTER 4

Digital expectancy:
It's all about
behaviour

Learner Outcomes

After reading this chapter, you should be able to:

- understand what is meant by the phrase 'digital expectancy'
- understand the six elements that drive digital expectancy
- understand how digital expectancy will changed teaching
- understand how the internet impacts on digital expectancy.

Key Terms

- digital divide
- digital expectancy
- knowledge-based society
- electronic era

Introduction

This chapter concludes and brings together all of the ideas and themes for Part 1. In Chapter 1 we set the scene for why a digital pedagogy was needed, making strong links to the current education systems and the digital expectations of students, parents, employers and the wider community. In Chapter 2 we examined theoretical underpinnings for the use of technology in education. Here, eleven theories were presented; some of them were theories of learning that had been re-shaped due to the addition of technology to learning, while others were new theories that have emerged as a result of digital technologies and their use in learning. In Chapter 3 we examined policy documents, both national and international examples, in order to see the current context of education systems regarding technology. From these three chapters, it is clear that there are a number of drivers behind the use of technology in teaching and learning:

- the changing nature of the world—the global information society within which we are placed
- the changing nature of the digital technologies themselves—more useable, mobile and applicable to learning contexts
- theoretical reform—how we learn has changed due to the impact of technology on our lives
- policy—policy documents concerned with the use of technology in education exist around the world, in both developed and developing countries, indicating the priority technology has within education systems
- research organisations—associations such as BECTA and JISC (Chapter 3), which produce research reports on the use of various technologies in educational settings.

This chapter examines one final driver behind this push for the use of technology in teaching and learning: digital expectations. As suggested in Chapter 1, students expect that their schooling will be rich in digital technologies. The non-schooling part of their lives is, and they expect their schooling to be likewise.

Increasingly, parents, employers and the wider community expect the education system to produce technologically fluent students who can use a wide variety of digital technologies, and who can adapt to emerging technologies. Parents are aware of the increasingly digital world and normally expect the teaching and learning their children engage in to include digital technologies. Schools are increasingly asked to bridge the **digital divide** between what the parents can afford and what they would like their children to experience or be fluent in. Employers are also digitally expectant. Whether their employees are students doing a part-time job during their secondary schooling or people leaving the education system for the world of work, employers expect them to be able to use digital technologies.

Background

Students today have been born into a digital world, but it is an unequal digital world. Not everyone will have had access to the same technologies, nor will they have the same understandings of technology. We might assume that Australian society is relatively classless, but in reality we have very distinct layers based upon socio-economic factors. We might assume that our students all know how to use a PC or laptop, that they can send a text using a mobile phone, can use email or can use common software programs such as Word or PowerPoint. Actually, the reality is far from this. Some interesting statistics to set the scene:

- Broadband is accessed by 62 per cent of households in Australia, with 86 per cent having internet access.
- The Australian Capital Territory has the highest proportion of internet connections (74 per cent of households), while Tasmania (49 per cent) and South Australia (54 per cent) have the lowest.
- If households have no children under 15, or have lower household incomes, they are significantly less likely to have an internet connection.
- Children aged 5–14 years use the internet for (in order from highest to lowest) educational activities (85 per cent) and online games (42 per cent).
- Of children aged 5–14 years, 42 per cent used the internet for 2 hours or less per week, while 4 per cent were online for 20 hours or more.
- Of children aged 5–14 years, 31 per cent had their own mobile phone, and of this group only 4 per cent used their phone to access the internet.
- Mobile wireless internet (excluding mobile handset) connections (44 per cent) now exceed digital subscriber line (DSL) connections (41 per cent) in Australia. Mobile wireless (excluding mobile handset connections) was the fastest growing internet access technology in actual numbers, increasing from 4.2 million in December 2010 to 4.8 million in June 2011

The statistics concerning ICTs in Australia tend to focus upon internet connections and mobile devices. Very little has been collected on how these devices are used and for what purpose, or who is using them. What is clear is that there is an increasing amount of internet connection in Australian homes. It would be useful to know the types of uses these internet connections have in Australian homes. Some ideas:

- internet browsing—for entertainment and personal reasons (for example, banking, bill paying, information from news sites, internet-TV, online gaming)
- email—communication for personal and work-related (including education) reasons
- communication—online chat and Web 2.0 applications (MSN, Facebook)
- telephone connection—VOIP phones
- Cable TV.

These are generally lifestyle tools, but they do contribute towards digital fluency and competency in several ways:

- familiarity with terms (for example email, Google, Bpay, Facebook)
- familiarity with some digital technologies
- a positive attitude towards digital technologies

- experience of the variety of uses and types of technologies
- developing skills and fluency in these technologies.

There is an important distinction to make here, and that is between the types of technologies we use in our private life and the types we use in our professional lives, including education and schooling.

Students in Australia

The current student population, from early years through to secondary school, have been born into a digital world. This generation is highly connected, as many of this generation have had life-long use of communications and media technologies such as the World Wide Web, instant messaging, text messaging, MP3 players, mobile phones and YouTube, earning them the nickname 'digital natives' (see Chapter 1). No longer limited to the home computer, the internet is now increasingly carried in students' pockets on mobile internet devices such as mobile phones. A marked difference between previous generational groupings and today's student generation is that members of the former remember life before the take-off of mass technology, while the members of the latter have been born into an era of mass technology, postmodernism and globalisation. Their parents are working part-time or becoming stay-at-home parents so that children are raised by them and other family members instead of a daycare facility.

However, today's students would be best described as having varying levels of digital experience. As we have suggested, there is a broad range of differing technologies in homes across Australia, and while the overall rate of connectivity (that is, internet connection) in homes is high, this is unevenly distributed. Lower socio-economic households do not have the same access to technologies as their middle and upper socio-economic counterparts. Also, the types of technologies and how they are used vary considerably across households, so the assumptions we make about digital fluency and skills must be cautious. What we can assume with confidence is an enthusiasm for and desire to use technology.

In October 2008 the Ministerial Council for Education, Early Childhood Development and Youth Affairs (MCEEDCYA) released the *National Assessment Program—ICT Literacy Years 6 and 10 Report*. This was the second sample assessment for ICT (the first was conducted in 2005), with 5604 year 6 students from 299 schools and 5322 year 10 students from 292 schools participating. The participating students were from both government and non-government schools. The assessment measured students' ability to access, manage, integrate and evaluate information, develop new understandings and communicate with others in order to participate effectively in society.

Results of the assessment show that, nationally, 57 per cent of year 6 students reached or exceeded the year 6 proficient standard and 66 per cent of year 10 students reached or exceeded the year 10 proficient standard. This represents improvement on the 2005 assessment results of 8 percentage points for year 6 students and 5 percentage points for year 10 students. The report also found that a student's socioeconomic background had the biggest effect on their performance, with 41 per cent of year 6 students whose parents are from the 'unskilled manual, office and sales' occupational groups attaining the proficient standard, compared to 72 per cent of students whose parents are from the 'senior managers and professionals' occupational group. In year 10, the corresponding figures are 52 per cent and 78 per cent.

CASE STUDY
Student expectations of teachers' use of technology

It is apparent that students expect to be taught via technology and as such expect their teachers to be able to use technology well. But it is not the random use of technology that is hoped for by students, but technology that enhances their learning that is appropriate to the learning objectives and has been carefully selected by the teacher to enhance their lesson.

Read the following case study—it describes the expectations of students in secondary school regarding teachers and their use of technology. It is based on a large-scale project conducted in America. As you read it, think about the Australian context. It is representative of the current generation regardless of geographical location.

Students' learning expectations begin with the expertise and passion of the teacher. The following student comments represent the general perspective of students:

- To me, my success in the classroom depends on the teacher. If the teacher is prepared and knowledgeable about their particular field, I know I can expect to learn from their knowledge as well as know what is expected of me.

- I love when I come back from a class where my teacher's knowledge of a particular field is astonishing.

- It's great when the professor is passionate about the field. They are usually knowledgeable about their field. In turn, that knowledge and passion rubs off on me, and that's my ideal class environment!

These students still view teachers who are committed to teaching as the key ingredient for learning success. However, they have high expectations for faculty members' technology knowledge and skill. Ranked in order of preference:

1. The teacher's experience and expertise.
2. The teacher's ability to customise the class using the current technology available.
3. The teacher's ability to professionally convey lecture points using contemporary software.

Given the technology expectations of Net G-ers, it is no surprise that they may also have significant expectations regarding the use of technology to support learning. However, those expectations appear tied to teachers and *their* ability to use technology correctly.

Based on: Oblinger & Oblinger (2005). *Educating the Net Generation.*

Now answer the following questions:

1. Do you agree with the quotes from students listed above?
2. What do you think is meant by the phrase 'customise the class using the current technology available'? How does this apply to your phase of

learning? Can you think of some examples of technology that you can use that would illustrate this point?

3. The emphasis would appear to be on the technology skills and digital fluency of the teacher—do you think that is correct? Why?

Digital expectancy

Students expect that their schooling, like the non-schooling part of their lives, will be rich in digital technologies. **Digital expectancy** is an attitude, and it is not necessarily negative. It is evidence of a positive engagement with the digital world and an eagerness to become a fully participating member of the **knowledge-based society**. It is the product of a number of factors:

- the **electronic era**—increasingly we are surrounded by more electronic devices than previous generations have experienced; this would include household, communication, recreational and work devices
- the knowledge-based society—knowledge drives the current economic model, and knowledge or information is electronic
- eConsumerism—we shop electronically, search for items and respond to trends electronically, and this has significantly changed our behaviours
- digital communication—the majority of our communication is conducted electronically.

All of these factors have contributed to a digital world in which our students wish to participate. It has produced a context that has resulted in the expression of digital expectancy.

The six drivers of digital expectancy are students, teachers, parents, employers, government and the wider community.

Figure 4.1: The six drivers of digital expectancy

These drivers are the typical stakeholders in the schooling system. They have interests in the outcomes, whether due to being or having children participating in education, working in education, being employers of the graduates from the education system, being directors and policy framers of education plans, or being part of the context within which the education system is situated. 'Digital expectancy' is a term that encompasses a lot of different views, by disparate groups that collectively seek the same objective, the development of digital fluency and skills in students within our education system. How do stakeholders express their digital expectancy?

- *Students* do so via discussions with teachers and peers, and providing feedback either formally or informally.
- *Parents* do so via parent/teacher interviews, discussions with the school management team, P & T meetings, and informal discussion with other parents and teaching staff.
- *Teachers* do so via discussions with peers, discussions and collaboration with students, requests for professional development opportunities and discussion with school management.
- *Government* does so via curriculum and syllabus reform, new focus areas and policy initiatives, training opportunities, press releases and enewsletters.
- *Employers* do so via feedback to government and schools, and reports in the media.
- *The wider community* does so via feedback to schools through local events, local newspaper reports, support staff, school–community discussion and via the media.

All of these channels of communication, sources of information and opportunities for discussion have created an environment where the expectations of all education stakeholders can be heard clearly.

Personal Reflection

How digitally expectant are you?

As a pre-service teacher, you are currently engaged in either an undergraduate or postgraduate program. You might be studying immediately upon completion of grade 12, you might have spent some time working prior to starting study or you might be re-training and hoping to enter teaching as a new profession. It is very likely that you have a different set of skills or level of digital fluency than your peers. Think about your expectations when you started this program, and study and answer the following questions:

- Did you have any expectations regarding technology and this program? For example, did you expect to learn using digital technologies?
- Did you expect to learn how to use digital technologies in your teaching? If so, have you been taught any of those skills?
- What level of technology is used in your program? Was it what you expected? Or did you expect more or less technology use?
- If you have been on a teaching practicum, did your supervising teacher expect you to be digitally fluent?

As discussed above, stakeholders have a variety of channels through which to communicate their expectations to schools and the wider education system. We have described this as being a general digital expectation that students will graduate from the education system digitally fluent and skilled.

But what, specifically, does this mean? In later sections of this book, we will look at how to develop digital fluency in learners in each phase of school and examine digital technologies that could be used in each phase. What skills does each stakeholder expect?

- *Students* expect skills to learn more effectively, more current and up-to-date information and the ability to use different technologies.
- *Parents* expect skills for their children to complete their education successfully and participate in the world.
- *Teachers* expect skills to teach in a more current, engaging and effective manner.
- *Government* expects skills that will equip members of society to participate in and share in the opportunities afforded by the global knowledge-based society.
- *Employers* expect skills that enable employees to be effective and help with the success of the company.
- *The wider community* expects skills that enable opportunities and assist the community itself.

Critical Reflection

What are the digital expectations of the different stakeholders?

The list of skills above for each of the stakeholders is crafted in general terms. Let's now take the opportunity to be more specific and aligned with your particular phase of learning. For your phase of learning, decide on the possible digital expectations each of these stakeholders may have. Try to be specific; list actual software programs, skills and experiences. An example has been provided to illustrate your task.

Stakeholder	Learning phase	Expected skills
Students	Secondary	How to use a word processor to produce a document
Students		
Teachers		
Parents		
Employers		
Government		
Wider community		

Now answer the following questions:

1. Were some of the stakeholders easier to do than others? Why?
2. Were you able to come up with something for each of the stakeholders? If not, why?
3. Was there a difference in the types of expectations each stakeholder group had? Or were they similar?
4. Do you think stakeholder expectations might influence your planning when you are a teacher?

How digital expectancy will change teaching

Digital expectancy will be responsible for driving change in teaching and learning. It is not a reactionary movement, but is built on theoretical research on the impact technology has on learning, the increasingly digital world in which we are situated and the expectations of all stakeholders in education. As we have suggested above, digital expectancy is not limited to students, but includes six stakeholder groups. All these drivers have particular emphases that will drive change.

Driver	Areas of emphasis
Students	Expect and desire to learn and be taught via a range of digital technologies.
Teachers	Desire to use digital technologies in their teaching and learning in order to engage and motivate learners, and equip learners with the necessary skills to succeed at school.
Parents	Expect their children will develop digital fluency and skills in different digital technologies.
Employers	Expect that their employee will have a breadth of experience and level of digital fluency that will support their work.
Government	React to electorate demands (i.e. those of parents, employers and the wider community). Aim to develop a digitally fluent workforce and life-long learners.
Wider community	Expect schools to develop digital fluency in learners and have a range of technologies for learners to use.

In 2011, JISC released an important document that was concerned with how teaching and education was undergoing change due to digital technologies, entitled *Emerging Practice in a Digital Age*. Within this document it was suggested that:

> *These technologies are changing the jobs people do. We need to use these technologies because they transform the nature of teaching and learning, and because the world people are going into—the jobs, the economy that education is supposed to be servicing and supporting—is being changed by these technologies. (JISC 2011, p. 44)*

So what actual changes could we expect as a result of digital technologies? There has been much research and publication on this topic: much that is speculative of new technologies emerging; some positive, heralding a new way of teaching and learning; some negative, prophesying the demise of teachers. It is often a highly emotive topic, but there are some aspects that we can confidently describe:

- Information will increasingly be used electronically—eBooks and websites—and costly printed texts will be less prevalent in the classroom.
- How we communicate with students and parents will be electronic—email, enewsletters, blogs and class websites will become more common.
- Classrooms will physically change—data projects, interactive whiteboards, computers, WiFi and networks will be typical.
- How we conduct assessment will be more electronic—ePortfolios, multimedia, electronic documents and electronic exams will replace current paper-based assessment practices.

- Teaching will be less teacher-centered and more collaborative, with students and teachers working together.
- Students will work more independently.
- Students will collaborate differently, aided by technology.
- The classroom will no longer be limited to a physical space; it will have links beyond its geographical constraints.
- Teachers will prepare lessons electronically—they may not present information in the same way; they may structure lessons differently; they may use different tools.

These are just some of the ways digital technology and digital expectations will change teaching. These are all largely concerned with physical aspects—how learning occurs and how lessons are delivered; but what about the content of those lessons? Will they also change due to digital expectations? Yes. We are already seeing change to our syllabus documents: as they undergo review, new phrases are appearing; and as new curriculum documents are drafted, technology is present in the objectives and anticipated outcomes. Let's examine this statement by closely looking at the Australian Curriculum. *The Shape of the Australian Curriculum, Phase 1* is a curriculum document that covers foundation to grade 10 in the areas of English, Mathematics, Science and History. Of the general competencies stated for the Australian Curriculum, the one pertaining to technology states:

> *Students develop ICT competence as they learn to use ICT effectively and appropriately when investigating, creating and communicating ideas and information at school, at home, at work and in their communities. (ACARA 2009, p. 19).*

This general competency is interpreted by the different subjects in a number of different ways. Some subject areas appear to emphasise the communication aspects while others are more concerned with skills in search for and understanding data. Below are the aspects of the Australian Curriculum pertaining to technology in the English, Mathematics, Science and History curriculums. It is surprising to note the differences between each of the subjects as they interpret the general competency statement above in their subject area.

The Australian Curriculum—statements pertaining to technology competency

English

6.4 The role of digital technologies

Australians conduct their routine daily activities through a wide and complex range of oral and written language and images. Our sense of belonging to local, institutional, national, and, increasingly, virtual communities, and our ability to contribute meaningfully to those communities, increasingly depends on how well we communicate.

Digital and online technologies continue to profoundly transform how members of Australian society work, meet, keep in touch, express themselves, share, build and store knowledge, and access material for pleasure and learning. Clearly, digital and online materials present the English curriculum with new teaching opportunities. Enhancing the access of all teachers and students to these resources is critical.

Mathematics

6.5 The role of digital technologies

6.5.1 An important consideration in the structuring of the curriculum is to embed digital technologies so that they are not seen as optional tools. Digital technologies allow new approaches to explaining and presenting mathematics, as well as assisting in connecting representations and thus deepening understanding. The continuing evolution of digital technologies has progressively changed the work of mathematicians and school mathematics (consider the use of logarithm tables and the slide rule), and the curriculum must continue to adapt.

(Continued)

The Australian Curriculum—statements pertaining to technology competency (*Continued*)

Mathematics (*Continued*)

6.5.2 Digital technologies are now more powerful, accessible and pervasive. For example, modern mathematical technologies (hand-held devices or computer software) support numerical, statistical, graphical, symbolic, geometric and text functionalities. These may be used separately or in combination. Thus, a student could readily explore various aspects of the behaviour of a function or relation numerically, graphically, geometrically and algebraically using such technologies. These approaches allow greater attention to meaning, transfer, connections and applications. Digital technologies can make previously inaccessible mathematics accessible, and enhance the potential for teachers to make mathematics interesting to more students, including the use of realistic data and examples.

6.5.3 The curriculum and associated assessment will allow teachers to use appropriate technologies in the classroom that support learning and teaching mathematics. The curriculum will advise on standards and expectations for parts of mathematics which are better done mentally, and the need for students to make appropriate choices about when to use technology. To give just one instance, it is reasonable to expect that school leavers will choose mental calculation to multiply or divide by 10 or 100, or to calculate a 10 per cent tip, and that nearly all will be able to accurately estimate 15 per cent of a quantity. In the senior secondary years, current courses allow appropriate use of computer algebra systems and dynamic geometry, and an option for this will be preserved in the new national mathematics curriculum.

Science

6.5 The role of digital technologies

While the Australian science curriculum will not mandate particular technologies it will be important to recognise in the curriculum the possibilities that digital technologies provide for helping students understand science. Some of the technologies available include: internet-based inquiry resources, digital images, computer simulations, probeware tools for science investigations and on-line data for scientific analysis. Use of digital technologies can help to engage and maintain the interest of students provided that the context of their use is relevant and interesting.

History

6.4 Role of digital technologies

An important consideration in the structuring of the curriculum is to embed digital technologies so that they are not seen as optional tools. There should also be recognition that the digital technologies available to enhance learning are rapidly changing.

Students and teachers have access to a growing range of online information critical for historical analysis and understanding. These include digitised online materials such as historical documents, books, newspapers, images and items from museum collections, as well as other online resources including databases, reference works (such as dictionaries of biography), and indexes to library holdings.

A range of computer applications provide new and less linear ways of thinking about, interpreting and representing data. These include new ways for capturing oral history, such as digital audio visual recording, and tools for the creation of online timelines and graphic organisers. A range of other programs and applications for data collection and management enhance opportunities for gathering, interpreting and presenting historical material. ICT tools such as wikis and blogs have the potential to enhance students' analytical thinking capabilities in their study of history.

The new curriculum should use and build upon resources such as online learning objects to provide support in navigating the ever-increasing amount of online materials available for historical inquiry.

© Australian Curriculum, Assessment and Reporting Authority 2012

The impact of the internet on digital expectancy

No one other technological innovation has had as much impact on the behaviours and expectations of the world population than the internet. It has changed how we search for information, how we interact with it (for example, cloud computing and eBooks) and success in life, be it professionally, educationally or personally relies upon your abilities to use the internet effectively. Yet, as teachers, we often overlook teaching our students the basics of this technology as we assume that everyone knows how to use it! The internet facilitates the sharing of ideas and these in turn feed feelings of digital expectancy. We share ideas, see what others are doing, hear about new and emerging technologies and we want to ensure that we have a place in this new emerging world. Traditional ways of doing things just don't compare with the examples we see in the flood of information at our fingertips. The statistics of internet use are interesting. We have seen that 86 per cent of households in Australia have an internet connection. If you examine the map below, we are not the biggest users of the internet.

Figure 4.2: Global use of the internet by households

	100,000,000+
	50,000,000 – 100,000,000
	20,000,000 – 50,000,000
	10,000,000 – 20,000,000
	5,000,000 – 10,000,000
	2,000,000 – 5,000,000
	1,000,000 – 2,000,000
	500,000 – 1,000,000
	100,000 – 5,000,000
	10,000 – 100,000
	– 10,000

(UNESCO 2006, Creative Commons)

Summary

This chapter brings together all of the ideas and themes of Part 1. In Chapter 1 we established why a digital pedagogy was needed, making strong links to the current education systems and the digital expectations of students, parents, employers and the wider community. In Chapter 2 we examined theoretical underpinnings for the use of technology in education. Here, eleven theories were presented: some of them were theories of learning that had been re-shaped due to the addition of technology to learning, while others were new theories that had emerged as a result of digital technologies and their use in learning. In Chapter 3 we examined policy documents, both national and international, in order to see the context of education systems regarding technology.

In this chapter we have explored in greater detail the concept of digital expectancy. This began with an examination of the current situation in Australian homes regarding internet access and a general snapshot of the characteristics of students in Australia. Digital expectancy was defined, and the six drivers of its impact on the education system were examined in greater detail. These were then examined to see how they would change teaching. The chapter concluded with one final aspect, an examination of how the internet impacts on digital expectancy. Currently, the internet has an enormous impact on the way we communicate and search for information, and this has carried over into how we learn. Increasingly, learning includes web-based resources; so, teachers need to teach learners skills in how to use the internet and how to critically evaluate the information they find.

Where to now? The following sections are concerned with the different phases of schooling. Part 2 (Chapters 5, 6 and 7) focuses on the early and primary years, exploring how technology could be used in these phases of schooling, examining several examples of technologies suited to these phases and then concluding by presenting the characteristics of a digital pedagogy for creative technologies. Part 3 (Chapters 8, 9 and 10) is arranged in a similar fashion, it starts with an exploration of the use of technology in the primary and early secondary phases of schooling, followed by examples of suitable technologies and then the digital pedagogy most suited to this phase. Part 4 (Chapters 11, 12 and 13) presents the secondary phase of learning, but as this phase of learning is divided into separate discipline areas, there are some significant differences in these chapters. There is still an exploration of the uses of technology in this phase, examples of suitable technologies and a digital pedagogy suited to teachers in this phase, but it is structured to accommodate the discipline-specific nature of secondary schooling.

FURTHER READING

DEEWR (2008). *Review of Australian Higher Education. Final Report.* [Online] From http://www.deewr.gov.au/HigherEducation/Review/Pages/Review ofAustralianHigherEducationReport.aspx.

Dye, J. (2007). *Meet Generation C: Creatively Connecting through Content.* [Online] From http://www.econtentmag.com.

Goldberger, P. (2003). *Disconnected Urbanism.* [Online] From http://www. metropolismag.com/html/content_1103/obj/index.html.

Lenhart, A., Madden, M., Ranking Macgill, A., & Smith, A. (2007). *Teens and Social Media.* Pew Internet and American Life Project. [Online] From http://www. pewinternet.org/pdfs/PIP_Teens_Social_Media_Final.pdf.

Lessig, L. (2002). *The Future of Ideas.* New York: Vintage Books.

Lorenzo, G., Oblinger, D. & Dziuban, C. (2006). *How Choice, Co-Creation, and Culture Are Changing What It Means to Be Net Savvy.* [Online] From http:// connect.educause.edu/Library/EDUCAUSE+Quarterly/HowChoiceCo CreationandCul/40008.

McNeely, B. (2005). Using Technology as a Learning Tool, Not Just the Cool New Thing. *Educating the Net Generation.* EDUCAUSE E-book. [Online] From http:// www.educause.edu/UsingTechnologyasaLearningTool,NotJusttheCoolNew Thing/6060.

Oblinger, D. G., & Oblinger, J. L. (2005). *Educating the Net Generation*. [Online] From http://www.educause.edu/educatingthenetgen.

Papert, S. (1993). *The Children's Machine: Rethinking School in the Age of the Computer*. New York: BasicBooks.

Pillay, H., Boulton-Lewis, G., & Wilss, L. (2004). Changing workplace environments: Implications for higher education. *Educational Research Journal*, 19(1), 17–42.

Prensky, M. (2001, October). Digital natives, Digital immigrants. *On the Horizon*. Vol. 9, No. 5: NCB University Press. [Online] From http://www.marcprensky.com/writing/.

Rheingold, H. (2002). *Smart Mobs*. Cambridge: Basic Books.

Tapscott, D. (2009). *Grown Up Digital*. New York: McGraw Hill.

Taylor, M. (2006). *Generation NeXt Comes to College: Today's postmodern student*. [Online] From http://globalcscc.edu/tirc/blog/files/Gen%20NeXt%20handout%2006%20oln.pdf .

Trendwatching. (2004). *Generation C*. [Online] From http://www.trendwatching.com/trends/GENERATION_C.htm.

Windham, C. (2007). *Father Google and Mother IM: Confessions of a Net Gen Learner*. Presented at ELI Annual Meeting, January 23, 2007. [Online] From http://connect.educause.edu/library/abstract/FatherGoogleandMothe/39228.

WEBSITES

The Digital Divide Network
http://www.digitaldivide.net/
The Digital Divide Network is the internet's largest community for educators, activists, policy makers and concerned citizens working to bridge the digital divide.

UNESCO—Education
http://www.unesco.org/new/en/education/
The UNESCO Education site has a wealth of maps, tables, and other comparative data for the world's developed and developing nations. It has very useful materials that could be used in lessons and the site is updated regularly. There are also some interesting research reports available for downloading.

Ted Talks
http://www.ted.com/
TED is a non-profit organisation devoted to Ideas Worth Spreading. It started out (in 1984) as a conference bringing together people from three worlds: Technology, Entertainment and Design. This website hosts the videos of the presenters at their two annual conferences. They are free to download, you can subscribe to them as podcasts, and they are often inspiring and motivational presentations. They are on a broader range of topics in recent years, and could be useful in the primary and secondary phases of schooling.

One Laptop Per Child Organisation—Australia
http://www.olpc.org.au/
The One Laptop per Child organisation was set up to oversee the creation of an affordable educational device for use in the developing world. In this case, its focus is on Indigenous Australians. It is included here as a website of interest, as it is an interesting philanthropic organisation that seeks to address the digital divide on a global scale.

PART 2

Creative Technologies and Learning

CHAPTER 5

The role of
technology in
emerging literacy
and numeracy

Learner Outcomes

After reading this chapter, you should be able to:

- understand the concepts of emerging literacy and numeracy
- know some of the imperatives that drive the current focus on emerging literacy and numeracy
- list the ways technology can be used to develop these skills in early years learners.

Key Terms

- emerging literacy
- emerging numeracy
- innumeracy
- mathematical literacy
- educational technology
- instructional technology
- technology of education

Emerging literacy and numeracy

You are probably quite familiar with the terms *literacy* and *numeracy*, having encountered them often in your studies. They are both areas that outside stakeholders focus a lot of attention and critical commentary on, particularly in this era of national standardised testing in Australia. Currently, in Australian education systems, there is a focus on early years curriculums, and literacy and numeracy standards. Early years programs have been the subject of research and reformulated policy documents in recent years, resulting in differences in many schools across Australia, some of which, in the case of Queensland, have established preparatory programs based on varied instructional paradigms. (The 'prep' year is the first year of formal schooling; children are five years of age.) There are many children who are entering these formal schooling programs with an apparent lack of 'school readiness' and below-expected literacy and numeracy skills, largely due to the lack of access to or lack of participation in pre-school programs. If you imagine a prep–year 1 class in a typical Australian school, you cannot assume that all of the pupils in that class have had the same pathways or pre-formal school learning. Some may have participated in kindergarten; some might have been at full-day or half-day childcare centres, which may or may not have offered a formal learning program. So the range of school readiness, and abilities in literacy and numeracy vary widely. This situation is made more complex by the multicultural nature of Australian society, with the result that many prep students come from homes in which Standard Australian English (SAE) is not the language spoken. Hence, the focus on **emerging literacy** and **numeracy** is quite valid.

Critical Reflection

What do we mean by 'emerging literacy and numeracy?

Look at the list below of elements concerned with emerging literacy and numeracy. Do you agree with this list? Are these the correct elements to be focusing upon during the early years of schooling? Is there anything you consider to be missing from this list?

- Awareness of words, syllables, rhyme, and sounds within words (phonemic awareness)
- Vocabulary and conversation skills
- Awareness of the functions and usefulness of print
- Emergent writing
- Identification of letter names and sounds, numerals, and shapes

- Enumeration and understanding of the quantities 0–10
- Measurement and estimation using standard and non-standard units
- Comparing, seriating, and categorising objects based on physical attributes
- Understanding concepts related to measurement and geometry, for example, length, weight, volume, area
- Independent play and exploration that uses reading, writing, and math

Select *six* of these elements and create a table with these elements all listed in one column. Then, for each of these six elements:

1. Think of creative, hands-on ways they could be covered in a prep–year 1 class. For example, for emergent writing, you might have a lesson based on the shape of the letter 'A'—copying the shape using stencils or practising writing the shape in notebooks. Or perhaps there is a more visual or play-based way this could be tackled in class.
2. List some of the problems or barriers you may encounter in a class with varying backgrounds and levels of skills.

Defining emerging literacy and numeracy

How do we define emergent literacy and numeracy? As the phrase suggests, they are skills just emerging or breaking through in children's development of formal language and mathematics. While they may at times be rudimentary approximations, they are important stages in development. You would naturally conclude that a sound grounding in emerging literacy and numeracy skills at this stage in children's development would set them up for successful learning. Imagine now a child in your class that has begun prep–year 1 after attending playgroup, kindergarten or a childcare program with a formal learning program. What would you expect of this child's emerging literacy and numeracy skills? You might expect them to recognise some letters and numbers, know what they sound like, perhaps be able to guess at meanings of words, be able to write some letters and words. These would be normal expectations. Imagine now a student who didn't attend any of these types of programs or who might have been at a childcare centre that didn't have a formal program of learning, or perhaps a child who speaks another language at home and for whom English is a second or foreign language. What would be your expectations of their emerging literacy and numeracy skills? Would you assume that, as they were of the same age as their peers, they would have similar skills? Possibly you might. It is important to understand that in any early years classroom the continuum of literacy and numeracy skills could vary considerably.

Emerging literacy and numeracy skills are the result of a number of different experiences that occur prior to formal schooling. Development in this area is not limited to school-based learning, reading with caregivers, understanding signs encountered, asking questions about meanings of words, word identification, sounding out words, listening to stories, reading stories with caregivers, counting and understanding meanings. These are just some of the activities the young learner engages in daily.

Personal Reflection

What was your literacy and numeracy journey?

Can you remember the stages of your development in the areas of literacy and numeracy? Answer the questions below—write your answers on a piece of paper.

Literacy	Numeracy
• When do you remember first being able to write? This could be recollections of copying shapes of letters or forming whole words. What grade at school were you in?	• When were you first conscious of numbers and the meaning they were associated with? What grade were you in at school?
• Do you remember any specific learning strategies you participated in? What grade were you in? For example, word cards that you put together to make sentences or reading comprehension cards.	• Do you remember any specific learning strategies you participated in, for example, whole class drills, copying numbers, flash cards? What grade were you in?
• Can you remember when you read your first book? What grade were you in at school?	• Can you remember specific mathematical milestones, such as the year in school you started learning tables, fractions, multiplication and percentages?
• Can you remember having particular stories or novels read to you? Write down as many as you can remember and the grade you were in at school.	• Can you remember any hands-on learning associated with numeracy, for example, using wooden blocks? What year at school were you in?
• Can you remember your first spelling test? What grade at school were you in?	• Did you ever participate in a particular numeracy program?
• Did you ever learn phonics? What grade were you in?	• What other numeracy milestones can you remember? Make a note of them.
• What other literacy milestones can you remember? Make a note of them.	

Looking back at your development, was there a point in your learning at which you felt 'literate' or 'numerate'? Was it a conscious feeling of achievement in learning—that you were equipped with the skills to face any challenge in these two areas? Or was it subconscious? Perhaps, you haven't really felt that you made the transition to being 'literate and numerate'. Or do you feel you are still developing? This is an interesting conundrum. Try answering the following question: When can a person be described as being literate?

A closer look at literacy

Literacy has traditionally been described as the ability to read for knowledge, write coherently and think critically about printed material, but in a digital world we need to make some changes to this traditional understanding. Literacy should be described as being the ability to read, write and think critically about text-based materials, which include both printed and electronic forms. The United Nations Educational, Scientific and Cultural Organisation (UNESCO) defines literacy as the

ability to identify, understand, interpret, create, communicate, compute and use printed and written materials associated with varying contexts. Literacy involves a continuum of learning in enabling individuals to achieve their goals, to develop their knowledge and potential, and to participate fully in their community and wider society. (UNESCO 2006, p. 29)

Emerging literacy is the beginning of this process of acquiring these abilities. Most people, when asked about their understanding of literacy, describe it as a process of reading and writing, but as we have suggested, it is also the ability to think critically about the materials engaged with. The ability to question, examine and understand what it is we are actually seeing or reading are important skills.

Literacy represents the life-long, intellectual process of gaining meaning from text. The key to literacy is reading development, which involves a progression of skills that begins with the ability to understand spoken words and decode written words, and culminates in the deep understanding of text. Reading development involves a range of complex language, including awareness of speech sounds (phonology), spelling patterns (orthography), word meaning (semantics), grammar, syntax, and patterns of word formation (morphology), which together constitute a necessary set of skills for reading fluency and comprehension. Once these skills are acquired, the reader can attain full literacy, which includes the ability to approach and interact with text critically, to write accurately and coherently, and to use information and insights from text as the basis for informed decisions and creative thought.

There are many approaches to teaching literacy; each is shaped by assumptions about what literacy is and how students best learn it. Phonics instruction, for example, focuses on reading at the level of the word. It teaches readers to attend to the letters or groups of letters that make up words. A common method of teaching phonics is synthetic phonics, in which a novice reader pronounces each individual sound and 'blends' them to pronounce the whole word. Another approach to phonics instruction is embedded phonics instruction, used more often in whole language reading instruction, in which novice readers learn about the individual letters in words on a just-in-time, just-in-place basis that is tailored to meet each student's reading and writing learning needs. In this approach, teachers provide phonics instruction opportunistically, within the context of stories or student writing that feature many instances of a particular letter or group of letters. Embedded instruction combines letter–sound knowledge with the use of meaningful context to read new and difficult words. Techniques such as directed listening and thinking activities can be used to aid children in learning how to read and understand what they read.

Critical Reflection
World literacy levels

The level of literacy in different countries varies greatly. If you look at the map below, you will see that countries that have achieved an adult literacy level of 95–100 per cent would represent only half the world.

Figure 5.1: World literacy levels

Source: United Nations Human Development Report 2007/2008

Think about the following questions:

- Of those countries that have achieved 95–100 per cent adult literacy, do they have anything else in common? Why do you think they have achieved this level of literacy? Are there any countries that surprise you within this group? What role do you think technology may play in literacy levels?

- Look at the countries that have achieved 70–79 per cent adult literacy. Are any of them surprising? What do you think are the barriers to these countries achieving 100 per cent adult literacy?

- Could you explain the levels of literacy in all the countries on this map? Do you think you have an understanding of the factors that might have contributed to these results?

A closer look at numeracy

The report *Numeracy, a Priority for All: Challenges for Australian Schools* (Department of Education, Training and Youth Affairs 2000) stated that:

> *In the early years of schooling the development of numeracy skills provides a crucial foundation for the later years to support and enhance future learning, at school, in the workplace and in everyday life. Within the school context, numeracy is needed to support learning in various curriculum areas. Interpreting data in graphs or tables, using a scale on a map or making critical judgments based on text containing quantitative information all require students to be numerate. (DEST 2000, p. 12)*

Numeracy is the ability to reason with numbers and other mathematical concepts. A numerically literate person can manage and respond to the mathematical demands of life. Aspects of numeracy include number sense, operation sense, computation, measurement, geometry, probability and statistics. The phrase 'numerical literacy' was first used in 1959 by the UK *Committee on Education*. **Innumeracy** is a lack of numeracy. *Numeracy* is a term that is defined in a number of different ways. *Numeracy*, having originated as an educational term in the UK, is commonly used in countries within the Commonwealth, such as Australia, New Zealand and Canada. Educators in other parts of the world use phrases such as 'school mathematics', 'quantitative literacy' or **mathematical literacy**. The use of a number of different phrases or terms has also resulted in a number of different definitions or understandings of what numeracy means.

The Australian Association of Mathematics Teachers (1997) stated that:

> *To be numerate is to use mathematics effectively to meet the general demands of life at home, in paid work, and for participation in community and civic life. In school education, numeracy is a fundamental component of learning, performance, discourse and critique across all areas of the curriculum. It involves the disposition to use, in context, a combination of:*
>
> > *underpinning mathematical concepts and skills from across the discipline (numerical, spatial, graphical, statistical and algebraic);*
> > *mathematical thinking and strategies;*
> > *general thinking skills; and*
> > *grounded appreciation of context (p. 17).*

While the OECD defined *mathematical literacy* as:

> *Mathematical literacy is an individual's capacity to identify and understand the role that mathematics plays in the world, to make well-founded mathematical judgements and to engage in mathematics, in ways that meet the needs of that individual's current and future life as a constructive, concerned and reflective citizen. (OECD 1999, p. 41)*

CASE STUDY

Read the following scenario and answer the questions that follow:

John is a prep–year 1 teacher in an inner-city school with a mix of students from low to middle socio-economic backgrounds. His class has a wide range of abilities, ranging from students who are able to read and pronounce words quite successfully, to those who are still sounding out each syllable of words and struggling to put them together. He has noticed that of all the reading activities his class engages in, the one they like best is when they are sitting on the mat listening to the teacher read aloud a storybook. Those who are weaker readers enjoy the discussion and questions associated with this activity, and those who are quite confident readers like to show their understanding of pronunciation and meaning by jumping in and being 'teacher'. Essentially, the activity was playing to the students' strengths but it wasn't really pushing them to improve their individual reading abilities.

John decided that he wanted to try an individual approach to reading and found a CD-ROM reading program that sounded out words and got the students to repeat sounds before it would move on. Each student could control the program themselves and was hooked up to the computer via a microphone. It would be self-paced, provide guidance and repetition when needed and provide constant positive feedback. So over a period of six weeks he tried the reading program.

1. What do you think the results of this program would be?
2. Would the learning needs of both groups of students be met?
3. What impact would the program have had on motivation and engagement?
4. What would be the disadvantages of this approach?
5. Do you have any other observations?

The role of technology in developing literacy and numeracy

There are three terms that need defining: **educational technology**, **instructional technology** and **technology of education**. They are commonly used when discussing the role or use of technology in learning.

1. *Educational technology* is the study and ethical practice of facilitating learning and improving performance by creating, using and managing appropriate technological processes and resources (Hlyna & Jacobsen 2009). Educational technology includes, but is not limited to, software and hardware, as well as internet applications such as wikis and blogs, and activities.

2. *Instructional technology* is the theory and practice of design, development, utilisation, management, and evaluation of processes and resources for learning (AECT 2001).

3. *Technology of education* is defined as an array of tools that might prove helpful in advancing student learning and may be measured in how and why individuals behave. In this case, 'technology' can refer to objects and tools such as overhead projectors, laptop computers and calculators.

The use of technology in early years literacy and numeracy programs has a growing body of research supporting its use. These studies have shown that early years learners have few difficulties operating hardware and are able to follow simple tailor-made software programs. Technology has a pervasive influence in modern life and children have a vast array of learning experiences, often with technology, before they start school. This exposure to technology at a young age facilitates a familiarity and confidence in these young learners. Interactions with their family and with technology combine to affect their literacy development. Computers and associated technologies help early years learners to develop fine motor skills, alphabet recognition, pre-mathematical skills, concept learning, cognition, self-esteem, social skills and school-readiness skills. It would be logical to conclude that early years learners who engage with technology have better learning outcomes, in particular, in literacy and numeracy skills, than their peers who do not.

An important aspect associated with technology for early years learners is the concept of 'play'. In this context, 'play' does not refer to random, unstructured engagement; rather, it describes creative, experimental and purposeful activity with which effective early years teachers can mediate to ensure that genuine learning occurs (see Figure 5.2). Software programs and hardware have been designed to be engaging and motivating to use, enabling learning to occur within the context of play. The framework shown in Figure 5.2 is an important tool in helping teachers understand and, more importantly, plan how to use technology in the early years. In Chapters 6 and 7 this is explored further, but it is important at this stage to familiarise yourself with the three types of activities technology can contribute to within early years settings: creative, experimental and purposeful activities.

Figure 5.2: The Technology and Play Framework

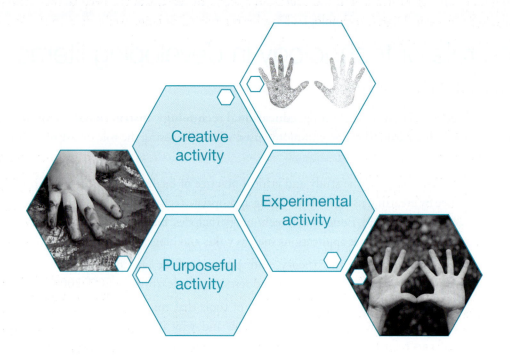

Critical Reflection
Learning and play

'Play' is a term that we probably assume that we understand; however, play within the context of education and learning can be a more complex concept to understand. According to Shipley (2008), play can be categorised into six different 'types':

- *Pleasurable play* is an enjoyable and pleasurable activity. Play sometimes includes frustrations, challenges and fears; however, enjoyment is a key feature.
- *Symbolic play* is often pretend, it has a 'what if?' quality. The play has meaning to the player that is often not evident to the educator.
- *Active play* requires action, either physical, verbal or mental engagement with materials, people, ideas or the environment.

- *Voluntary play* is freely chosen. However, players can also be invited or prompted to play.
- *Process-oriented play* is a means unto itself and players may not have an end or goal in sight.
- *Self-motivating play* is considered its own reward to the player.

Brainstorm examples that illustrate each of the six types of play listed above. Keep the examples within the early years context. Now revisit those examples and think of a technology that could be used. What impact does that technology have?

The value of technology within early years programs is clearly beneficial to emergent and, indeed, developing literacy and numeracy. As the global world economy, with its characteristic emphasis on digitality affects Australia and the education system, the extent of the need to include digital technologies is clear. Digital technologies have been reported as being well-suited to the learning styles of early years students regardless of cultural or ethnic background.

Personal Reflection
What have you learnt through play?

Play is an activity that can teach us many different things. Think back over your schooling during the early years and up to primary school. You would have engaged in a lot of different types of play, both formally within a classroom and informally away from the classroom setting. Some of those lessons might have been positive; some might have been negative! Think of one example and then list what you learned from that experience as a child. Were you aware that you had 'learned' something? Did the experience lead you to change your behaviour or modify your understanding of something?

Play-based learning is an effective strategy that we continue to engage in throughout our lives. It would be incorrect to assume that play is limited to 'children' or a certain age group, or particular time in our development. Play is something we continue to engage in; perhaps we might re-label it but, as adults, we do engage in activities that are play-based. Think about the following types of activities we engage in as adults:

- playing sport for fun; for example, local teams and informal games with friends
- updating your Facebook page
- Skyping friends.

Try filling in the table below, based on your current activities.

Type of play	An activity you do that illustrates this type of play
Pleasurable	
Pleasurable	
Symbolic	
Active	
Voluntary	
Process-orientated	
Self-motivating	

CASE STUDY

Read the following scenario and answer the questions that follow:

As a young teacher, I decided to try and use some technology in my prep–year 1 class. I had decided to try using LEGO Robotics with my class and, as they were all familiar with Duplo blocks I thought I should probably introduce them to smaller LEGO blocks first. For two weeks I set aside time for the students to work on the mat and build anything they liked with the LEGO blocks. I didn't want to direct them to build something specific, as I didn't want them to 'learn' how to use them, I wanted them to engage in pleasurable play and try to work out how to build things, pull them apart, become familiar with the different shapes and how to construct things, all without too much guidance. I hoped that by the end of the two weeks, they would be familiar enough with the LEGO bricks to be able to move on and build the robots I had planned.

During the first week I set aside two, possibly three, times for play with the LEGO bricks. I set the tubs down on the floor and students were asked to sit in their working groups and see what they could build. There was a lot of trying new things, lots of frustration in trying to separate the blocks or in clicking them together. Some groups argued over what to do, with self-nominated 'experts' (those with older siblings who had LEGO at home) leading the group. I observed a mixed response from the students—some enjoyed it; some found it too difficult. I felt I had probably interfered too much in trying to get them to work in groups, so I tried a different strategy. The next two days, if students finished their work early or if they had earned a reward, they could go over to the mat and play with the LEGO bricks themselves. This was very motivating for students; they had the freedom to do what they liked, by themselves or sometimes working with friends, to build with and explore the LEGO bricks.

After the success of this 'free-time' with the LEGO, I decided to try it as a whole class strategy. One afternoon after lunch, I announced that we were going to have free time to play with the LEGO bricks. The only scaffold I set in place was time; they had 30 minutes to do whatever they liked with the bricks. Well, amazing things happened—gardens were built, new cars were invented, swimming pools were very popular (we had read a class story earlier in the week about a swimming gala) and lots of interesting new houses. All of the LEGO constructions were placed along the windowsill and the students could see them there and often went to visit them, show their friends and parents, talk about what they had built and why they used the bricks they did. They were having wonderful learning conversations! So, the following week, I followed this model. Students were given free time to engage in pleasurable-play. We used the constructions in a different way this time: we asked each student to show their construction to the rest of the class and describe or explain what they did. Their peers also asked them questions and gave them advice.

Answer the following questions:

1. What did the students actually learn? Be specific and list everything you think they might have learnt.
2. What did the teacher learn?
3. What were the learning outcomes for the following:
   - social skills
   - literacy
   - numeracy
   - technology skills?

Summary

The development of emerging literacy and numeracy in the early years is an area where technology can play a role in the classroom. The broad range of prior experiences that students have, courtesy of pre-formal schooling programs, has meant that learners start the early phase of schooling with a broad range of abilities in literacy and numeracy. This can present as quite a complex issue for teachers, as the first year of schooling becomes concerned with ensuring that students are equipped with a sound grounding in literacy and numeracy. When learners are starting from different developmental points, teachers need strategies that can meet all of their learners' needs; technology may be a useful tool.

Understanding what we mean by the term 'literacy' is also quite complex. Perhaps in the past we might have associated literacy with the ability to read, but it is a much more complex series of skills. Our understanding of what makes a literate person has also undergone some adjustment and, on that account, how we teach literacy has changed. Literacy is the ability to identify, understand, interpret, create, communicate, compute and use printed and written materials associated with varying contexts. Numeracy has been revealed as a complex skill; it is not merely the ability to compute mathematical equations or count. Different countries and different education systems view numeracy differently. It's also termed differently. While in Australia we commonly use the term 'numeracy', in the USA it's more often described as 'mathematical literacy'. Numeracy is the ability to reason with numbers and other mathematical concepts. Some technologies in particular offer rich learning opportunities for early years learners, for example, interactive whiteboards (IWBs) have a plethora of software programs designed for early numeracy.

This chapter has also explored some of the understandings we have of the concepts that have emerged as technology became embedded within teaching and learning practices. Concepts such as educational technology, instructional technology and technology of education have been explored. There are subtle differences between these concepts, but essentially they are all concerned with describing the ways in which technology can support teaching and learning. The use of technology in the early years has increased recently and there have been numerous studies showing the benefits. It can be certain that our students will arrive at this stage of schooling more digitally experienced than their predecessors. This is not to suggest they are digitally fluent nor that they are digital natives, but that they are *aware* of technology. They see it around them, they see other people using it, they hear about it from family members, they see it on television. They might not possess the actual skill base for digital fluency but they are aware of it and find it engaging. This predisposition towards technology is a wonderful resource for teachers to capitalise on.

Play-based learning has been shown as a highly appropriate teaching strategy for this phase of learning. There are six types of play-based learning approaches—pleasure, symbolic, active, voluntary, process-orientated, self-motivating—and technology is able to facilitate all types. What has been proposed in this chapter, which has resonance for the following chapters, is the Technology and Play Framework. This framework suggests that there are three main types of activity that technology can support: creative activity, experimental activity and purposeful activity.

FURTHER READING

Association for Educational Communications and Technology (AECT). (2001). *What is the Knowledge Base?* [Electronic document] http://www.aect.org/standards/knowledgebase.html.

AAMT. (1997). *Numeracy = Everyone's Business, Report of the Numeracy Education Strategy Development Conference*, AAMT, Adelaide.

Bers, M. (2008). *Blocks to Robots: Learning with Technology in the Early Childhood Classroom*. New York: Teachers College Press.

Clements, D.H., Sarama, J. & DiBiase, A. (2004). *Engaging Young Children in Mathematics*. New York: Routledge.

COAG. (2009). *The National Early Childhood Development Strategy*. [Online] From http://www.coag.gov.au/coag_meeting_outcomes/2009-07-02/docs/national_ECD_strategy.pdf.

DEEWR (2009). *Belong, Being and Becoming. The Early Years Learning Framework for Australia*. [Online] From http://www.deewr.gov.au/Earlychildhood/Policy_Agenda/Quality/Documents/Final%20EYLF%20Framework%20Report%20-%20WEB.pdf.

DEST (2000). *Numeracy, a Priority for All: Challenges for Australian Schools.* [Online] From http://www.dest.gov.au/NR/rdonlyres/AA01AA6A-4EF5-4D1B-93BA-B1ED1392BC6C/3991/numeracy.pdf.

Hlyna, D. & Jacobsen, M. (2009). What is educational technology anyway? *Canadian Journal of Educational Technology.* [Online] From http://www.cjlt.ca/index.php/cjlt/article/view/527/260.

OECD. (1999). *Measuring Student Knowledge and Skills: A New Framework for Assessment*, OECD, Paris.

Shipley, D. (2008) *Empowering Children. Play Based Curriculum for Life-long Learning.* (4th edition) USA: Nelson Education.

UNESCO (2006). *Education for All: Global Monitoring Report.* [Online] From http://www.unesco.org/new/en/education/themes/leading-the-international-agenda/efareport/reports/2006-literacy/.

United Nations Human Development Report 2007/2008. [Online] From http://hdr.undp.org/en/data/map/.

Van Scoter, J. & Ellis, D. (2001). *Technology in Early Childhood Education.* [Online] From http://www.netc.org/earlyconnections/byrequest.pdf.

WEBSITES

http://www.earlychildhoodaustralia.org.au/eylfplp/play_based_learning_and_the_eylf.php
This website is a presentation by Lennie Barblett on play-based learning and the early years learning framework. It has a video embedded of the presentation, the PowerPoint file and links to an online discussion. These are all useful if you are keen to explore this teaching strategy further.

http://www.nsn.net.au/digi_kids_snapshot_no_1
This is a digital snapshot of a program conducted by Lynda Page, a teacher at Coolum Beach State School. Lynda is a keen supporter of including digital technologies in early years programs, and this website demonstrates some of the ways she has done this.

http://playinginprep.wordpress.com/2011/07/30/technology-in-the-early-years-a-philosophical-discussion/
An interesting blog, hosted by WordPress that examines different topics associated with 'playing in prep'. This link will take you to the posting on technology in the early years, but there are other interesting postings to explores.

http://teachingliteracy.global2.vic.edu.au/2011/07/12/using-technology-in-the-literacy-block/
This is a useful website concerned with teaching literacy in the year years, and the use of technology to achieve that. The content is updated fairly regularly so it's worth bookmarking and checking back to see what has been posted.

CHAPTER 6

Creative
technologies
and play

Learner Outcomes

After reading this chapter, you should be able to:

- understand the concept 'creative technology'
- know some of the ways that technology can enable play
- list the types of technology most suited to the early and primary phases of learning and some of their uses in the classroom.

Key Terms

- digital camera
- digital image
- creative technology
- play
- iPad
- interactive whiteboard (IWB)
- tablet PC
- LEGO Robotics
- touch tables
- web-based learning
- Bee-Bot Robotics

What is a 'creative technology'?

We should have a clear understanding of what we mean when we say 'technology', digital technology is perhaps the phrase most commonly heard which incorporates any technology that is digital (as opposed to tradition, analogue or perhaps the new android technologies emerging). A term still popular and commonly seen in education is 'Information and Communications Technology' (ICT). This was a very big step forward in the field. Prior to this term emerging, technology was viewed as being something connected to computers. But by adding the phrase 'and communications' to it, suddenly it incorporated technologies such as mobile phones, smartphones, Web 2.0 (online chat, social networking, RSS feeds) and any technology that enabled the communication between people or with information. You can see how the understanding of what 'technology' means has been evolving to match newly emerging developments. At present we seem to be sitting under a very large collective umbrella term, 'digital technologies'. But what happens when we put the word creative in front? It narrows the collection significantly to technologies that are concerned with creating something—the user makes a product, creates something digitally so that technology is a tool in this situation. Imagine a **digital camera** or perhaps a software program that enables you to edit and change, or create something with the **digital image** you have taken with your camera. These are both creative technologies.

The idea of technologies enabling creativity has been something considered by educational researchers for several years. You are probably familiar with terms such as 'gen X', 'gen Y', the 'internet generation' but have you heard of 'gen C'? 'Generation C' was a term first offered by the internet site, Trendwatching.com in 2004 and builds on the work of social commentator Lawrence Lessig (2002), who suggested that

> *Technology could enable a whole generation to create—remixed films, new forms of music, digital art, a new kind of storytelling, writing, a new technology for poetry, criticism, political activism—and then, through the infrastructure of the internet, share that creativity with others. (Lessig 2002, p. 9)*

Here, 'generation C' is defined as those who typically produce and share digital content (Trendwatching 2004), such as blogs, digital images, digital audio or video files, and SMS messages. These people are digitally fluent and fearlessly use new forms of technology as they are released. They fluently use computers, mobile telephones, the internet and other associated technologies.

Most were born in the late 1980s and early 1990s but, importantly, gen C is not limited to a narrow age range. As Dye (2007) says of these people, 'they aren't categorised by age, they're categorised by behaviour. And it's very much about content-centric communication, how they share, store, and manage content' (p. 38). They are a 'generation that spans across the age divide to encompass the growing population that creates, shares, and is connected by its own user-generated content' (Dye 2007, p. 38).

So what does this all have to do with learners in the early and primary years? Well it's a pretty simple idea: these phases of learning perhaps more than any others are concerned with learning activities that are creative and play-based. Can technology participate in this? Absolutely. Can technology enable this? Yes. **Creative technology** fits the aims and objectives of the early years and primary phase of schooling. What this section of the book would like to suggest is that technologies for these phases of learning should be creative; they should enable learners to create something, and that something should be a rich learner task that is complex, embedded in the curriculum and offers opportunities for development that are beyond knowledge acquisition. Sounds like an ideal rather than a reality, doesn't it? Well, let's now explore the idea of **play** and technology, and then examine some examples of creative technologies that offer all of these things.

Technology and play

As we have seen in the previous chapter, an important aspect associated with technology for early years and primary learners is the concept of 'play'. In this context 'play' does not refer to random, unstructured engagement; rather is describes creative, experimental, and purposeful activity with which effective early years and primary teachers can mediate to ensure genuine learning occurs. Software programs and hardware have been designed to be engaging and motivating to use, enabling learning to occur within the context of play (Brooker 2003; Chantel 2005). Technology researchers have been interested in the idea of combining play with technology; for example, consider the early work of Seymour Papert, who created Logo as a tool to improve the way that children think and solve problems. A small robot called the 'Logo Turtle' was developed and children used it to solve problems that were mathematically based. This is an example of an early use of technology in play-based learning. Extending from this idea was Mitch Resnick's work that explored how technology was suited to the kindergarten approach to learning (see Figure 6.1). In this approach, learners moved through a cycle of imagining, creating, playing, sharing, reflecting and then back to imagining. Technology can support this approach to learning if used appropriately and selected wisely. If you examine each of these stages in the spiral below, you can imagine a type of technology that would support it. For example, imagining could be supported seeing a small robot perform a simple task on a video; creating could be supported by planning how to build a similar robot using different materials or tools; playing could be the process of seeing if the design works; sharing could be achieved via digital images uploaded to blogs or email; reflecting could be short commentaries or blog postings. The interpretations are endless.

Figure 6.1: The kindergarten approach to learning

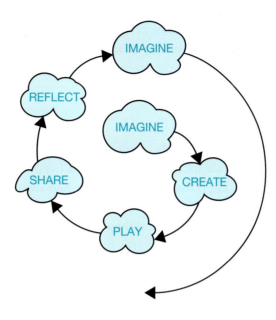

(Resnick 2007, p. 2)

Thus technology and play-based learning are synchronistic—they support the teaching and learning strategies of the teacher and can help achieve the desired learning outcomes. Let's now look at some examples of creative technologies.

Creative technologies for the early and primary years

Figure 6.2: The Technology and Play Framework

The remainder of this chapter explores different examples of creative technologies. While the list is not exhaustive, it does offer a variety of ideas that could support a wide range of creative projects and technology-based play. Each of the creative technologies is described with suggestions for use, followed by lesson ideas, then a brief overview of the creativeness of the technology and other benefits for development that are beyond the acquisition of new knowledge (for example, social skills or group work).

Digital cameras and images

Digital cameras, both for still images and video recordings, are rich learning tools ideally suited to the early and primary years. While the inclination is for the teacher or teacher aide to use the camera and take images, there are now cameras that are simple to use, and are designed specifically for early and primary years learners. The development of cameras with larger buttons, and the use of the large screen on the camera to frame shots has meant that the incidence of taking the typical 'headless' shot of the past is dramatically reduced. Also, considering that most mobile phones have a camera built in, most students will have had some experience using some type of digital camera. Some issues to consider when selecting a camera for use with early years learners:

1. Match the camera to the size of the child. Small children have small hands and need a lighter camera to use.

2. Look for an easy-to-use interface. Are the symbols on the LCD screen logical? Easy to see? Easy to understand?

3. The LCD screen should be robust—large enough to see clearly, be able to be used indoors and outdoors, and have clear, strong, vibrant colours.

Figure 6.3: A digital camera

4. Think about the zoom range you will need—at this stage a good basic 2x optical zoom would probably suffice. How easy is it to zoom? Is the button easy to reach, how do you reverse back after zooming?

5. Memory cards—are they affordable and are they common? This is important, as you do not want to purchase a digital camera that has a unique memory card that computers or laptops are not able to read or, more importantly, needs an expensive card reader.

6. Is there a cable that can connect the camera to the computer via USB? This is a much easier way to download images than taking out and potentially damaging or losing cards.

7. Adequate video capacity—this will depend on your memory size, either HDD or your memory card. Children love making videos; make sure you have the capacity.

8. A visually attractive camera—does it look fun to use?

9. Make sure the camera comes with a re-charger—rather than using disposable lithium batteries, find a model that has a re-chargeable battery.

10. Make sure there is a strap, preferably a neck strap. If you get the students into the habit of putting this on around their necks, any dropped cameras are saved from hitting the floor.

11. Think about purchasing waterproof covers—they do add weight, make access to buttons tricky and can be cumbersome, but look at your options here. Accidents happen and it's amazing how water and children attract each other!

Once you have explored the options and decided on the digital camera, think about quantity. You do not need a class set or one between two students. A class can be transformed by the purchase of one camera. Be sensible; in an average class two to four cameras would be transforming. So, how much instruction do the students need? There will be some basics that need to be covered, such as:

1. how to hold the camera so fingers don't cover the lens or flash

2. how to switch the camera on and off

3. using the zoom control

4. where the battery/batteries and memory card go

5. how to switch the flash on and off.

You may need to discuss framing an image, size and quality, but remember the aim here is to try and develop basic skills in taking digital images suitable for use in further learning activities.

Lesson Ideas

Some ideas for using digital cameras and images in the classroom

Some suggestions for literacy:

- Narrative writing (describe what is portrayed in the picture)
- Practising past tense—write about what students have done
- Describing a process—what we did and why
- Describing what is in the image—using new words or parts of speech
- Learning about processes—using a series of images to show how something was made or the steps in completing a particular task
- Creating a class diary—evidence of activities that the class participated in, with commentaries
- Using the images for posters, jigsaw activities or diary/journal entry
- Using the images for parent–teacher conferences.

We can see from the above that digital cameras and digital images are well-suited to early years learners. There are two types of learning that are supported: process learning, such as the technical skills of using a camera and taking an image; and content learning, such as understanding what is being framed and why. As the devices themselves have been designed for smaller hands and younger learners, they are well-suited technologies to include in the classroom.

A quick overview of digital cameras

What's creative about their use?	Opportunities for development beyond knowledge acquisition...
Their creativity is limited by your imagination! They are creative because they do not have one particular output such as a still image; they can be used for movie making and they can be used in different situations and contexts. For example, students can use them to create personal storybooks, record class events, create short movies, create artwork.	Fine and gross motor skills as they learn how to manipulate the digital camera. Process skills—how to take a photograph, how to frame, how to edit. Technological skills—fluency in a common technology device, perhaps also in editing, how to transfer images to the computer.

Digital storybooks

What is a digital storybook? A digital storybook is essentially a collection of digital images, placed in a particular order to tell a story, which is accompanied by an audio narration. The simplest way to envisage a digital storybook would be via the programs PowerPoint or MovieMaker. It is a mini-movie that is made out of still images. It can have text accompanying it but, most simply, it is a purposefully crafted movie. They are quite powerful tools, as they can tell the story of a shared experience or a special event; and for early and primary years learners, the fact that they have participated in the experience and created a visual record of it is a powerful learning tool.

Figure 6.4: A digital storybook

Options for formats

Readily available software programs

PowerPoint—most schools should have this program available on their computers.
MovieMaker—a free download from Microsoft. Very easy to easy, click and drag images into a movie reel, add a sound file and the program will complete the movie for you.
Web-based programs
Apple **iPad** app—StoryKit

Collections of digital stories online

http://www.creativenarrations.net/stories

http://www.mrsp.com/

Steps to a digital storybook

There are some steps involved in creating a digital storybook:

1. Decide on the theme or topic for the storybook. Sometimes this is opportunistic. Perhaps the class is participating in a particular activity, such as sports day, and you have decided that if you take some digital images of them participating in that activity they could write a narrative for the images. Or perhaps you are preparing a new unit of work and it is about the local community, so you decide what aspects or images might be interesting. Either way, a theme or topic is decided.

2. Create the storyboards. How will your digital story look? Is there a particular program you want to use—PowerPoint is very simple and easy to use, or perhaps MovieMaker?

3. Import your images into the chosen program.

4. Add the narrative—this could be a spoken recording of the students describing what is in the image, it could be a scripted or non-scripted recording, it could be a written narrative under the images.

5. Add special effects and transitions—sparingly. Resist these; they really are not necessary. Let the images speak for themselves. Remember PowerPoint presentations that have been over 'special-effected'? A terrible distraction!

6. Think carefully about how the digital story will be exported—use software with more common file extension formats, such as Windows Movie (wmv) and resist new formats as you cannot be sure that everyone will be able to play them. Also consider burning them on a DVD or ask every child to bring in a USB stick (of suitable memory capacity, as they vary greatly).

Lesson Ideas

Some ideas for using digital storybooks in the classroom

- Literacy—focusing on words, pronunciation, writing scripts, writing narrations or stories
- Rich task—could potentially cover many different discipline areas and involve many different approaches to learning: writing, speaking, using technology and content knowledge
- Reading—recording student narrations, playing back the recordings and listening to words, word recognition, pronunciation and practice at reading
- Digital storybook of field trips, special events, culmination of units of work, projects (focus on the processes), to demonstrate new knowledge (for example, prepositions 'in' and 'on'—imagine a storyboard with a toy that is inside a box, on top of a box, and so on).

Digital storybooks provide a technology-based option for writing and literacy development. They combine visual images with other supporting information such as narrations, recordings, soundtracks, visual addition (for example, adding title pages) and subtitles, and build on the skills students have acquired learning how to use digital cameras.

A quick overview of digital storybooks

What's creative about their use?	Opportunities for development beyond knowledge acquisition...
• There are multiple opportunities for creative expression when students create digital storybooks—the story, script, narration, the images to be taken or collected, ordering, visuals, soundtracks—all of these aspects have the opportunity for students to create something that is personal and individual.	• Technology—how to use a particular software program to build a digital storybook, the steps involved in taking, uploading and ordering images • Experience different formats for stories—not just print-based storybooks • Learning new uses for digital images students have taken • New ways to display information.

Interactive whiteboards

An **interactive whiteboard (IWB)**, is a large interactive display that connects to a computer and projector. A projector projects the computer's desktop onto the board's surface, where users control the computer using a pen, finger, stylus or other device. The board is typically mounted to a wall or floor stand. They are used in a variety of settings, including classrooms at all levels of education, in corporate boardrooms and work groups, in training rooms for professional sports coaching, in broadcasting studios and others.

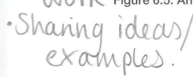

Figure 6.5: An interactive whiteboard in use

Uses for interactive whiteboards may include:

- running software that is loaded onto the connected PC, such as a web browser or proprietary software used in the classroom
- capturing and saving notes written on a whiteboard to the connected PC
- capturing notes written on a graphics tablet connected to the whiteboard
- using as an online whiteboard
- controlling the PC from the white board using click and drag mark-up to annotate a program or presentation
- using OCR software to translate cursive writing on a graphics tablet into text
- using an audience response system so that presenters can poll a classroom audience or conduct quizzes, capturing feedback onto the whiteboard.

In some classrooms, interactive whiteboards have replaced traditional whiteboards or flipcharts, or video/media systems such as a DVD player and TV combination. Even where traditional boards are used, the IWB often supplements them by connecting to a school network digital video distribution system. In other cases, IWBs interact with online shared annotation and drawing environments such as interactive vector-based graphical websites. The software supplied with the interactive whiteboard will usually allow the teacher to keep notes and annotations as an electronic file for later distribution either on paper or through a number of electronic formats.

In addition, some interactive whiteboards allow teachers to record their instruction as digital video files and post the material for review by students at a later time. This can be a very effective instructional strategy for students who benefit from repetition, who need to see the material presented again, for students who are absent from school, for struggling learners, and for review for examinations. Brief instructional blocks can be recorded for review by students—they will see the exact presentation that occurred in the classroom with the teacher's audio input. This can help transform learning and instruction.

Figure 6.6: A handheld 'clicker'

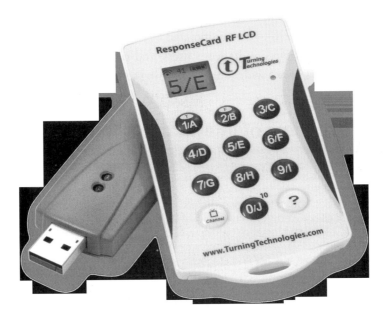

Some manufacturers also provide classroom response systems as an integrated part of their interactive whiteboard products. Handheld 'clickers' operating via infrared or radio signals, for example, offer basic multiple-choice and polling options. More sophisticated clickers offer text and numeric responses, and can export an analysis of student performance for subsequent review.

By combining classroom response with an interactive whiteboard system, teachers can present material and receive feedback from students in order to direct instruction more effectively or else to carry out formal assessments. For example, a student may both solve a puzzle involving math concepts on the interactive whiteboard and later demonstrate his or her knowledge on a test delivered via the classroom response system. Some classroom response software can organise and develop activities and tests aligned with state standards.

Lesson Ideas

Some ideas for using interactive whiteboards in the classroom

- The potential use of IWBs is limited only by your confidence as a teacher. Remember, the students are fearless and will come up to the board and tap, point or touch it while they work out how it functions. There are numerous programs already developed that you can access and load up on the computer, ready to use in class. Start with these until you become confident in using them, then try making your own.
- IWBs work with a variety of organisations: whole class, small groups, individual learning—so try using them in different ways. Set up learning centres and rotate the class around several different technologies, including IWBs, so that students have some hands-on time with them.
- They cater for different learning styles; for example, hands-on or visual. So, try basing a lesson on a different approach to learning and use the IWB; set yourself the challenge.
- Use the IWB for making PowerPoint presentations, searching for information on the internet, sending emails to other classes around the world, learning writing genres via whole-class constructions.

IWBs are tools that are prevalent in schools across all phases of learning. They should be seen as interactive tools rather than screens to be manipulated by the teacher only. Due to their size, IWBs provide opportunities for multiple simultaneous users, and the types of software programs being developed mean that teachers have a wide range of learning tools.

A quick overview of interactive whiteboards

What's creative about their use?	Opportunities for development beyond knowledge acquisition...
• They allow multiple users. They are a technology device not limited to one subject or one way of being used. As software programs develop, more creative options will be available. Interactive whiteboards are well suited for use by both teacher and students.	• Technology skills—how to touch and manipulate the screen • Fine and gross motor skills, coordination skills.

Laptops, tablet PCs, iPads

Individual Work Apps filming

Most classrooms have either one or two PCs, or they have access to a set of computers. At the very least, the teacher has a laptop. But how can we use these types of machines (PCs, laptops, **tablet PCs**) with early and primary years learners? These learners don't know how to operate them, do they? No. In short, we use them in exactly the same way we would with older users. The technology industry has been slow to build purpose-built machines for this phase of learning, and schools, when they do get the funding for technology purchases, tend to buy 'traditional' laptops. This is fine, and still effective, but let's think for a moment and imagine the possibly of purchasing age-specific devices. What is out there? What are the choices? While a traditional laptop with a keyboard and large screen are logical choices, there are some other concerns that we should consider:

- rugged and spill-resistant keyboard
- not too heavy for children to lift and move around

- robust screens that can cope with finger, pokes and jabs
- a touch-sensitive screen—provides another way for operating it apart from the keyboard or mouse.

Figure 6.7: A laptop

Tablet PCs offer a lot of extra options—if they are attached to a laptop, then the screen can pivot around and transform the machine into a writing tool, touch screen or simply a different shaped tool for ease of sharing or moving.

Figure 6.8: A tablet PC in use

The iPad and iPad2 are increasingly popular but are limited by the apps that are purchased. However, their size, weight and user-friendly operating systems have seen them being popular additions to the classroom. As new apps are developed, their usefulness in the classroom will expand.

Figure 6.9: An iPad

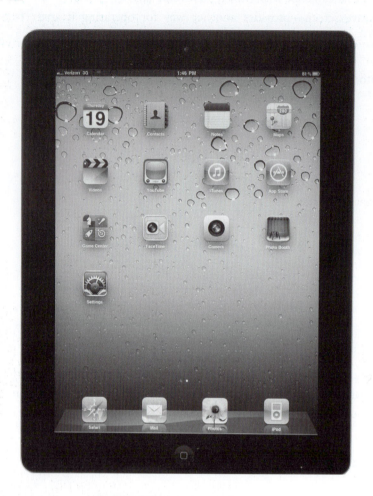

Lesson Ideas

Some ideas for using laptops, tablet PCs and iPads in the classroom

- Reading—eBooks
- Games—educational and recreational
- Drawing—using simple programs such as Paint
- Group work—these devices are mobile, so learners can be grouped more comfortably and share devices
- Drill work—via programs or online sites, learners can practise teacher-selected skills and content
- Music—listen to songs, sing along
- Taking images—most devices have built-in cameras
- Searching for information.

The strengths of using laptops, tablet PCs and iPads are their mobility and size. They can be moved around the room, and students are not restricted as to where they use them. They are also easier for group or pair work and can be used individually, so suit all modes of organisation. If they have software loaded or are WiFi-enabled, then their applications are limitless.

A quick overview of laptops, tablet PCs, iPads

What's creative about their use?	Opportunities for development beyond knowledge acquisition...
• Students are not restricted to being in a particular physical space. • They can be used in a variety of groupings—whole class (hooked up to a projector), pairs, small groups, individuals. • They allow for personal self-paced development • They are creative as they are tools that need opening, using, creating with—they are not creative themselves; they provide opportunities for creativity by their use.	• Fine and gross motor skills—how to use touch pad mouse, how to use touch screens, how to coordinate their fingers and mouse movements. • Technology—knowledge and experience that will be used throughout their schooling.

LEGO Robotics

The **LEGO Robotics** system is comprised of several different programs (RXT, LEGO Mindstorms NXT, Mindstorms NXT 2.0, WeDo). The program most useful for the early years is LEGO WeDo. The Mindstorms Robotics Invention System was created in the MIT Media Lab in 1994. The original kit contained two motors, two touch sensors and one light sensor. The educational version of the products is called 'Lego Mindstorms for Schools',

and comes with the ROBOLAB GUI-based programming software, developed at Tufts University. The name Mindstorms is after the book *Mindstorms: Children, Computers, and Powerful Ideas* by Seymour Papert.

Schools purchase 'kits', which comprise approximately 600 pieces, including Lego pieces, motors, sensors, cables, USB connection cables and the programmable NXT Brick. There are also extra accessory pieces that can be purchased.

LEGO WeDo was launched in 2008, and is a simpler version of the robotics program aimed at younger learners (aged 7+). The WeDo kit contains 150 elements, including a motor, tilt sensor, motion sensor, LEGO bricks, gearing mechanisms and easy-to-use software. It includes a collection of sample projects—everything from an alligator that snaps its mouth shut when anything comes near (using the motion sensor) to an airplane that plays different sounds as you move it (using the tilt sensor). The easier-to-use software is a key point, as the screen is more visual and uses readily recognisable images to program the robot's movements.

Lesson Ideas
Some ideas for using LEGO Robotics in the classroom

- Science—learning about simple science concepts i.e. how machines move
- Technology—designing machines, robots and animals that perform tasks
- Engineering—how machines work i.e. gears and pulleys
- Mathematics—counting practice, problem-solving
- Literacy—building robots based on the characters in a story, re-create a scene from a story.

LEGO Robotics can appear intimidating, but with the new WeDo program, which is aimed for younger learners, it can be easily included in the classroom. An actual working robot that engages and inspires the learners to progress through hurdles and difficulties lends itself to rich, complex learning tasks. With the current focus on STEM in schools, including robotics would provide opportunities for this phase of learning to experience fun, play-based STEM activities.

A quick overview of Interactive LEGO Robotics

What's creative about their use?	Opportunities for development beyond knowledge acquisition...
- Hands-on construction - Colourful LEGO bricks - Creating working robots - Modifying robots after trialling them - Programming robots to move in any way the students wish.	- Building skills - Fine motor skills—manipulating bricks, using a mouse - Technology—understanding - the mechanics of robotics - Group work and social skills—cooperating with peers to complete tasks.

Touch tables

We are familiar with touch screens that function with single points of contact, such as a single finger, or at most two fingers manipulating the content on the screen. Starting to emerge onto the technology market are multi-touch screens, screen that can have limitless points of contact at one time. Imagine ten finger tips at once, or perhaps a collaborative group of four students, all touching a screen and manipulating different text, images or actions at the same time. It's an exciting prospect, and one that will be appearing in classrooms soon. At present, the market is dominated by several key players—larger companies already dominant in other technologies—and it's a technology that is being rapidly picked up by schools. The tables are designed to be used comfortably by groups of four (one person seated at each side) and software programs specifically designed for the technology are being developed. As with the interactive whiteboards, the first wave of software has been designed for numeracy and mathematics. It would appear that IWB software had been quickly adapted in order to get these products out into the marketplace. There have been a lot of games designed for the **touch tables**, but another more interesting use of their touch tables is with image-editing suites. By using index fingers to pull out and push in the image, users can re-size, cut, colour and paste it into a document—all of the options currently available with editing software in more tradition computing formats. Several demonstration videos are circulating on the internet, and this is where the more interesting uses are being shown—data mining on a large scale, using meta-search engines, such as Google, to find images, zoom in on maps, change profiles of images (for example, maps switching to satellite view and then 3D view)—these are exciting new developments. Some of the examples available already are:

Microsoft Surface http://www.microsoft.com/surface/en/us/default.aspx

TouchTable http://touchtable.com/

Lesson Ideas

Some ideas for using touch tables in the classroom

- Grouping items together physically
- Editing images or drawings
- Collaborating with peers to create presentations
- Playing educational games
- Manipulating software programs that have been designed for the touch table

While this has been largely speculative, as we do not have cheap or commonly accessible touch tables, the technology is one that will appear in classrooms over the next decade. Already, touch tablets such as eBook readers, iPads and tablet PCs are providing opportunities for students not to be tied to keyboards but to use their hands to manipulate the devices. As the tables and large multi-touch screens become available to schools, there will be some exciting opportunities ahead for learning.

A quick overview of touch tables

What's creative about their use?	Opportunities for development beyond knowledge acquisition…
• In their present format, touch tables are as creative as the software programs they come with—so gaming, photo editing, searching for information and word processing are all possible. Their creative strength is as a tool for collaboration, enabling multiple users at one time to work on a digital artefact.	• Fine and gross motor skills, hand–eye coordination • Technology—experience with a new tool • Developing stronger skills in touch techniques • Collaboration and cooperation skills.

Web-based learning programs

The internet is a rich learning tool, but not one often thought of as usable with this phase of learning. What would be a powerful skill for students to learn would be how search engines work! Imagine if you hooked up a computer to a data projector or whiteboard and, as a whole-class exercise, looked for information together. If this became a habitual behaviour, what learning might occur? At the very least, students would know that if you want to find something on the internet, then you type in a word on a page called 'Google' and a big list emerges with blue and black writing. They would also know that after you type in the word you need to hit the enter button on the computer—pretty powerful knowledge for prep–year 3 learners, not to mention older primary learners. Talking them through what you are doing each time models new learning; asking for help with ideas for words to write or how to spell words would reinforce prior learning—all rich learning experiences. I wonder what would happen if you let them try for themselves? So, I think the message here is that we should not underestimate the interest or ability of early years and primary learners.

Some skills are needed if **web-based learning** is to be successful. This is an opportunity to teach students the basics. The list below is a guide only:

- How to switch on the computer
- How to turn off a computer (PC or Apple)
- How to use a two-button mouse or a mouse pad on a laptop
- How to open a particular program
- How to type text (this could be on a document page, into a program which might need you to first click the mouse in a box and then type)
- Navigating a keyboard—what is a space bar for? When do we use enter?

These are all important skills that need to be taught before you use computers or laptops with your students. Remember, assume nothing! While some of your class might have computers at home, many will not. Once the basic operating skills have been taught, then the online learning tools you have at your disposal are endless. How do you select an appropriate website? Some hints here:

- Ask fellow teachers—what do they use? How do they use them (for example, whole-class, individual, small groups, pairs)?
- Read professional magazines; they are a rich source of ideas.
- Government websites—tailor-made for different phases of learning. Don't limit yourself to Australia. I find there are a huge number of really useful sites from the United Kingdom, in particular.
- Search for them yourself—but be careful, try them exhaustively yourself before you let a class use them, as you don't want any surprises!
- Make sure your online sites can be saved or the work exported into a format that can be used.
- Make sure the sites are age-appropriate and safe. Look at the URL—'edu', 'org', or 'gov' are the safest options.

At the end of this chapter are some interesting sites to start you off!

Lesson Ideas
Some ideas for using the internet in the classroom

- There are numerous CD-ROMs and software programs available for purchase in each of the subject areas covered by the curriculum. Your school will have purchased some, but make sure you are on the mailing lists of some of the publishers to make sure you are up to date with new programs.
- Basic typing can be used for producing letters, sentences and writing captions to digital images.
- Drills can be used in basic mathematics, spelling, grammar and reading comprehension at the level for each of the students in your class; this can be for remedial purposes or as a special reward for fast finishers.
- Web-based programs and sites can be used—almost any topic imaginable has a resource available online. Make sure that you use sites that have 'edu', 'org' or 'gov' in their URL; check carefully the sites you use.
- Whole-class searches can be done—use the IWB or screen to project your searches for information, make it a whole-class activity, brainstorm key words, look at sites together and see if they are suitable, model good search techniques and how to evaluate the information you find. Don't limit searches to text-based information; try searching for images and use this to introduce a new topic or discussion about the image.

There are several reasons you should include web-based learning programs, but primarily because they will provide your students with the opportunity to develop and refine skills they will use throughout their schooling. Basic computer operation is important; so too are skills in searching for information, how to insert CDs and how to open programs. These are things we might take for granted, but they need to be taught at this stage. Don't assume that learners are able to do these tasks; many students will be imitating older family members and not fully understanding what they are doing and why.

A quick overview of the web-based learning

What's creative about their use?	Opportunities for development beyond knowledge acquisition...
- The computer is a tool that is limited only by the operator. Students should be able to create many different types of learning artefacts via interacting with the computer - The rich web-based learning resources represent a limitless source of creative activity to engage in. The only warning is that teachers guide and select resources or sites carefully.	- Mechanical process skills—how to use the tools, how to operate them, understanding how things need to be done and in what order - Fine motor skills and coordination - Opportunities for cooperative learning - Peer mentoring—helping those who have trouble - Building an awareness of the internet, and the wider world.

Bee-Bots

Bee-Bots are simple robots that are programmable and designed to be used on the floor. They were designed in the United Kingdom and have been purpose-built for use with early phase and primary students. Their features include:

Figure 6.10: A Bee-Bot

- sounds and flashing eyes that let students know that their instructions have been entered
- the ability to remember up to 40 instructions or steps entered by students
- the ability to move accurately in 15-cm steps and to turn in 90° increments
- bright buttons for the students to use to input instructions
- a friendly and happy design that appeals to young learners (and teachers).

The Bee-Bot comes with software, and the robot can be programmed via a computer or via the buttons located on its head. There are floor mats available that can be used with the robots, such as simple street scenes, maps, letter charts and number grids, and the robot can be programmed to move around the mats.

Figure 6.11: Creative Bee-Bot and floor mat

Alternatively, an obstacle course can be designed and the students can program the robot to go left, right, forward, backwards, around and over, to work its way around a course. As you could imagine, the opportunities for learning are rich. The Bee-Bot's simple and child-friendly layout is a perfect starting point for teaching control, directional language and programming to young children. This open-ended resource allows teachers to use the Bee-Bots as a tool to enhance learning of curriculum content, and processes such as literacy (including storytelling and recounting), science (including experiments and problem solving) and numeracy (including sequencing, counting, direction and estimation). The Bee-Bot has a limit of remembering 40 instructions, but this is plenty to navigate around a course or to spell out a word. Bee-Bots are increasingly being used in prep–year 1 classrooms across Australia, and learning support sites have lesson ideas and resources available (for example, The Learning Place). While the Bee-Bot is a recognisable yellow beetle, many teachers have 'dressed' the robot in other ways so that it resembles a different animal, character from a storybook or even a dinosaur!

Lesson Ideas

Some ideas for using the Bee-Bots in the classroom

- Learning numbers and ordering via floor mats that the robot moves around
- Building obstacle courses that allow for rich learning opportunities—such as prepositions, positional language (for example, 'under the table', 'around the chair')
- Learning directional phrases (for example, 'turn right', 'go straight ahead')
- Act out a story—create the background and floor mats, then program the robot to move through while narrating the story

Bee-Bots are an interesting and very popular robot to use with early years learners. The options to either use a computer or the buttons on the top of the robot to program instructions are good. Bee-Bots run on AA batteries, they are colourful, suited to the age group and they can operate on the floor. All of these aspects make them attractive to use. As a simpler introduction to robotics, these would be an easier technology, but their simplicity might also be a limitation.

A quick overview of Bee-Bots

What's creative about their use?	Opportunities for development beyond knowledge acquisition…
• As they are 'toy'-like and are designed to be used on floor mats, they have a strong play aspect, which makes them potentially very creative tools—various different worlds can be created for them on the floor and they can then be moved around in them. This is potentially very rich. The machines themselves could have paper sleeves or decorations stuck on them transforming how they appear.	• Art—backgrounds and floor mats can be created for the robots, providing opportunities for painting, drawing and design • Technology—experience in working with programmable robots • Cooperation and collaboration as students work in small groups.

Summary

To conclude, this chapter has presented eight examples of creative technologies that you can use in the early years classroom. As you can see, they vary in complexity and the types of activities they facilitate. As you will see in the next chapter, teachers working in this phase of learning need a specific set of skills within their digital pedagogy to use these technologies effectively.

FURTHER READING

Brooker, L. (2003). Integrating new technologies in UK classrooms: Lessons for teachers from early years practitioners. *Childhood Education*, 79(5), 261–7.

Chantel, R. (2005). Computers use in preschool: Trixie gets a screen name. *New England Reading Association Journal*, 41(2), 49–52.

Dye, J. (2007). *Meet Generation C: Creatively Connecting through Content*. [Online] From http://www.econtentmag.com.

Judge, S., Puckett, K., & Bell, S. M. (2006). Closing the Digital Divide: Update from the early childhood longitudinal study. *Journal of Educational Research*, 100(1), 52–60.

Lessig, L. (2002). *The Future of Ideas*. New York: Vintage Books.

Resnick, M. (2007). *All I Really Need to Know (About Creative Thinking) I Learned (By Studying How Children Learn) in Kindergarten*. ACM Creativity & Cognition conference, Washington DC, June 2007 [Online] From http://web.media.mit.edu/~mres/papers/CC2007-handout.pdf.

Trendwatching. (2004). *Generation C*. [Online] From http://www.trendwatching.com/trends/GENERATION_C.htm.

WEBSITES

BBC KS1 Bitesize
http://www.bbc.co.uk/schools/ks1bitesize/literacy/
An activity-rich website designed by the BBC in the United Kingdom. It has great resources that you can rely on for being correct, safe to use and engaging. They have been designed in collaboration with teachers working in this phase of learning.

Online Games for Early Years Learners
http://www.miniclip.com/games/kindergarten/en/
Miniclip has some interesting games and video clips that can be used in the classroom. Explore all the different topics and games available.

Jumpstart
http://www.jumpstart.com/free-online-game.aspx?pid=googpdau&cid=kinder
garten%20online%20games&gclid=CIKilLr6o6wCFYSI4godcSyO2A
An interesting portal for online learning games aimed at early years learners.

Funschool
http://funschool.kaboose.com/
This is a commercially produced site for educational games, so there is a fair amount
of advertising on this website. However, there are some nice activities for students to
try, particularly the science games.

Kindersite
http://www.kindersite.org/Directory/DirectoryFrame.htm
A useful site with songs, games and stories. They are clearly labelled which age group
they are suited for and do get updated regularly.

CHAPTER 7

Developing a digital
pedagogy for
creative technologies

Learner Outcomes

After reading this chapter, you should be able to:

- understand that digital fluency in the early years is a combination of skills and experiences
- know how the Technology and Play Framework can be used to develop a digital pedagogy
- list the skills required for a digital pedagogy in the early years.

Key Terms

- digital fluency
- purposeful activities
- digital pedagogy for the early years
- creative activities
- experimental activities

What does digital fluency look like in the early years of schooling?

In Chapters 5 and 6 we looked at the role technology might play in early years learning and some examples of technology that build on the strengths of this phase of schooling. It's important to pause and re-examine what **digital fluency** looks like in this phase of schooling. We need to consider what skills, aptitudes and abilities we are hoping learners in prep to year 3 will acquire during these years. It is clear from the first two sections of this book that there is a national imperative behind the embedding of ICTs across the curriculum and phases of learning, and the learners in this stage are developing important sets of skills that will carry them through the schooling system and into the world beyond school. It is important that those who might be lagging behind in exposure to digital technologies, either due to the digital divide or because they have not had access to pre-school programs prior to starting prep, catch up. So while we might not usually associate the term 'digital fluency' with this phase, it's important that we view children's learning outcomes in the area of digital technology in this way. To illustrate, examine the two case studies below. One illustrates a digitally fluent learner at the end of year 3, and the other illustrates a learner who has had a different technological journey up to year 3.

CASE STUDY 1: MICHAEL

Michael is just finishing term 4 in grade 3. He has completed four years of formal schooling (prep and years 1–3). His teacher has a data projector hooked up to a laptop, a printer and three PCs set up along one wall of the room. There is a TV and DVD player on a trolley that gets wheeled around the classroom into different positions. There is one interactive whiteboard in the school (in the grade 2 classroom) which he experienced for one year. These facilities are typical for all of the classrooms in his school and represent what he has had access to during his studies. Michael's school is enthusiastically exploring the use of technology in teaching and learning. His teachers have all incorporated basic technologies and would, on average, use technology one or two times per day. As a consequence, Michael's digital fluency includes the following skills and experiences:

- He knows how to turn on and shut down a PC and laptop.

- He can navigate around a PC, click on Start, open up Internet Explorer, start programs loaded on the PC and, as a result, try new programs.

- He can use a two-button mouse and a laptop mouse, and understands the connection between the mouse, clicking on a space and typing words.

- He can work independently with technology.

- He can type words and understands how to 'go back' and correct a word.

- He knows if he wants to find something on the internet, he uses Google. He knows where to put the word into the search engine and then to press Enter.

- He has used other digital technologies—a digital camera and digital movie camera. He can use zoom and a DVD player.

- He has use web-based learning programs selected by his teachers—some required click and drag skills, some required typing in words or numbers and some required him to select the best answer.

- He has used Bee-Bot robots to learn directions—he has built obstacle courses and learnt how to program the robot.

- He has used an iPad to read a book.

His teacher would describe him as enthusiastic with technology. He is quite confident and enjoys problem-solving his way out of hurdles or in experience with technology. He often volunteers to help set up equipment, help put equipment away and is naturally curious about new technologies.

CASE STUDY 2: DAVID

David is just finishing term 4 in grade 3. He has completed four years of formal schooling (prep and years 1–3). His teacher has an interactive whiteboard hooked up to a laptop, a printer and four PCs set up along one wall of the room. There is a TV and DVD player on a trolley that gets wheeled around the classroom into different positions. These facilities are typical for all of the classrooms in his school and represent what he has had access to during his studies. David's school is reasonably well equipped with technology. His teachers have all incorporated basic technologies and would, on average, use technology one or two times per day. As a consequence, David's digital fluency includes the following skills and experiences:

- He knows how to turn on and shut down a PC and laptop. He has watched his teacher and teacher aide do this regularly.

- He hasn't learnt how to navigate around a PC, click on Start, open up Internet Explorer nor start programs loaded on the PC, as the program he is going to use in a lesson is always open and ready for him to use.

- He can use a two-button mouse and a laptop mouse, and he understands the connection between the mouse, clicking on a space, and typing words, as long as someone is modelling this or is nearby to help when he gets confused.

- He cannot work independently with technology; he has only ever worked supervised.

- He can type words and understands how to 'go back' and correct a word.

- He has watched his teacher use Google; he understands where to put the word into the search engine.

- He has seen his teacher use other digital technologies—a digital camera, digital movie camera and DVD player.

- He has use web-based learning programs selected by his teachers—some required click and drag skills, some required typing in words or numbers and some required him to select the best answer.

He has teacher would describe him as familiar with technology. He is quite able to use certain types of technology.

What is the key difference between these two case studies? Clearly, both schools have technology devices in their classrooms, but the difference is the teacher. Michael's teacher would appear to be enabling the development of skills in the class in an active, hands-on manner, while David's teacher would appear to be modelling the use the technology to the class, permitting only a passive engagement with the devices themselves. As a result, there are distinct differences between the learning outcomes of these students. We have probably all encountered variations of the type of teacher David has experienced—perhaps not technologically fluent or confident in their own skills, using technology in the classroom because they know it's the right thing to do or because they feel pressure to do so, but still fear the devices. It's a common problem, but one that can be avoided if you have a digital aptitude or, more importantly, a digital pedagogy.

So, let's get back to the original question we asked at the start of this chapter—what does digital fluency look like in the early years of schooling? The case studies above showed us the differences in learning outcomes between two students who experienced very different uses of technology in their learning and different abilities and aptitudes of teachers during those years. Digital fluency in this phase of learning is comprised of two specific characteristics: skills and experiences. The skills are concrete learnings of actual abilities (for example, how to use a digital camera) but the experiences are more complex. The experiences are the actual uses of different technologies and their educational applications, such as how they enhance writing development or literacy skills.

A quick overview of digital fluency in the early years

Skills	Experiences
• Basic operations associated with PC and laptop computers (turning on/off, navigating around the screen, use of a mouse, how many 'clicks' of a mouse button)	• Familiarity with terms associated with computers (for example, names of programs, 'Windows', 'Word', 'PowerPoint', 'Start', 'My Computer')
• Basic web-searching (understanding what a search engine is, key words for searching)	• Understanding how to use key words to find information

(Continued)

Skills	Experiences
• Use of commonly used programs (Word and PowerPoint, how to create a new document, how to save)	• Knowing some terms associated with the internet (for example, 'Google', 'Internet Explorer', 'Firefox')
• How to use a digital camera and associated skills (use of buttons, framing pictures, zoom, how to transfer pictures to a computer)	• How to frame images—considering how to set up a shot, what you trying to take, visual literacy
• How digital movies are made (either hands-on or assisted)	• Social experiences—working in pairs or groups, turn taking and sharing
• How to record your voice	• Literacy experiences—language associated with content, new terms associated with technologies
• How to play a DVD—steps in operating the DVD player and TV	• Fine motor skill development (manipulating devices)
• How to save something on a computer	• Complex problem-solving (working out how to do something associated with a particular program)
• How to use more complex technologies (for example, LEGO Robotics, Bee-Bots)	• Rich tasks (for example, LEO Robotics that incorporates science, mathematics, engineering and technology)
• How to use a touch pad (for example, iPad)	• Learning via modelling—watching, practising and then using skills and techniques
• How to use an interactive whiteboard (with a pen or finger), how to use particular programs.	• Conversations with peers about technology—what they can do, what they have seen, new uses.

This list of the attributes of digital fluency in the early years of learning is only a starting point, a suggested list of basic skills that you would hope learners had acquired after four years of formal schooling. It should be expected that the list would vary dramatically based upon the skills, aptitudes and enthusiasm of the teacher and students. Use it as a guide to understanding the basic expectations of learners at this phase of schooling. It's certainly not a finite list that, once achieved, you can 'tick' off digital fluency from your learning outcomes for your class! Remember, this is the initial stage of acquiring digital skills that will be used throughout children's schooling. So, we have a clearer understanding of what digital fluency in this phase of learning is, we know the types of technologies children should be engaging with, but importantly, how is this to be achieved? For this to be achieved, teachers need a digital pedagogy. In each phase of learning, this is a different set of skills or areas to focus upon. Let's examine what a digital pedagogy for early years teachers comprises.

Personal Reflection

What levels of digital fluency have you observed?

You are currently engaged in a pre-service teacher education program, which you may be undertaking either as an undergraduate or postgraduate student. During your studies, you will have experienced a number of teacher practicums. Hopefully, as you are specialising in early childhood, you have had some practicum teaching experience in this phase of schooling or have at least observed classes. Think about those classes and the levels of digital fluency you might have observed. Answer the following questions:

- What types of digital technologies did you see the students use or did you see available for use around the classroom?
- Did the class teacher use any technologies? If so, what types? This could be a simple PowerPoint presentation, a handout or worksheet created using Word, the IWB or something similar.
- What were the responses of the students to the use of digital technologies?
- Does the school have a lot of technology resources for teachers to access?
- If you observed the students using technology, answer the following questions:
  - How digitally fluent was the class?
  - What impact did the use of technology have on the learning outcomes?
  - What other impact did the use of technology have on the learning experience? For example, better group work, learning how to share learning tools.
  - Did you make any other observations?
- How would you describe the technology skills and the teacher's attitude towards technology use in the classroom?

Developing a digital pedagogy for early years teachers

In Chapter 5 we explored the idea of learning with technology in the early years. It was suggested that the type of learning activities that typically occur in the early years of schooling are built on solid curricular foundations that incorporate creativity, play and exploration or experimentation. The Technology and Play Framework was suggested as a model to base the inclusion of technology in teaching and learning in the early years (see Figure 7.1).

Figure 7.1: The Technology and Play Framework

It's timely to revisit these ideas, as they form the cornerstones to the digital pedagogy required by teachers working in the early years. Let's first consider *creative activity*—this brings to mind hands-on learning that results in the production of an artefact, something tangible and real. It could be the creation of a painting, a finger puppet, or it could be a robotic animal that opens and closes its mouth. *Experimental activity* is concerned with creativity, but also with processes, with how things work, with how something might change if you move this or change that. Learners engage in a process of trying to understand how something functions. This could also be concerned with problem-solving. For example, what happens to a glass of water when we put something in it, or how we get the digital camera to take a close-up picture. Finally, there is *purposeful activity*. It could be assumed that this is concerned with the hard learning associated with the curriculum and the acquisition of specific content knowledge, but purposeful learning is mainly concerned with the acquisition of a specific 'chunk' of knowledge. For example, it could be how to write the letters A–E, upper and lower case, or it could be learning how to turn on a computer and open a particular program. All three of types of activities are concerned with a combination of content and process knowledge; all three can be applied to technology-based learning or non-technology based learning.

Critical Reflection

Let's consider the types of technology suggested for this phase of learning from Chapter 6; these are presented in the table below. Examine each type of technology and decide if it could be used in creative, experimental or **purposeful activities** within an early years classroom. Think of a specific activity for each to illustrate your point.

Type of technology	Creative activity	Experimental activity	Purposeful activity
Digital camera and images			
Digital storybooks			
Interactive whiteboards			
Laptops, tablets and PCs			
LEGO Robotics			
Touch tables			
Web-based learning			
Bee-Bots			

Are there any of the technologies that you consider could not be used for these purposes? If there are, explain why you think they could not be used for that purpose.

So, we are beginning to see that a **digital pedagogy for the early years** is concerned with three elements: creative activity, experimental activity and purposeful activity.

A digital pedagogy for creative technologies

As we explored in Chapter 1, a digital pedagogy is a complex blend of skills and aptitude. We have suggested that there are three elements that are central to the development of digital pedagogical skills in teachers who specialise in the early and primary years of learning (prep to grade 7). But what does this really look like? Figure 7.2 demonstrates how each of these types of activity is associated with an aspect of technology that is particular to these phases of learning.

Figure 7.2: Activities and their associated technologies

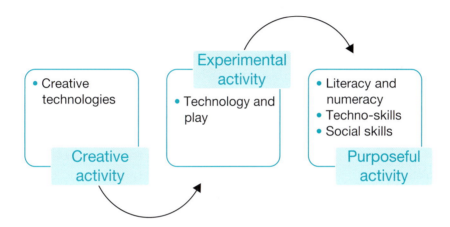

To be pedagogically prepared, teachers need to acquire skills and experience in the types of technologies most likely to be found or that create learning opportunities that suit a particular type of activity. It is assumed that an effective digital pedagogy starts with a positive aptitude towards technology, which could be either nervous acceptance of its place in the classroom to enthusiastic embracing of different kinds of technology. We all start somewhere along this continuum. However, to develop a set of pedagogical skills that will allow you to use technology effectively in your teaching and learning activities in the early years classroom, you need to develop a set of skills that are quite specific. The majority of teachers would have completed their pre-service teacher qualification using computers to generate assignments, search for information and communicate with lecturers and peers; they would have used online learning programs (for example, Blackboard) quite regularly for two to four years. While on teaching practicum, they would have used a computer to produce lesson plans, handouts, worksheets and newsletters. This list is endless. So we can assume there are some common basic technology skills present in all teachers. But private use of computers and technology is quite different from teaching with them in front of a class or setting up individual, pair or group work for students using digital devices. In order to ground the development of a digital pedagogy on a specific set of skills, the table below lists the skills required to use the technologies presented in Chapter 6.

Table 7.1: Skills required for particular types of technology

Type of technology	Types of skills required
Digital camera and images	How to operate a digital camera (particularly the model you are using with the class)
	How to zoom, transfer files from the camera to a PC
	Familiarity with a basic image editing program—most cameras come with a program—ensure you have installed it on the computers you wish to use. Practise using the program—can you re-size, fix red eye, save, export in different sizes and formats?
Digital storybooks	How to operate the program you are using to create your storybook; for example, MovieMaker, PowerPoint
	How to load images, add sound files, re-order images, add title and credit slides, add text narration
	How to export your storybook into a format that can be used (a common movie format)
	How to burn your storybook onto a DVD or CD, or transfer to a USB device
Interactive whiteboards	How to use the IWB with different programs that are available in your school—how to fix basic technical problems
	Basic IWB skills—how to turn on/off, save work, move objects on the screen, how to use the pen or your finger to manipulate objects
Laptops, tablets and PCs	All very dependent on the make and model of your device, but some suggestions are:
	for laptops—how to use the mouse pad and be able to describe to students how to use it, how to open and close the laptop programs, how to connect the laptop to data projectors, TVs or other viewing devices
	for tablet PCs—how to calibrate the screen, how to use the touch pens, how to load programs, turn the screen around on the PC
	for iPads—how to open apps, how to navigate settings, how to save work, how to go back
LEGO Robotics	How to build basic robots—practise using the step-by-step instructions, how to describe instructions to the class, how to explain the mechanisms and science, how to program the robot using the software, how to troubleshoot if the robot fails to move
Touch tables	How to open and close programs, how the programs work, how to save work
	Familiarise yourself with how many points of touch are able to be used at one time
Web-based learning	How to conduct a simple search (for example, using Google) and explain what you are doing
	How to use basic truncation
	How to select an online site to use with the class
	Basic computer operations—on/off/enter button, typing, mouse work
	Specific skills or familiarity with the programs or websites you are using
Bee-Bots	How to program the robot, both using a computer and the buttons on the top of the robot
	How to direct the robot to move in different directions
	How to navigate around a floor map or chart
	How to problem solve if the robot does not move
	How to change the batteries

Let's examine each of these three types of activity in greater detail to see the specific types of skills needed.

Creative activity: The use of creative technologies

Creative activities, like their name would suggest, are possibly the hardest to define for a specific set of skills, as they are limited only by the teacher's imagination of which type of technology to use with their class. Of course this might be constrained by the types of technology they have access to within the school or funding available to purchase, but the use of the imagination plus access to the internet can mean that there are limitless opportunities that present themselves for use. So what is the most import skill required for this aspect of your digital technology? Techno-fearlessness! Be brave, try anything and everything, be led by your students' interests and what is popular at the time. Remember you are not using technology just for the sake of including it in the lesson; it should be a pedagogically sound choice, grounded in the curriculum and the learning objectives. As long as you meet those criteria, the opportunities are limitless.

Critical Reflection—part 1

Let's focus on creative activities that use technology. Above are listed the types of skills you would need to use eight examples of technology. Let's now re-examine those skills through the lens of creativity. What are some of the creative applications of those technologies and what types of skills would you need to be able to use them? Think outside of the box. Be careful with what you think of, as you will be repeating this task for experimental and purposeful activities.

Type of technology	Example of a creative use of that technology	The specific skills required
Digital camera and images		
Digital storybooks		
Interactive whiteboards		
Laptops, tablets and PCs		
LEGO Robotics		
Touch tables		
Web-based learning		
Bee-Bots		

Experimental activity: Technology and play

As suggested above, experimental activity is concerned with creativity but also processes how things work, how something might change if you move or change it, how learners engage in a process of trying to understand how something works or functions or it could also be concerned with problem-solving.

So what sets of skills do teachers need to be able to facilitate **experimental activities** in their classroom? There are four interrelated skills required:

1. Good analytical abilities: Can you break down a process into a series of understandable steps? Can you explain change and differences clearly? Do you understand how a particular object functions, works or can be modified? These are aspects that can be learnt; you are not necessarily good or bad at this, but you can learn how to do this more effectively. Try setting out the processes or steps, then trialling it on someone. Could they follow? Did they complete what you wanted them to successfully? We have all taught what we thought was an effective lesson, only to realise that we have either left the class behind or they have not fully understood the processes. A suggestion for developing good skills in describing or taking a class through a process would be to start at the very beginning, assume no knowledge and work together. Model the steps first, then talk the class through step-by-step (scaffolding), then let them work independently. Remember: model, scaffold, then independent learning.

2. Problem-solving skills: Can you work out solutions to problems during lessons or do you get flustered and grind to a halt? The ability to problem-solve and keep a lesson going is crucial to experimental learning. A lesson cannot stop just because a problem has been encountered. This is particularly important with technology, so you need a calm problem-solving approach when you strike problems.

3. Skills in inquiry-based learning: When students are engaged in inquiry, they are engaged in complex learning tasks. While a teacher may plan for specific learning outcomes and the type of activities they wish the class to engage in, often with inquiry-based learning new directions are taken and the learning is student-led. So how will you set this up in an early years classroom? You will have to consider the specific skills of the students involved, the resources, and amount and type of guidance or scaffolding needed to ensure that students are engaged in inquiry. All of these are skills required by the teacher to ensure that the learning progresses. Think of inquiry-learning within an experimental activity as being focused on answering key questions: How? Why? What happens if …?

4. Skills in play-based learning: Play-based learning is a key activity in this phase of learning. While some might describe it as learning by stealth, play is underestimated as a learning tool by teachers who do not work in this phase of learning. Exploring a particular technology, or building something and using the computer or digital camera to record it, are all play-based activities. Imagine the robots described in Chapter 6, LEGO robots built out of LEGO bricks or the Bee-Bots, small yellow 'bugs' that run around the floor following your commands. It looks like play, but is in fact serious learning. So you need to develop skills in designing learning opportunities that are play-based but are strongly aligned to achieving curricular goals.

Personal Reflection
Play-based learning

A couple of years ago I had decided to learn Japanese. I had decided that I wanted to focus on spoken skills, so that when I was travelling in Japan I would be able to make myself understood and also understand what I was hearing. So, I started attending night classes twice a week to learn the language. They were fairly traditional language lessons. Lists of new words were given out each week; we memorised them, learnt how to pronounce them, practised drills in class and slowly worked our way up to learning whole sentences and questions. Our language teacher was an Australian who was married to a Japanese person now living in Australia. All was going well; it was a struggle, but I felt I was progressing. Then in term 2 we had a new teacher. This teacher had a background in early childhood education and approached instruction in a completely different way.

One night I turned up to class ready to tackle the tricky topic of directions—how to say 'turn left', 'turn right', 'go straight ahead', and so on. The teacher arrived with several large rolls under her arm and an ice cream container. It turned out that the rolls were large floor mats with streets printed on them and in the ice cream container were small cars. We were sorted into groups and had to give each other directions to move our cars around the mats. It was a really fun lesson and we played with our cars for the duration, telling each other to turn left, go past the library and so on.

When I eventually travelled to Japan, I caught a taxi from the airport to my hotel. Unknown to me, this was not a common thing to do as the distance from the airport was quite a lot. So, the taxi driver didn't know where to go! As I had been to the hotel several times I was able to direct him, but how I did was I imagined myself back in that classroom, sitting on the floor with my mat and toy car! We managed to arrive at the hotel easily and the taxi driver congratulated me on my Japanese skills. Ten years later, that lesson is the only one that I really remember in detail and can still remember the language necessary to direct someone. So the value of play-based learning is not to be underestimated.

- Can you remember a play-based lesson you experienced as an adult?
- What impact did it have on your learning?
- Can you remember the content still?
- What about your level of enjoyment?

Critical Reflection—part 2

Let's now focus on experimental activities that use technology. Above are listed the types of skills you would need to use eight examples of technology. Let's now re-examine those skills through the lens of experimental learning. What are some of the ways these technologies could be used in experimental learning and what types of skills would you need to be able to use them? Think outside of the box. Be careful with what you think of, as you will be repeating this task for purposeful activities.

Type of technology	Example of how that technology could be used in experimental learning	The specific skills required
Digital camera and images		
Digital storybooks		
Interactive whiteboards		
Laptops, tablets and PCs		
LEGO Robotics		
Touch tables		
Web-based learning		
Bee-Bots		

Purposeful activity: The use of technology to acquire specific skills

Finally, purposeful activity, as suggested above, is concerned with the hard learning associated with the curriculum and specific content knowledge, but mainly with the acquisition of a specific 'chunk' of knowledge. This type of activity requires a combining of your understanding of the curriculum and syllabus documents with your skills in technology. As you design and plan your units of work, this is an opportunity for you to decide:

- Which types of technology could be used to achieve these learning outcomes?
- Which technologies would support the learning of the students?
- Which technologies could be used to meet the needs of a variety of learning styles?
- How could technology be used to introduce, engage and motivate the class to the new topic?
- If a technology is being used, what technological learnings will the class engage in?
- If a technology is being used, what learning outcomes particularly associated with that technology can be listed?
- How could technology be incorporated meaningfully?

Critical Reflection—part 3

Let's focus on the final type of activity that uses technology, purposeful activity. Above are listed the types of skills you would need to use eight examples of technology. Let's now re-examine those skills through the lens of purposeful activity. What are some of the applications of those technologies and what types of skills would you need to be able to use them? Think outside of the box.

Type of technology	Example of how that technology could be used in purposeful learning	The specific skills required
Digital camera and images		
Digital storybooks		
Interactive whiteboards		
Laptops, tablets and PCs		
LEGO Robotics		
Touch tables		
Web-based learning		
Bee-Bots		

Summary

This chapter is the final in the section pertaining to early and primary years and technology. It ties together all of the concepts explored in Chapter 5, such as the use of technology in emerging literacy and numeracy, and combines those understandings with the examples of creative technology presented in Chapter 6. In this chapter we have brought these ideas together so that they form the basis upon which a digital pedagogy specifically geared towards the early phase of schooling can be based.

Digital fluency in the early years is a combination of skills, to be learnt, and experiences. The experiences are equally as important as the skills, as they will facilitate a positive aptitude towards technology and enable learners to continue to use digital technologies in their learning. It is important that a basic grounding in technology skills is developed in this phase of schooling, as children will form the basis for later technology-based learning. It is an important phase, as learners enter the schooling system with differing levels of technology experience and skills but, hopefully, by the end of their first four years of schooling, they have a sound set of skills and a wide range of technology experiences.

The Technology and Play Framework has formed the basis upon which technology has been presented as an effective tool for learning in the early years, and will continue to be applied in the primary and secondary phases in this book. It is a useful scaffold to demonstrate the different ways that technology can be used and the different types of learning activities that can be developed.

As we have stated often, a digital pedagogy is based on a positive attitude and aptitude towards technology. You do not have to be technologically fluent, just technologically enthusiastic. The skills and ideas presented in these three chapters are only the starting point; the potential for technology in the early years is far greater than has been presented. What is hoped is that this will provide you will the basis to get started and develop your digital pedagogy throughout your teaching career.

FURTHER READING

Arthur, L., Beecher, B. & Downes, T. (2001). Effective Learning Environments for Young Children Using Digital Resources: An Australian Perspective. *Information Technology in Childhood Education Annual*, 2001(1), 139–53. Norfolk, VA: AACE. [Online] From http://www.editlib.org/p/8493.

Brooker, L. (2003). *Integrating New Technologies in UK Classrooms: Lessons for Teachers from Early Years Practitioners*. [Online] From http://www.freepatentsonline.com/article/Childhood-Education/104520645.html.

Carrington, V. & Robinson, M. (2009). *Digital literacies: Social learning and classroom practices*. [Online] From http://books.google.com.au/books?hl=en&lr=&id=AAe7vnChUsoC&oi=fnd&pg=PR5&dq=early+years+%2B+digital+

pedagogy&ots=oGDhUTnI1X&sig=xIRdSn-GH7m-uZZP8OJ4jPZzxjU#v=
onepage&q=early%20years%20%2B%20digital%20pedagogy&f=false.

Exley, B. (2008). *Communities of Learners: Early Years Students, New Learning Pedagogy and Transformations.* [Online] From http://eprints.qut.edu.au/17360/.

Levy, R. (2009). *You Have to Understand Words ... but Not Read Them: Young Children Becoming Readers in a Digital Age.* [Online] From http://onlinelibrary.wiley.com/doi/10.1111/j.1467-9817.2008.01382.x/full.

Willett, R. (2007). *Technology, Pedagogy and Digital Production: A Case Study of Children Learning New Media Skills.* [Online] From http://www.tandfonline.com/doi/abs/10.1080/17439880701343352.

Zevenbergen, R. (2007). *Digital Natives Come to Preschool: Implications for Early Childhood Practice.* [Online] From http://www.wwwords.co.uk/pdf/freetoview.asp?j=ciec&vol=8&issue=1&year=2007&article=3_Zevenbergen_CIEC_8_1_web.

WEBSITES

Research for Teachers
http://www.gtce.org.uk/tla/rft/pedagog0103/

This website contains some interesting and practical research reports. They emphasise making the link between what is happening in the education research world with teaching. It is a UK-based organisation with some interesting articles available.

Digital Pedagogies
http://education.qld.gov.au/smartclassrooms/dp.html

This is the portal for the Queensland Depart of Education and the various professional learning programs, initiatives, classroom activities and other technology-based projects conducted by the department. Rich with ideas and resources.

QSITE: Digital Pedagogy
http://www.qsite.edu.au/keywords/digital-pedagogy

QSITE is the Queensland Society for Information Technology in Education. It is a useful association to join if you are located in Queensland, but it also has a number of reports, resources and links to professional development programs.

ACEC
http://acce.edu.au/

ACEC is the Australian Council for Computers in Education. A useful organisation that has a professional journal, bi-annual conference and holds other professional learning programs throughout the year. Its membership is comprised of teachers and educational researchers.

PART 3

Creative, Purposeful and Experimental Learning with Technology

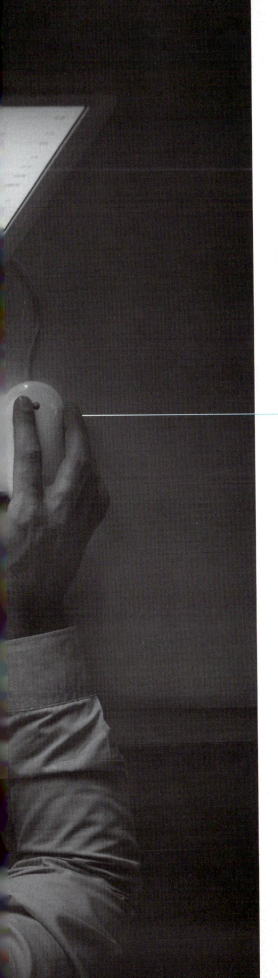

CHAPTER 8

The role of
technology in the
primary and
early secondary
classroom

Learner Outcomes

After reading this chapter, you should be able to:

- understand the concepts creative activity, experimental activity and purposeful activity as they relate to the primary classroom
- have a clear understanding of what it means to be digital content creator and how that can be developed by teachers
- understand the important of developing digital fluency in primary and early secondary-aged learners
- list the ways that teachers can create opportunities for students to become technology innovators.

Key Terms

- technology neophyte
- digital fluency
- digital content creator
- technology innovator
- wiki
- html
- metacrawler
- data mining
- truncation
- blogging
- mLearning
- diffusion of innovation

The primary classroom

Part 2 of this book explored the use of technology in the early years, defined as the first four years of formal schooling (prep to grade 3). The focus for technology in this phase is in three key areas:

1. to assist in the development of emerging literacy and numeracy skills
2. to offer an alternative tool for use in creative, experimental and purposeful activity
3. to develop a strong set of basic skills to be built upon throughout schooling.

We also saw that a digital pedagogy for this phase of learning was designed to support these three areas. So how do the uses of technology in primary and early secondary school differ?

First, let's define what we mean by 'primary'. In the majority of states in Australia, the primary phase of schooling is taken as grades 4 through to 7, but this is starting to become more complicated. Some states in Australia have adopted a middle-school model, which means grades 5 through to 8 are together on a separate campus, while in other states grade 7 is being 'moved' up to secondary school. For the purpose of simplicity, primary school for our purposes will be taken as grades 4 through to 7. Our inclusion of early secondary is important due to the types of learning students engage in within this stage of schooling. The term 'early secondary' refers to grades 8 through to 10.

The primary and secondary phases of schooling have undergone some changes in recent years, apart from the incoming Australian Curriculum, there has been a constant wave of reform, new policy, curriculum and syllabus review, and new programs being grappled with by teachers and being implemented in schools. Change is common. Situated within this context have been technological reforms such as the National *Digital Education Revolution*. Within this program have been the high-profile programs such as laptops for teachers, computers for schools and the National Broadband Network. Individual departments of education across Australia have drafted technology guidelines, professional development programs or accreditation for teachers in the area of technology; the stream of information, training and new programs has been endless. Consequently, primary and secondary classrooms have seen the greatest uptake of technology in any of the three phases of schooling (early years, primary and secondary). The primary phase has also seen more investment in technology than any other phase, as there has been a sense of 'catch-up' with the technology resources available in secondary schools. To be a primary or secondary school teacher in this climate has been both exciting and challenging.

Critical Reflection

Technology in the primary and early secondary classroom: past and present*

This is a time for you to reflect upon the technology you experienced as a student in primary or early secondary school. Remember, technology is not limited to digital technologies or computers; it could be something as rudimentary as a tape recorder, overhead projector or camera. Your task:

1. Write down a list of all the technologies you can remember experiencing when you were in primary or secondary school.

2. Write down how they were used. Were they used in a lesson? How was the class organised (for example, did you work individually, in pairs or as whole class)? Who used the technology (for example, the class teacher or a specialist teacher)? What impact did the technology have on you as a learner (on your learning and your subjective responses)?

Hopefully, you have a list of at least five to six items, perhaps more. It's important to write down how they were used, as the way we use technology has changed dramatically. Do you know how the first computers were used in schools? They were dramatically different machines to the ones typically found in classrooms now, and operated using an MS-DOS format.

Now we are going to repeat this experience based on the schools you have visited as a prac student. Your task this time is:

1. Write down a list of all the technologies you have either seen, seen your supervising teacher use or you have used while on prac.

2. Write down how they were used. Was it in a lesson? How was the class organised (for example, did students work individually, in pairs or as a whole class)? Who used the technology (the students, class teacher, teacher aide or yourself)? What impact did it have on you as a teacher and what observed impact did it have on the students?

*Compare these two reflections—what are the key differences? Are there any similarities?

One final aspect that needs to be considered in relation to primary classrooms is organisation. The traditional model of having one class teacher for all subjects is not the only mode of transmission adopted by schools. Increasingly, curriculum experts support class teachers, stepping in to take particular subjects or lessons each week in their area of specialisation. Most classrooms are supported by a teacher aide (often two, if they job share), and some class teachers are released from the classroom, as they may have a management role within the school, so a second class teacher is responsible for the class on certain days. Then, added to this mix, could be job sharing, a class split between two teachers, or it could be a blended class such as prep–year 1 or a combined grade 2–3 class, so the students in these classes not only have different levels of instruction, but will also have that class teacher for two years. All very complicated when compared to the traditional model of the past, where a class had one teacher for all subjects for the entire school year. These elements need considering when we are thinking about primary classrooms; we need to be clear about the variations and differences between classrooms across Australia.

Starting grade 4: The technology neophyte

Let's examine what skills a student entering grade 4 might have. Remember, when students begin the early phase of schooling, their experiences of learning programs vary greatly, some students enter formal schooling having come from pre-school programs that have strong learning programs, some do not. So a problem faced by early years teachers is this wide-ranging continuum of skills. In grade 4, the students have experienced four years of formal schooling and should have a set of similar skills. Obviously students will differ in their levels of proficiency and fluency, but they will have shared a common journey to this point and should have experienced a similar set of learning activities. What are we hoping the students are able to do by this stage?

- They will be able to turn and turn off a computer, start commonly used programs (for example, Word or Internet Explorer) and perform basic tasks.
- They will be able to use a PC and a laptop.
- They are able to use a mouse (and have a clear understanding of its buttons and movement).
- They should be able to use a digital camera, frame photographs, use the zoom button, transfer images to a computer and perhaps do some basic editing.
- They will be able to use Google (or something similar) to perform basic internet searches; they will understand the use of key words in searching for information; they will know how to find pages and open them.
- They might have experience in more creative and complex technologies such as robotics (for example, LEGO Robotics and Bee-Bot).
- They should have an enthusiastic attitude towards technology.

These would be the basic expectations we would have of students at this stage; the minimum we would expect them to have experienced over four years of schooling. Clearly, there would be students who might, due to technologies available at home, be significantly more fluent in technology. But at this stage in their education, we could describe the students starting in grade 4 as **technology neophytes**; they are beginners who have a solid grounding in the basics and are ready for more complex learning experiences with technology. It should be noted, that the skills and fluency in technology that we are describing here are all pertaining to those encountered and situated within a formal learning context; it would be possible to assume that some of the students at this stage are fluent users of digital technologies that are associated with gaming; for example, Nintendo DS, PlayStation, Xbox and Wii. These are a very different set of skills and, while they do feature in some classrooms, at present we are concerned with developing learning technology fluency in students. More about games and their use later! We started this section with the term 'technology neophyte', meaning a technology beginner. At the end of primary school, what term would be most suitable for the level of experience and skill displayed by the learners? It would be great to describe them as digitally fluent—that is what we are aiming for—digitally fluent and digitally able learners.

Technology in the primary and early secondary classroom

We now have a clearer understanding of the types of skills we expect the students will be entering this stage of schooling with. The next four to eight years of schooling, in terms of **digital fluency**, are years of consolidation and building on the skills already acquired, and exposure to a wider range of technology tools. Figure 8.1 shows the application of the Technology and Play Framework introduced in Chapter 5, and discussed further in Chapter 7, in the context of early years learning to the new context of primary and early secondary school learning. In this new context, it is transformed from being a framework within which technology can be *included* within the early years learning context, into aspects of *effective* learning with technology in the primary and early secondary context.

Figure 8.1: Aspects of effective learning with technology in the primary and early secondary phases of schooling

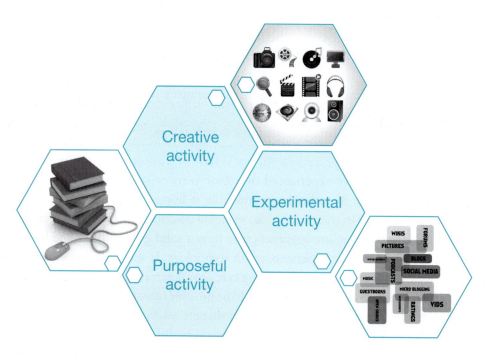

This provides a framework for the development of digital fluency in learners engaged in these phases of learning, and provides the scaffold for understanding the different types of technologies and their learning applications. What does this mean? Well, let's expand on each of these aspects.

Creative activity—digital content creators

As the name would suggest, the technologies that primary learners would engage with would be concerned with the creation of an artefact, preferably a digital artefact. Creative activities would involves a wide range of skills, would be rich learning tasks, perhaps built around problem-solving or inquiry models of learning. There would less teacher-led learning and more collaborative, peer-supported learning. Students would have the basic skills to engage in creative activities but during the completion of the task would find they were extending their skill sets, acquiring new skills and knowledge and applying previously taught knowledge to new contexts. As this type of activity is connected with creativity, it is easy to understand if you view the participant students as **digital content creators**. The types of activities they are engaging in result in the creation of some type of digital content.

Experimental activity—technology innovators

While this type of activity is closely associated with creative activity, the distinguishing difference, as we saw in the previous section, examining early years learning, is that there is an additional focus on processes. For example, how things work, how something might change if you move this or change that, learners engage in a process of trying to understand how something works or functions, it could also be concerned with problem-solving. This becomes more complex and independent in the primary phase of learning, as students engage in discovery learning activities—not only are they trying to understand or discover how something works, they are also trying to discover how to *make* something work—a key difference that builds on them being digital content creators. However, technology is not so much the central aim in this type of activity; rather, it is a tool to achieve the learning objectives, not the learning objective itself.

Purposeful activity—developing digital fluency

The types of technologies students would be engaging in with these types of activities are largely building upon prior skills. In this category there would be a purposeful plan to acquire experience and fluency in particular technologies, programs, sets of skills and understandings as they become more digitally fluent. The activities would be closely tied to the curriculum and there would be clearly established learning outcomes for the types of content knowledge and skills that are to be acquired.

We are starting develop a picture of the aim for the use of technology in the primary and early secondary phases of learning. Clearly, it is built upon the groundings of the early years, but there is a distinct difference. While the students engage in the same categories of activities (creative, experimental and purposeful), the outcomes are quite different. At these stages in children's development, the aim is to develop digital content creators, **technology innovators** and digitally fluent learners. These concepts are explored in greater detail below.

Figure 8.2: Learning outcomes of technology-rich learning in primary and early secondary schooling

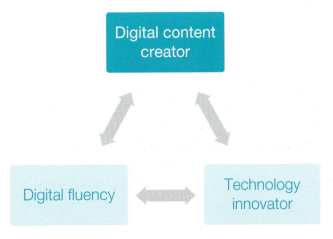

Digital content creators

What do we envisage when we say digital content creator? In 2004, Trendwatching.com coined the term 'Generation C'. They prophesied that the next generational grouping would be quite different from previous ones. Whereas groupings such as Gen X and Gen Y were specifically a generational cohort (born during the same period and exhibiting the same characteristics), this new generational cohort would be quite different. Gen C would be the digital content creators, not limited to a specific timeframe or generation, but defined by abilities and behaviour. Gen C would be a behavioural, not a generational, grouping. These technology users were developing podcasts, digital video and other digital content and uploading them to the internet—a significant change in the direction of the information. No longer merely downloading or taking information from the internet; they were contributing to it—creating its content. This is a trend that has continued. While the term 'Gen C' failed to gain popularity or become widely known or used, the idea behind its conception, that we are now becoming digital content creators, does have resonance. So, what do we envisage that digital content creators are able to do? See Table 8.1 for some ideas.

Table 8.1: What can digital content creators create?

What can digital content creators create?
• Videos made from still images (i.e. using programs such as MovieMaker)
• Embedding narration or soundtracks on videos
• Create moving objects via robotics
• Create clay animation movies
• Create and maintain a blog—perhaps to chart a project or to communicate with others on a topic

But what does this mean for primary and early secondary learners? It changes the learning outcomes in two significant ways. The product becomes a focus of the activity—so the processes that are involved in the creation of the artefact, plus the actual artefact itself, become important but, significantly, there are new forums and new 'end' points for the artefact. Artefacts can be shared online with other learners, they can be posted for a wider audience to see and comment on, they can be uploaded to a variety of different websites (both private and public) and learners develop a set of skills that expand the types of learning outcomes they can participate in.

Personal Reflection
Are you a digital content creator?

Let's re-examine the prediction of a new behavioural grouping, Gen C, emerging, made by Trendwatching.com. What was behind this new grouping? According to Trendwatching.com (2004), two main drivers fuelled this trend:

1. Each consumer undeniably possesses creative urges. We're all artists, but until now we neither had the guts nor the means to go all out.

2. The manufacturers of content-creating tools relentlessly push us to unleash that creativity, using—of course—their ever-cheaper, ever more powerful gadgets and gizmos. Instead of asking consumers to watch, to listen, to play, to passively consume, the race is on to get them to create, to produce and to participate.

- Do you agree? If you reflect on the types of digital content you have created, do you think it puts you in the category of being Gen C?

- List the types of digital content you have created—where did you keep that content? Is it stored on your computer or a USB stick? Or did you post it on a blog, upload to YouTube or share it in a **wiki**?

Technology innovators

An innovator is a person who develops something new. Children are continually innovating as they work within their worlds, learning to understand how things work. It is no different with technology. As children engage with the technologies they are exposed to, they may initially follow instructions or modelling by the teacher, but at some point they independently engage with the technology and start innovating as they try to work out how something works, what it can do and what it cannot. They discover new uses for technology as they attempt to understand processes and as they engage in inquiry learning or problem-solving. Innovation is a form of discovery learning, and all of these approaches clearly require the learner to be engaged in higher-order thinking. How do we encourage our students to become technology innovators? We need to provide them with access to a variety of different technologies and provide them with the opportunities to solve problems independently. Real innovation occurs when peers collaborate. A group of learners engaged in solving a problem or producing a particular artefact will innovate. Opportunities to have free use of these tools will result in powerful learning experiences. Overly teacher-led or highly scaffolded learning does not allow for innovation; freedom to try does. So the point for teachers here is to allow students the freedom to try. Step back and take a role of resource, someone students can access for help or guidance, but allow learning to be mainly student-led.

CASE STUDY

The Epic Citadel Project by Ringwood North Primary School

The following is an example of innovative technology, in this case iPads and an app called The Epic Citadel. The iPad formed the basis of a technology challenge given to grade 4 and 5 students.

Background

Ringwood North Primary School began the iPads for Learning Trial in semester two, 2010 with 136 year 4 and 5 students. As a leader in the integration of technology into learning, Ringwood North continues to innovate and share its journey with a worldwide audience.

Ringwood North Primary School is located in the outer eastern suburbs of Melbourne. The school has a reputation for its use of digital technologies, and its visual and performing arts programs. The use of information communication technologies is integrated in all curriculum areas, particularly in the senior years. A whole-school focus on literacy and numeracy aims to improve students' knowledge, understanding and application of these study areas.

The Project

Teachers at Ringwood North Primary School created the Epic Citadel Challenge. The Epic Citadel Challenge involved educators and students collaborating to create a digital story based on the Epic Citadel environment and then sharing the story and reflections globally. The Epic Citadel app is an 82.2Mb free download where players navigate in a dynamic fantasy setting, exploring the world, from the bridge overlooking the river to the mysterious cathedral at the centre of town. The Epic Citadel app is available for the iPhone, latest iPod touches and iPad.

Here's the Epic Citadel Challenge students were set:

- Create a digital story utilising photos from the app Epic Citadel.

- The digital story may include text, or it may not. It may be a collage, a poem. It is entirely up to you, as long as it tells some sort of story.

- Use any apps you like to create your story.

- Your story must be no more than three minutes.

- All finished stories must include a short reflection by the student before being uploaded.

- Please answer these questions:

  - How did you create your story?

  - What worked well? What didn't?

  - What skills do you think you have learnt in completing this task?

- Some ideas to help you get started:

  - Sequence your pictures in Keynote in order to add text to your snapshots.

  - Create a short film in Reel Director where you can include transitions, audio and even record a voiceover.

  - Use Doodle Buddy to stamp new characters over the top of the pictures.

  - Use Strip Design to create a comic. Insert pictures into frames, add text and speech bubbles.

  - Use apps that allow you to compose your own music to create a soundtrack or ambience.

You can see the results online at http://ipadtrial.posterous.com/

(This case study was taken from iPads for Learning, an initiative of the Victorian Government http://www.ipadsforlearning.vic.edu.au.)

This case study illustrates the rich, complex problem-solving activities that create an environment where students can become technology innovators. If possible, look at the student work online. Now answer the following questions:

1. What specific skills would students have needed to complete this task?
2. What skills would students have acquired after completing the task?
3. What was the role of the teacher?
4. Are you familiar with all the programs/apps listed above (for example, Keynote, Reel Director, Doodle Buddy, Strip Design)? Go and find out about them.

Digital fluency

At this stage, students have a sound grounding in the basics; for the next four years of schooling these need to be built on and refined. The level of digital fluency students start with is generally basic; these students were described as technology neophytes, or beginners. Here begins the shift toward becoming digital fluent. There should be a sense of not only moving towards the skills needed in senior secondary schooling but a developing proficiency in key programs and digital technologies. As mentioned, students have probably achieved a level of proficiency in recreational technologies such as gaming consoles, so they have a level of ability and aptitude towards technologies. What students need to focus upon now are the learning technologies. At the end of these four years of schooling, students should be digitally fluent in a wide range of technologies, as set out in Table 8.2.

Table 8.2: A digital fluency checklist

A suggested checklist of digital fluency by the end of primary and/or early secondary school
• Be able to use proficiently Word, PowerPoint, Excel, Publisher
• Be familiar with some higher level technology programs, such as FrontPage, Dreamweaver, Flash, some programming languages (**html**)
• Be able to create digital artefacts, for example, videos and podcasts
• Be proficient in web searching: experience in **metacrawlers**, **data mining**, **truncation**, how to refine searches, understand the different types of websites (for example, edu, gov, org, com)
• Have a developed understanding of digital literacy: know the limitations and strengths of hypertext, eBooks, how to critically evaluate electronic sources of information
• Be experienced in and understand the strengths and weaknesses of Web 2.0 (social networking and online communication)
• Be experienced in **blogging**, wikis, podcasts, RSS feeds
• Have experience in more complex technologies: **mLearning**, robotics
• Understand the associated language—terminology and meanings

So what does this mean for teachers working in these phases of learning? Clearly, there is a list of skills and abilities that we need to be mindful of and be working towards achieving across the four years. There is significance in developing a proficient level of digital fluency at these stages in schooling; it will have a direct impact on students' abilities to cope with and work in the secondary phase of schooling, but it will also form the basis of the skills they will learn post-formal schooling. Many of our policy documents mention the requirement for schools and the education system as a whole to prepare individuals to be life-long learners. Digital fluency is central to achieving this, as the majority of information we access is electronic. The internet will play an increasingly important role in our lives and it is the first place people log on to find information. Being digitally fluent will mean that learning is a process students continue to engage in.

Technology terms

We have mentioned quite a few different types of technologies above and some terms that are associated to digital devices. Just in case you are unsure of some of these there is a quick guide below:

A quick guide to...mLearning

What is mLearning? A simple definition is: any sort of learning that happens when the learner is not at a fixed, predetermined location, or learning that happens when the learner takes advantage of the learning opportunities offered by mobile technologies. To put it in more colloquial terms, mLearning is learning that occurs using a mobile device. What types of devices enable mLearning?

- Smartphones (phones with internet browsing, email)
- iPads
- Laptops
- eBooks
- MP3 players (e.g. iPod).

A quick guide to search terminology

Metacrawlers are metasearch engines that blend the top web search results from Google, Yahoo!, Bing, Ask.com, About.com, LookSmart and other popular search engines. A MetaCrawler also provides users the option to search for images, video, news, yellow pages and white pages.

Data mining is the process of discovering new patterns from large data sets. It is the process of looking for differences and similarities. For example, a survey of students in your class on a particular topic, when you analyse the spread of answers you are engaged in data mining.

Truncation is a searching technique used in databases in which a word ending is replaced by a symbol. For example, when typing into Google 'red + ginger', the search engine will find incidents of these two words together. Other popularly used symbols are '*' and '?'.

HTML stands for HyperText Markup Language and is the main language used for building web pages. HTML is written in the form of tags that are enclosed in angle brackets, for example, <html>. Web browsers read and transform them into visible web pages.

A quick guide to blogging

A blog (a blend of the term 'web log') is a type of website or part of a website supposed to be updated with new content from time to time. Blogs are usually maintained by an individual with regular entries of commentary, descriptions of events, or other material such as graphics or video. Entries are commonly displayed in reverse-chronological order. Many blogs provide commentary on a particular subject; others function as more personal online diaries. A typical blog combines text, images, and links to other blogs, web pages, and other media related to its topic. The ability of readers to leave comments in an interactive format is an important part of many blogs. Most blogs are primarily textual, although some focus on art (art blog), photographs (photoblog), videos (video blogging or vlogging), music (MP3 blog) and audio (podcasting). Microblogging is another type of blogging, featuring very short posts. As of 16 February 2011, there were over 156 million public blogs in existence (The Nielsen Company; BlogPulse).

A quick guide to wikis

A wiki is a website that allows the creation and editing of any number of interlinked web pages via a web browser using a simplified markup language or a WYSIWYG text editor. Wikis are typically powered by wiki software and are often used collaboratively by multiple users—this is the key distinguishing feature of a wiki as compared to a blog which is created by an individual. Perhaps the most commonly used wiki in the world is Wikipedia.

Critical Reflection

Technology in the primary and secondary school teacher: Diffusion of Innovation

Diffusion of innovations is a theory that seeks to explain how, why, and at what rate new ideas and technology spread through cultures. Everett Rogers, a professor of rural sociology, popularised the theory in his 1962 book *Diffusion of Innovations*. He said diffusion is the process by which an innovation is communicated through certain channels over time among the members of a social system. The origins of the diffusion of innovations theory are varied and span across multiple disciplines. The rates of adoption are shown in the graph below:

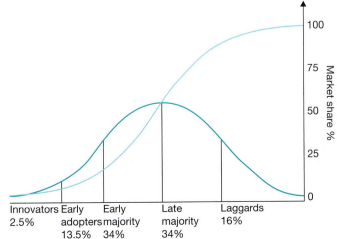

This theory has made a sizeable impact on education. Some of the terminology can be heard in conversations we have about technology uptake in the classroom. 'Be an early adopter not a laggard' was typical. Your task:

1. Define each of the following terms in relation to technology and teaching:

2. What is an innovator-type teacher? What is an early-adopter teacher, an early-majority teacher, a late-majority teacher, a laggard teacher?

3. Think of a teacher you have experienced or know who might illustrate each of these types—what are the learning experiences of the students in their classes with regard to technology?

4. Define yourself as a teacher—where do you fit on this scale? Where would you like to be on this scale?

Summary

This chapter presents a number of different ideas that are built on the concepts expressed in Part 2. Technology has a role to play in the teaching and learning activities within each phase of schooling. We have seen how technology can be used in three different ways, to engage students in three different types of learning activities:

- creative activities
- experimental activities
- purposeful activities.

All of these activities have different skills and content knowledge associated with them. We have seen how, in the primary and early secondary phases of schooling, there is a significant up-skilling of students. While in early years classrooms there is a concern for students to learn the basics and develop a positive attitude towards technology, in the primary and secondary phases there is a considerable increase in the knowledge and expertise needed by teachers to meet the continual development in digital technologies. The aims in these phases of learning are to develop students as:

- digital content creators
- technology innovators
- digitally fluent users of technology.

This might give an impression that lessons will be dominated by technology, that we need to crank up the amount and variety of technology used in our teaching and learning and, more importantly, that teachers need to be technological marvels. Not at all! We do need to be open and enthusiastic educators, who embrace and do not resist technology. That is a mindset we can all adopt. In Chapter 9 we go into greater detail about specific types of technologies for primary and early secondary classrooms.

FURTHER READING

Bruns, A. & Jacobs, R. (Eds) (2006). *Uses of Blogs.* New York: Peter Lang Publishing.

Burnett, C., Dickinson, P., Myers, J. & Merchant, G. (2006). *Digital Connections: Transforming Literacy in the Primary School.* [Online] From http://extra.shu.ac.uk/bvw/Cambridge%20Journal%20piece.pdf.

Dwyer, J. (2007). *Computer-based Learning in a Primary School: Differences between the Early and Later Years of Primary Schooling.* [Online] From http://www.tandfonline.com/doi/abs/10.1080/13598660601111307.

Graham, L. (2008). *Teachers are Digikids Too: The Digital Histories and Digital Lives of Young Teachers in English Primary Schools.* [Online] From http://onlinelibrary.wiley.com/doi/10.1111/j.1467-9345.2008.00476.x/full.

Howard, S. (1998). *Wired-Up: Young People and the Electronic Media.* [Online]. From http://books.google.com.au/books?hl=en&lr=&id=oYfcY3On8fwC&oi=fnd&pg=PP1&dq=primary+school+%2B+digital+pedagogy&ots=twqL-_5Eo7&sig=-hWWH76XOY5VFrlPRrkQdoYPz18#v=onepage&q&f=false.

Leask, M. & Meadows, J. (2000). *Teaching and Learning with ICT in the Primary School.* [Online] From http://books.google.com.au/books?hl=en&lr=&id=Cz08wZ4duigC&oi=fnd&pg=PR10&dq=primary+school+%2B+digital+pedagogy&ots=6qzTqJrFPZ&sig=SvlEp1-25PHWOanL09mXBRqd7as#v=onepage&q&f=false.

Trendwatching. (2004). *Generation C.* [Online] From http://www.trendwatching.com/trends/GENERATION_C.htm.

Selwyn, N., Potter, J. & Cranmer, S. (2008). *Primary Pupils' Use of Information and Communication Technologies at School and Home.* [Online] From http://onlinelibrary.wiley.com/doi/10.1111/j.1467-8535.2008.00876.x/full.

Willet, R. (2007). *Technology, Pedagogy and Digital Production: A Case Study of Children Learning New Media Skills.* [Online] From http://www.tandfonline.com/doi/abs/10.1080/17439880701343352.

WEBSITES

Primary school
http://www.primaryschool.com.au/learningtech.php
A useful website with links to other sites all sorted into categories and school grades. The list of resources is comprehensive, for example, web-based tools such as Google Sketch-up and resources for interactive whiteboards.

Blog site for Kathleen Morris, a Primary School Teacher in Victoria
http://primarytech.global2.vic.edu.au/
This is a remarkable site as it inspires teachers to try new technologies. It is a blog of a primary school teacher in Australia, who explores the use of blogs, Web 2.0 tools and technology use in her classroom.

Newspaper article

http://www.smh.com.au/lifestyle/back-to-school/technology-in-the-classroom-20100119-mhn3.html

An interesting article from *The Sydney Morning Herald* detailing some technology-based learning in primary classrooms.

Woodvale Primary School

http://www.woodvaleps.wa.edu.au/Information%20Technology/Information%20technology.html

A school website detailing the different information technology projects that students are engaged in. Shows the possibilities and range of projects primary-aged students are capable of.

CHAPTER 9

Developing digital
fluency in learners

Learner Outcomes

After reading this chapter, you should be able to:

- understand how technology can be included in all classrooms
- know some of the ways that technology can enable; digital content creation, technology innovation and digital fluency
- list the types of technology most suited to the primary and secondary phases of learning and some of their uses in the classroom.

Key Terms

- word processing
- publishing
- spreadsheets
- advanced web-searching skills
- WebQuests
- animation
- presentation software
- podcasting
- blogging
- Web 2.0
- making a video or movie
- web design

Technology for primary schools

In the previous chapter we explored the basic skills that students entering grade 4 would hopefully possess. The objective for primary and, indeed, secondary school teachers is simple: to consolidate and build on these skills in order to develop digital fluency. Effective learning with technology in the primary and lower secondary school phase of learning is still anchored to creative activity, experimental activity and purposeful activity; but now the focus of the outcomes of these activities is to develop digital content creators, technology innovators and digitally fluent users of technologies. The range of digital technologies that can be used in the primary classroom is wide. There is still an emphasis on creative technologies, but there is also a building up of a repertoire of skills that can be used in the later secondary school phase of learning. This chapter will present a mixture of technologies aimed at building skills and those aimed at expanding learners' digital experiences.

Word processing (Word)

Word processing is a basic and important skill needed by students throughout their formal schooling. From grade 4 it would be expected that students are able to use a word processor to produce documents. The level of expertise in word processing should increase as they progress through primary school. Associated with using a word processor are other important skills:

1. Students should be able to save documents (both to the hard drive of a computer and to an external device such as a USB stick), save them in different formats and understand what those formats mean.

2. Typing skills could be explicitly taught via a software program, but how to navigate your way around a keyboard is an important skill. Trying to use both hands and all fingers takes time, but there are fun drills and online resources that students can use to practise. Understanding the different types of keyboards is also important.

3. Students should know how to send a document to the printer—how to change preferences, page size, colour or black and white—all are important concepts to understand.

These are important skills to teach students. But what about the word processing program itself? What word processing skills should students exit primary school with? The list below is a guide:

- Changing font, font size, bold, italics, highlight and font colour
- Justifying, changing spacing, indenting
- Setting up bullets and numbers and re-starting numbered lists
- Inserting and modifying a table
- Inserting a blank page and understanding why this is used (not just hitting 'Enter' multiple times)

- Inserting a picture—embedding it tightly with text, understanding how to re-size and re-position it
- Inserting graphics, tables, smart art, symbols
- Inserting a hyperlink, setting how the linked page opens
- Understanding how to set up a header, footer, page numbers
- Setting margins, knowing which is the standard setting, changing page orientation, setting up columns
- Using templates—there are some that would be more useful such as tri-fold brochures, newsletters.

An interesting way to set these skills up in learners is to make the process of using the program part of the assessment. Their proficiency or ability in using the program can form part of the assessable content. Set up specifics that you wish students to use, such as how a page is to be set out, make it a little different from the standard settings in the program and see how they achieve this. Think outside the box regarding submission; for example, older primary students could submit their documents electronically—if not via email, then on a USB stick—how revolutionary!

A note on the selection of a word processing program—be mainstream in your selection, for example Word—as you want to set up a set of skills and experiences in your students that transfer beyond your classroom or particular school environment.

Lesson Ideas

Some ideas for using Word in the classroom

- Creative writing
- Journals
- Letter writing
- Templates—the wide variety of templates available make many different formats possible, for example, newsletters, calendars
- Simple desktop **publishing**
- Creating tables
- Creating graphs, smart graphics and charts using the templates

Proficiency in word processing is one of the core basic skills students will continually use throughout their schooling. Careful instruction in the basics in primary and early secondary school will provide students with the skills to be more creative and innovate with the program. It is likely that your students will surprise you with what it is possible to produce using a word processing program.

A quick overview of word processing

How do students develop as digital content creators?	How do students develop as technological innovators?	How does word processing aid digital fluency?
They develop skills in producing text-based digital artefacts that can be shared, uploaded or printed.	They apply new skills to creating artefacts that are beyond the task description or in new formats.	Core skills will be used throughout schooling and will be built upon as students become more experienced in the software programs.

Spreadsheets (Excel)

Spreadsheets are particularly undervalued by teachers and often dismissed as being too difficult or limited to 'accounting type' activities. Nothing could be further from the truth. Spreadsheets can be used for simple mathematical computations such as addition, division and subtraction; they can be used for more complex computations too. They are useful tools for presenting data, particularly columns of numbers that need to be sorted or added together. They are also very good for alphabetical data, such as names, places or other information. With some of the more complex rich-learning tasks that have been suggested throughout this book, a spreadsheet is often a good tool for helping to organise the information that is collected or the planning that occurs. As with word processing, there are some skills that are associated with spreadsheets that need to be learnt:

1. Students should be able to save documents (to the hard drive of a computer and to an external device such as a USB stick), save them in different formats and understand what those formats mean.

2. Typing skills—these could be explicitly taught via a software program, but how to navigate your way around a keyboard is an important skill. Trying to use both hands and all fingers takes time, but there are fun drills and online resources that students can use to practice. Understanding the different types of keyboards is also important. Importantly, here with spreadsheets, use of the number keys on the right side of the keyboards and the symbol keys is important.

3. How to send a document to the printer—how to change preferences, page size, colour or black and white—all are important concepts to understand. This is quite tricky with spreadsheets as areas for printing need to be selected.

These three aspects are important skills to teach students. But what about the spreadsheet program itself? What spreadsheet skills should students exit primary school with? The list below is a guide:

- Setting up columns, changing column size, inserting or deleting rows and columns
- Using basic formulas (for example, AutoSum and functions)
- Changing font size, colour, type, designating a label to font (for example, heading), wrapping text
- Inserting a pivot table and understanding what such tables are used for, converting data into a graph and knowing what the different types of graphs (column, line, pie, scatter, bar) are used for
- Inserting an image, clip art, shape, smart art
- Modifying margins and orientation, inserting titles.

Again, a note on the selection of a spreadsheet program—be mainstream in your selection, for example, Excel—as you want your students to have a set of skills and experiences that transfer beyond your classroom or particular school environment.

Lesson Ideas
Some ideas for using spreadsheets in the classroom

- Different formats for a variety of data, not necessarily numeric, mean that spreadsheets could be used in many different content areas.

- Collate and present information collected by a survey.
- Analyse information in a table or chart format.
- Do mathematical computations of both small and large sets of data.
- Create name lists, special rewards lists and attendance registers electronically with the help of students.
- Create data logs for characters in a story or sports day results.

Spreadsheets are not limited to mathematics. This is an important point for teachers to remember, as we often regard such tools as being useful for mathematics only. Consider spreadsheets as useful databases; be creative in your use of them.

A quick overview of spreadsheets

How do students develop as digital content creators?	How do students develop as technological innovators?	How do spreadsheets aid digital fluency?
They learn creative applications of spreadsheets beyond mathematics.	They apply new skills and knowledge to new situations and content areas. They learn to think of new ways to program formulas, produce graphical representations of data.	Spreadsheets help students learn useful skills that can be used throughout schooling. As a commonly used program outside of education spreadsheets will assist students beyond school.

Advanced web-searching skills

Previously, we have suggested that students acquire basic familiarisation and skills associated with web searching and the internet. So we could assume that the students in your class are familiar with search engines such as Google and know how to type in keywords, know what key words are and know how to hit 'Enter' to get results. It is important that these skills are built upon so that students become proficient at searching for information on the internet and able to analyse critically the information they find. When we say **advanced web-searching skills**, there are two aspects that need to be covered: practical skills that assist in searching efficiently for information; and critical skills in analysing the information that is found.

1. Practical skills

- There are some aspects that need to be acquired so that web searching is more efficient. These are:

- Boolean operators and truncation—higher level truncation skills need to be taught that move the students beyond the use of '' and +. Boolean Operators such as AND, OR, NOT; Truncation symbols such as *, "", #, +, & and the use of synonyms for search engines. A great skill that can be fun to learn is how to turn sentences or questions into keywords and then synonyms—all useful techniques for learning how to put terms into the search engine that will result in the types of information you want to find.

- Knowing how to read URLS—what the difference is between 'http' and 'https'; what 'www' means and 'W2' means.
- Searching techniques—how to limit the results via the use of 'site:'.

2. Critical skills

- Understanding domain names and what they mean; knowing which are more trustworthy; knowing which are more useful for information and research:

    - '.gov' government agencies
    - '.edu' educational institutions
    - '.org' organisations (nonprofit)
    - '.com' commercial business
    - '.net' network organisations
    - '.mil' military
    - '.int' international

- Critical literacy skills—evaluating the quality of websites and the information they present—understanding bias and subjectivity.

Beyond these skills are also wider concepts such as:

- different types of search engines, for example, 'Google, Ask!.com'
- meta-search engines, for example, 'Dogpile.com'
- terminology, such as 'webcrawling', 'indexing', 'cache'.

Lesson Ideas
Some ideas for using advanced web-searching in the classroom

- Searching for specific types of information—be specific so that the focus is upon search skills rather than end points; for example, an online treasure hunt for certain sites.
- **WebQuests** http://webquest.org/index.php—see this site for online search activities.
- Research-rich tasks that support class themes—set them as homework?
- Website critiquing—make a fun activity working out the quality of a site. Ask students to write a review justifying their criticisms.

Advanced web-searching skills are a combination of practical and critical learnings. They are important skills, as they will be used increasingly as students' progress through the school system. As information and research is increasingly electronic, efficient skills in searching for and critically evaluating information are important.

A quick overview of advanced web-searching

How do students develop as digital content creators?	How do students develop as technological innovators?	How does advanced web searching aid digital fluency?
They acquire the ability to locate sources of information, download, understand the mechanics of various sites.	They develop skills in searching for information, learn short cuts and gain understanding of what they see.	Efficient information searching, knowledge of search engines, truncation, Boolean operators, evaluating websites are all skills that aid students' fluency and make them efficient information users.

Animation—clay, drawing

Animation is the rapid display of a sequence of images of 2-D or 3-D artwork, or model positions in order to create an illusion of movement. The effect is an optical illusion of motion due to the phenomenon of persistence of vision, and can be created and demonstrated in several ways. The most common method of presenting animation is as a motion picture or video program, although there are other methods. These can be simple projects or they can become quite complex, but an advantage is their complexity. Students are involved in a series of processes as they produce their animation:

- Crafting a story
- Planning the story on storyboards—involves sequencing, drawing
- Planning materials
- Planning the filming—position of camera, background, lighting, framing of shots
- Collecting the digital images, either as video footage or still shots and then editing them into a movie via a software program (for example, MovieMaker) or **presentation software** (for example, PowerPoint)
- Finishing off the visual footage and then recording a narration or soundtrack
- Writing a script for the narration or soundtrack
- Merging the visual footage with the sound files
- Finishing the final product and exporting it into a format that is easily used—this might involve converting into another format.

This is an abbreviated list of the steps involved to produce an animation, but it does provide you with an idea of the complexity and tasks involved. There are several different media that can be used to produce an animation, and these are limited only by what you might have available:

- Background scenes painted or drawn by the students
- Background images selected by the students (could be compiled from images found, storybooks or other sources)
- Characters and animation action can be created via modelling clay or using LEGO, puppets, toys, painted scenes or drawings.

Lesson Ideas

Some ideas for using animation in the classroom

- Creating original animated movies
- Entering online animation competitions
- Re-creating scenes from stories or poems studied in class
- Create an animation that illustrates a current issue e.g. global warming

Creating animations with students is a rich learning task due to the different aspects associated with producing the short movie. Students will be engaged and find the end product extremely motivating. A small warning to teachers is the time this type of activity may take—think about setting it as a term-long project and dedicate one afternoon per week. There are a number of stages, and these need to be carefully planned and completed.

A quick overview of animation

How do students develop as digital content creators?	How do students develop as technological innovators?	How does animation aid digital fluency?
Creative outputs such as animated movies will develop a number of skills in the students, but the end product is evidence itself of their ability to create digital content.	The potential for innovation in the development of animation is high, particularly in editing the film, how scenes are set up and framed, and other additions to the final product.	Creating your own animated movie, with all the skills required to plan, implement and complete such a task is demonstrable of high levels of digital fluency.

Podcasting

What is **podcasting**? It is a term that we use regularly but probably don't have a clear definition of what it actually is. The term is the result of the combination of broadcasting and Apple's iPod—first used in 2004 by *The Guardian* newspaper journalist Aled Williams. A podcast (or non-streamed webcast) is a series of digital media files (either audio or video) that are released episodically and often downloaded through web syndication. Essentially, we mean an audio file that is placed in a publically accessible website and that can be downloaded. For a school setting, it could be an audio recording placed on the class website. The most common format is MP3, though increasingly due to the popularity of Apple products, MP4 is increasing in popularity. Podcasts are designed to be played via a portable media player—such as an MP3 player. However, in recent years, there has been some change in how we view podcasts and how we use them. Many people use the term synonymously with 'audio file'.

How do you create a podcast?

- Plan what you are going to say—with a class of students, it might be best to write out a script.
- You will need some equipment: computer, microphone, some type of audio recording software. There are plenty of free software program available, a good one is Audacity.
- Record your show—try using some introductory lead-in music.

- Save your show in MP3 format.
- Edit your file—remove any background noise, dead air time or other noises. If something needs re-recording, then add it to the main file. There are many programs that can be used here and they are very simple; don't worry that it's going to be very technical and beyond your skills.
- If you are putting it on a Class blog or website, you can publish your podcast as an RSS feed (Feedburner.com will help you with this, step by step). Otherwise, upload your audio file or podcast. It's that easy.

Lesson Ideas
Some ideas for using podcasting in the classroom

- Interviews—recorded by the students
- Class radio show—set up as a podcast
- Monthly podcast for parents, 'what we have done this month'
- Podcasts as a form of communication with other schools around the world—rather than an email exchange, podcast
- As an assessment item—rather than produce a text, produce a podcast, use it to check pronunciation and speech patterns

Podcasting is a popular and useful tool that is easy to include within the classroom. The types of technology devices needed are minimal, and the end product is an engaging and motivating artefact for students. There is something quite appealing for young learners to hear themselves in a recording.

A quick overview of podcasting

How do students develop as digital content creators?	How do students develop as technological innovators?	How does podcasting aid digital fluency?
Podcasting is one of the most common digital contents created and hosted on the internet. Skills in this will allow students to participate in this behaviour online.	The content of the podcast, how it is used, where it is out and how it is edited all allow space for innovation.	Students become familiar with the use and creation of a common digital artefact.

Presentation software (PowerPoint, Keynote, Prezi)

Presentation software is commonly used in education settings—teachers will often present lessons using either PowerPoint or Keynote, and students often use them for assessment. They can be wonderful learning tools if used well, or they can be boring experiences if overused or used badly. School is perfectly placed to develop these skills in students. There should be some scaffolding on the types of presentations that students prepare, starting from basic text or visual slides, up to more complex multimedia presentations. Suggestions are to avoid overuse of particular aspects (for example, transitions or animations) and to avoid overly long presentations. Set very clear guidelines, for example:

1. maximum of five slides
2. one image per slide
3. only two animations in total
4. text must be black, but background colours are up to you
5. no audio files or film clips.

This might appear to be strict and stifle creativity, but at times you need to focus on particular skills being developed, and you need to control the length and complexity of the final product.

There are two software programs most commonly used: PowerPoint and Keynote. As with word processing and spreadsheets, there are some skills that are associated with presentations that need to be learnt:

1. Students must learn how to save documents (both to the hard drive of a computer and to an external device such as a USB stick), and to save them in different formats and learn what those formats mean.
2. Students need typing skills—these could be explicitly taught via a software program, but navigating around a keyboard is an important skill. There are drills that are fun and online resources that students can use to practise using all fingers and both hands. Understanding the different types of keyboards is also important.
3. Students need to learn how to print handouts and notes sheets.

What about the presentation programs themselves? What presentation software skills should students exit primary school with? The list below is a guide:

- How to select a layout, insert new slides, slide formats (selection and changing them)
- How to change font, font size, colour, bold, italics, justify, insert bullets, numbered lists, indenting, slide orientation
- How to insert a table, image, clip art, smart art, graphic, movie, sound file, hyperlink
- How to design your own slide design
- How to use animations—selecting these carefully so that they support the presentation and not distract from it
- How to create handouts and notes pages.

There are also presentation programs available for use on the internet. One that is particularly popular is Prezi (http://prezi.com/). This is a web-based presentation program that offers a very different format for users—the templates and final products are very professional and, importantly, the program is free to sign up to. The presentations are stored on the Prezi website, so are available to use from any computer with a web connection. Internet presentation programs are very worthwhile using due to their popularity with young learners, and would be an ideal project for grades 6 through to 9 to try using.

Lesson Ideas
Some ideas for using presentation software in the classroom

- Individual and group presentations
- As a different format for assessment tasks
- As portfolios of work
- Short information presentations

Presentation software is a much complained-about technology, 'death by PowerPoint' is an often-used phrase. But use of presentation software is still an important skill for students to acquire. Presentations do not need to be long and boring, but should be short, effective and engaging. Clear guidelines are always needed; set limits and try to develop skills in multimedia. Web-based presentation sites are increasing and might offer new ways for presenting information in the future.

A quick overview of presentation software

How do students develop as digital content creators?	How do students develop as technological innovators?	How does presentation software aid digital fluency?
Students are creating a digital artefact, the presentation itself.	The format and multimedia used in the presentation provide multiple opportunities for innovation.	As group and individual presentations become more common and are assessment tasks, students using presentation software for these tasks become more fluent in key skills needed in school.

Blogging

A blog (a blend of the term 'web log') is a type of website or part of a website that is supposed to be updated with new content from time to time. blogs are usually maintained by an individual, with regular entries of commentary, descriptions of events, or other material such as graphics or video. Entries are commonly displayed in reverse-chronological order. Although not a must, most good quality blogs are interactive, allowing visitors to leave comments and even message each other via widgets on the blogs, and it is this interactivity that distinguishes them from other static websites.

Many blogs provide commentary on a particular subject; others function as more personal online diaries. A typical blog combines text, images, and links to other blogs, web pages, and other media related to its topic. The ability of readers to leave comments in an interactive format is an important part of many blogs. Most blogs are primarily textual, although some focus on art (art blog), photographs (photoblog), videos (video **blogging** or vlogging), music (MP3 blog), and audio (podcasting). Microblogging is another type of blogging, featuring very short posts.

There are several sites that offer secure blog spots such as:

- EduBlog (specifically designed for education, that is, schools and universities) http://edublogs.org/

- WordPress http://wordpress.com/
- Tumblr (mainly a photo blog https://www.tumblr.com/
- Blogger (a free blog tool from Google) www.blogger.com

Alternatively, school websites can have blogs built into them. There are some elements that need to be considered when blogging:

- What is posted is public—anyone can read the posting; granted, they need to find the blog first, but it should be remembered it is out there in the public domain.
- Little things matter—make sure that spelling and grammar are checked.
- Blogs offer an interesting new space for writing and literacy development—blogs are written!
- Blogs work well with independent and group learning.
- Blogs have the potential to connect schools globally—many schools in the USA and UK use blogging so the opportunities to make connections with another class are high. As we are all citizens of a global and interconnected world, blogs have enormous potential to connect different cultures, promoting intercultural awareness. Also, the use of blogs by non-English speaking background (NESB) students around the world makes them a useful learning tool in Languages Other than English (LOTE) education.

Lesson Ideas

Some ideas for using blogging in the classroom

- Blogging can work two ways—as a site you read and follow, or as a site you create yourself. Select a suitable blog for the class to follow—build activities around it.
- Create a class blog—use it as a site for writing, updates on activities, future activities and have blog monitors who are responsible for writing entries.

Blogging is an interesting way to create opportunities for your class to be digital content creators. They will build their on their literacy skills as they write blog entries, but they will also be entering the world of publishing and all that entails. Blogs should be secure, safe environments so, if they can be attached to the school website or set up in a secure site such as EduBlog, any concerns parents or the wider community has should be alleviated.

A quick overview of blogging

How do students develop as digital content creators?	How do students develop as technological innovators?	How does blogging aid digital fluency?
Students are creating digital online journals that are shared publically.	The format and content of the blogs are able to be changed, personalised, added to—there is a lot of room for innovation.	Students gain familiarity with a common digital tool. Students gain experience in creating digital content that is shared online.

Web 2.0 (social networking)

Web 2.0 has received a lot of criticism from the media and some aspects of society. Some of it is well earned, but it should be remembered the negative is created by individuals who *use* the tools available, it is not the tools themselves. When you hear the term Web 2.0, do you know what it means? The term Web 2.0 is associated with web applications that facilitate participatory information sharing, interoperability, user-centred design, and collaboration on the World Wide Web. A Web 2.0 site allows users to interact and collaborate with each other in a social media dialogue as creators (prosumers) of user-generated content in a virtual community, in contrast to websites where users (consumers) are limited to the passive viewing of content that was created for them. Examples of Web 2.0 include social networking sites, blogs, wikis, video sharing sites, hosted services, web applications, mashups and folksonomies. Two of the most popular Web 2.0 programs currently are Twitter and Facebook.

Twitter is an online social networking and microblogging service that enables its users to send and read text-based posts of up to 140 characters, informally known as 'tweets'. Twitter was created in March 2006 by Jack Dorsey and launched that July. Twitter rapidly gained worldwide popularity, with 200 million users as of 2011, generating over 200 million tweets and handling over 1.6 billion search queries per day. It is sometimes described as 'the SMS of the internet.'

Facebook is a social networking service and website launched in February 2004, operated and privately owned by Facebook, Inc. As of July 2011, Facebook has more than 800 million active users. Users must register before using the site, after which they may create a personal profile, add other users as friends, and exchange messages, including automatic notifications when they update their profile. Additionally, users may join common-interest user groups, organised by workplace, school or college, or other characteristics, and categorise their friends into lists such as 'People From Work' or 'Really Good Friends'. The name of the service stems from the colloquial name for the book given to students at the start of the academic year by some university administrations in the United States to help students get to know each other. Facebook allows any users who declare themselves to be at least 13 years old to become registered users of the site.

Do social networking sites have any place in the classroom? Yes. But it is strongly suggested that you think carefully about how you will use them, how to set them up, the types of permissions you will need (from the school and parents), your reasons for using them and what they will be used for. All this really means is that you must plan carefully. There are many reasons why you should embrace Web 2.0: currency, popularity, teaching students how to use social networking sites responsibly, and the natural enthusiasm and motivation your class will have towards them. Are they being used in schools within Australia? Yes.

Some examples of schools that use Web 2.0:

1. Woolsthorpe Primary School http://woolsthorpeps.global2.vic.edu.au/2011/10/14/twitter/

2. St Francis of Assisi Primary School http://stfa.act.edu.au/communication/twitter.html

3. Fremantle Primary School http://www.fremantleps.wa.edu.au/text/facebook_link_b9cu.htm

4. Kadina Primary School http://www.kadinaps.sa.edu.au/

5. Christies Beach High School http://www.facebook.com/pages/Christies-Beach-High-School/38270765422

6. Canley Vale High School http://www.facebook.com/CanleyValeHS
7. Healesville High School http://www.healesvillehs.vic.edu.au/
8. Elanora State High School http://elanorashs.eq.edu.au/wcms/

Lesson Ideas
Some ideas for using Web 2.0 in the classroom

- Twitter—Twitter has been used in several ways by schools—classes on excursions use it as a means of keeping in touch, as a treasure hunt tool and for quizzes
- Facebook—class Facebook pages, which parents, caregivers, school management could join—Facebook has a Group Page function, so a class page is easily created. It can be a closed page, so no public access
- Tumblr—digital images with short titles, which could be produced after class field trips and camps, in order to share experiences with the wider community

Web 2.0 has received a lot of negative comments in the media and, often, rightly so. It is open to abuse but it can also be useful if you are mindful of potential problems. Don't be put off using it, and do be guided by your class. Sometimes you have a class and a set of parents who are very enthusiastic users, so it would be a new technology that would receive a lot of support. Be prepared to explain how you will use it, how you will ensure safety and how you can link it to the content you want to cover with your students.

A quick overview of Web 2.0

How do students develop as digital content creators?	How do students develop as technological innovators?	How does Web 2.0 aid digital fluency?
Students are participating in digital content that will be used to communicate online	How the digital content is created, how words are selected and Web 2.0's format, all allow for innovation.	Fluency in common digital behaviours such as social networking, an awareness of Web 2.0 applications and an understanding of how it works contribute to students' digital fluency.

Publishing

Publishing programs such as Microsoft Publisher are extremely useful tools for students to learn during primary schooling. Many of the formats and templates tend to match the learning outcomes of units of work; for example, brochures, flyers and newsletters. They offer students easy-to-use templates that result in highly professional and polished outputs. There is a strong feeling of achievement and pride in the end product when students use programs, such as Publisher. As with word processing and spreadsheets, there are some skills that are associated with Publisher that need to be learnt:

1. Students should learn to save documents (both to the hard drive of a computer and to an external device such as a USB stick) and learn about the format documents are saved in. This has ramifications for the types of programs students can use; generally Publisher files are saved as '.pub' which means only that program can open the file. Publisher files can be exported as text files, but much of the formatting is lost.

2. Students need typing skills and should learn to understand the different types of keyboards.

3. Students should learn how to print the finished product—often publications are designed to be double-sided, so how paper is put in the printer becomes complicated, as does paper size and working out where perforations should be placed.

What about the program itself? What publishing skills should students exit primary school with? The list below is a guide for use with the program Microsoft Publisher:

- How to select a publication type—from the template list, then the different formats and variations of each template
- Understanding the language associated with publishing, for example, 'perforation', 'template', 'flyers'
- How to determine the best layout—strengths and weaknesses of each design
- Selecting font schemes—no longer a simple task of selecting one font type, they have been grouped together for aesthetic reasons
- Selecting a colour scheme—again from a pre-selected list
- Understanding page objects, for example, mailing lists, logos sign-up forms, order forms and response forms
- How to insert images
- How to change the template.

Lesson Ideas

Some ideas for using publishing in the classroom

Professional-looking:
- newsletters
- brochures
- reports
- letters
- posters.

All of these could be used in many different content areas for formative and summative assessment, display, parent information nights and community events.

Skills in publishing software build on those acquired in the use of word processing but result in more professional, finished products. There are a lot of skills and knowledge associated with using such programs, particularly in the areas of formatting, genre, and different types and styles of writing that make them attractive inclusions in the classroom activities.

A quick overview of publishing

How do students develop as digital content creators?	How do students develop as technological innovators?	How does publishing aid digital fluency?
Producing digital content such as electronic newsletters—the potential range is quite broad.	While the formats and templates provide a scaffold for students, the actual content, visual design and finished product have enough scope for innovation.	Students learn more proficiency in skills that are beyond basic word processing skills.

Making a video or movie

Making a video or movie requires two sets of skills—those needed for the actual filming and those needed for editing. It is a complex process but extremely rewarding as students have an end product that they can see and show to others. There are three stages involved in process of making a video or movie:

1. Pre-filming preparation

   - Importantly, a story must be decided on and a script written.
   - Once the script has been written, the filming needs to be planned shot-by-shot via a storyboard.
   - Lots of rehearsal time should be scheduled, so that lines can be learnt, positions can be worked out and an idea gained of what footage will look like when it is being filmed.
   - Costumes should be decided on—and practised.

2. Filming

   - It would be a good idea to allocate roles to different students and teach the class about these roles; that is, what they do and what their responsibilities are, as you do not want too many experts!
   - If you can have several students do the filming and directing—it makes it more of a collaborative project and that way more people can learn more skills.
   - Practise shooting—learn the hard way about lighting and position by filming a scene then examining it. Remember you are not after an Academy award—don't try for perfection.
   - Decide on a shooting schedule and make sure everyone knows what it is. Filming is a slow process that doesn't involve everyone at the same time, so decide on what tasks others can be doing.
   - Try using a combination of handheld camera shots and shots using a tripod.
   - Don't shoot a long film—think of breaking a story up into different sections and let one group do each section.
   - Once you have finished filming for the day, download the film off the camera and save in two places (just in case).

3. Editing

   - Use a simple program that is visual and logical—don't purchase complex, sophisticated programs that require expert knowledge. I like to use MovieMaker.

- Spend some time editing the movie—deleting re-takes, erasing sounds, changing the levels of brightness and so on.
- Hopefully you have recorded the voices at the same time as you filmed, so check sound levels and see if any adjustments are needed.
- Add title and credit pages—think out a music track here.
- Save the film, and then export it into a useful format.

Lesson Ideas
Some ideas for using video or movie making in the classroom

- Creating a movie based on a story or poem covered in class
- Writing an original script
- Having a movie awards night—invite parents, guest speakers, award prizes
- Record a movie review program
- Create your own television series

The production of a video or movie is a process that is quite complex involving, planning, filming and editing. These three stages each have their own sets of skills and knowledge, thus making for a rich learning task. The end product, the movie itself, is motivating for students as it is a real, authentic artefact.

A quick overview of video and movie making

How do students develop as digital content creators?	How do students develop as technological innovators?	How does video and movie making aid digital fluency?
Students create a digital movie that they have scripted, filmed and edited.	Room for innovation is vast—how the video or movie is written, how it is filmed, the backdrops, settings, casting, special effects, editing.	The production of a finished movie requires a high level of digital fluency and the development of new skills will be considerable due to the various stages in the process.

Web design

Web design is the process of planning and creating a website. Text, images, digital media and interactive elements are shaped by the web designer to produce the page seen on the web browser. Web designers can use a mark-up language, such as html for structure and CSS for presentation to develop pages that can be read by web browsers. In simple terms, html is the language used to build a web page and CSS are templates for how the pages are set out. This is the complicated way of building a web page, there are easier options! There are several programs that are easy to use and appear to be like a word processor, except that they are actually creating a web page. There are three that I would recommend:

(1) Dreamweaver

This is perhaps the most professional of the options, but it can also be quite intimidating for the novice user. A lot of the language and formatting is new and specific to the program itself. That said, once you have tried Dreamweaver yourself a couple of times, you should find it reasonably easy to use. The only problem is that it is an expensive program, so if it is not already loaded on the computers at school you might be put off purchasing it.

(2) FrontPage

This is a slightly easier program to use, and as it comes from Microsoft, if you are familiar with their other programs such as Word or Publisher, you would find it very easy to work out how to use. This program has been the one most commonly used by schools as it is logical and builds on the knowledge students already have.

(3) Word

Yes, Word will let you build web pages. You create a normal document but save it as an html file. Very easy.

Another option would be web-based sites. Often when you search for build-your-own websites, after purchasing a domain name there are web page templates that you can use that only require you to fill in the information you wish to display. There are also free webhosting sites.

Why should you bother with teaching this skill to school-aged learners? Because it will push them beyond their current levels of digital fluency, because they can do it and because the sense of achievement after they have completed their own web page is outstanding. If you are a fluent web designer or have your own web page, perhaps the focus is not upon creating their own web page but learning some of the coding language? Perhaps teaching them some of the html tags and commands would be an interesting lesson?

Lesson Ideas

Some ideas for using web design in the classroom

- Class web pages
- Web pages for a particular issue being covered in class (social activism)
- Individual web pages as an ePortfolio tool
- Web pages designed partly by the teacher for a particular unit of work—which contains all the materials and resources—teach the unit electronically!
- Historical websites—of a particular event, time or person
- Celebratory websites—events, people in the class, local community

Websites might be intimidating, but with the number of web-based templates available you can create sites quite easily. Be sure to investigate school restrictions—you might need to use a particular program, host, or not be able to hang a website off the existing school web page.

A quick overview of web design

How do students develop as digital content creators?	How do students develop as technological innovators?	How does web design aid digital fluency?
A website is a sophisticated digital artefact.	How it is designed, what is included, colour, structure, contents all can be opportunities for innovation.	The production of a website is demonstration of high levels of digital fluency. Students gain familiarity with html coding, programs and hosting.

Summary

This chapter has presented a wide range of digital technologies for the primary and secondary phases of learning. The focus at this stage in school is to build on the skills developed in the early years and develop the digital fluency of learners. It is also aimed at developing digital content creators and technology innovators. The mixture of the types of technologies presented in this chapter allows for the development of skills and also the expansion of experiences with different types of technologies.

FURTHER READING

Bruns, A. & Jacobs, R. (Eds) (2006). *Uses of Blogs*. New York: Peter Lang Publishing.

Burnett, C., Dickinson, P., Myers, J. & Merchant, G. (2006). *Digital Connections: Transforming Literacy in the Primary School*. [Online] From http://extra.shu.ac.uk/bvw/Cambridge%20Journal%20piece.pdf.

Dwyer, J. (2007). *Computer-based Learning in a Primary School: Differences between the Early and Later Years of Primary Schooling*. [Online] From http://www.tandfonline.com/doi/abs/10.1080/13598660601111307.

Graham, L. (2008). *Teachers are Digikids Too: The Digital Histories and Digital Lives of Young Teachers in English Primary Schools*. [Online] From http://onlinelibrary.wiley.com/doi/10.1111/j.1467-9345.2008.00476.x/full.

Howard, S. (1998). *Wired-Up: Young People and the Electronic Media*. [Online] From http://books.google.com.au/books?hl=en&lr=&id=oYfcY3On8fwC&oi=fnd&pg=PP1&dq=primary+school+%2B+digital+pedagogy&ots=twqL-_5Eo7&sig=-hWWH76XOY5VFrlPRrkQdoYPz18#v=onepage&q&f=false.

Leask, M. & Meadows, J. (2000). *Teaching and Learning with ICT in the Primary School*. [Online] From http://books.google.com.au/books?hl=en&lr=&id=Cz0 8wZ4duigC&oi=fnd&pg=PR10&dq=primary+school+%2B+digital+pedagogy &ots=6qzTqJrFPZ&sig=SvlEp1-25PHWOanL09mXBRqd7as#v=onepage&q& f=false.

Trendwatching. (2004). *Generation C*. [Online] From http://www.trendwatching. com/trends/GENERATION_C.htm.

Selwyn, N., Potter, J. & Cranmer, S. (2008). *Primary Pupils' Use of Information and Communication Technologies at School and Home*. [Online] From http:// onlinelibrary.wiley.com/doi/10.1111/j.1467-8535.2008.00876.x/full.

Willet, R. (2007). *Technology, Pedagogy and Digital Production: A Case Study of Children Learning New Media Skills*. [Online] From http://www.tandfonline.com/ doi/abs/10.1080/17439880701343352.

WEBSITES

Kidsview: parliament in focus
http://www.peo.gov.au/kidsview/menu.html
Explore parliamentary concepts and processes through fun and educational games and interactives. Learn about representation, law-making, democracy, Parliament House and parliamentary treasures. Includes teachers' notes for teachers and parents. Kidsview is designed for upper primary students and is a sub-website of the Parliamentary Education Office.

KidsHQ
http://www.awm.gov.au/kidshq/
Kids HQ is a website designed by the Australian War Memorial education team mainly for upper primary students; however, the site also offers an introduction to the study of Australia's military history for secondary students. The site includes stories, animals in wartime, military technology, and wartime military and home front occupations.

ABC for kids
http://www.abc.net.au/abcforkids/
Activities for children of all ages, including kids' TV guide, chat rooms and games.

SuperClubsPLUS Australia
http://www.scplus.com/d/index.php
SuperClubsPLUS Australia is the only Australian age-verified and actively protected social learning network where young children can meet friends, make new ones, have fun and learn cool stuff. And they can do all these things knowing they are completely safe!

CHAPTER 10

Developing a digital pedagogy for creative, purposeful and experimental learning with technology

Learner Outcomes

After reading this chapter, you should be able to:

- understand the concepts creative activity, experimental activity and purposeful activity as they relate to the primary classroom
- have a clear understanding of what it means to be digital content creator and how that can be developed by teachers
- understand the importance of developing digital fluency in primary-aged learners
- list the ways that teachers can create opportunities for students to become technology innovators
- know what a digital pedagogy for primary teachers comprises.

Key Terms

- technology neophyte
- digital content creator
- technology Innovator
- digital fluency
- diffusion of innovation
- innovator
- early adopter
- early majority
- late majority
- laggard

The primary classroom

Chapters 8 and 9 explored the types of technologies that might be used in primary classrooms and the types of skills we are trying to develop in learners at this stage of schooling. We need to briefly re-cap these points as they form the cornerstones to the digital pedagogy we need to develop as primary school teachers. As we are building on the skills developed during the early phase of learning, our students are at the **technology neophyte** stage. From this point we are aiming to develop their skills in three main ways:

1. The inclusion of technology-rich *creative activities* in order to develop students into **digital content creators**

2. The inclusion of *experimental activity*, rich learning tasks that potentially use technology in order to encourage our students to become **technology innovators**

3. The use of *purposeful activity* in order to develop **digital fluency** in our students.

These three types of activity will form the basis of our digital pedagogy in the primary phase of learning—while they are based on the same types of activity used in the early years, a significant difference will be the level of skills and engagement with the types of technologies. Previously the focus was upon developing a sound grounding in basic technologies; now the focus is on developing digitally fluent learners. So what does an effective digital pedagogy look like? Chapter 8 introduced the idea of **diffusion of innovation**. We can all be categorised somewhere on the graph below:

Figure 10.1: Diffusion of innovation

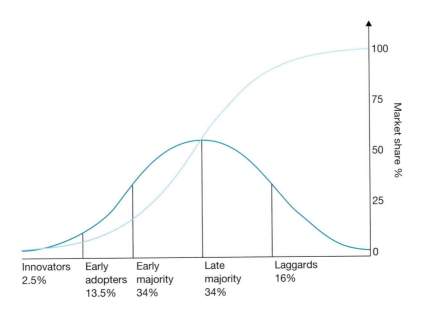

Innovators

Innovators are the first individuals to adopt an innovation. Innovators are willing to take risks, are the youngest in age, have the highest social class, have great financial lucidity, are very social and have the closest contact to scientific sources and interaction with other innovators. Risk tolerance has them adopting technologies which may ultimately fail. Financial resources help absorb these failures.

Early adopters

This is the second fastest category of individuals who adopt an innovation. These individuals have the highest degree of opinion leadership among the other adopter categories. **Early adopters** are typically younger in age, have a higher social status, have more financial lucidity, advanced education, and are more socially forward than late adopters. More discrete in adoption choices than innovators. Realise judicious choice of adoption will help them maintain central communication position.

Early majority

Individuals in this category adopt an innovation after a varying degree of time. This time of adoption is significantly longer than the innovators and early adopters. **Early majority** people tend to be slower in the adoption process, have above-average social status, have contact with early adopters, and seldom hold positions of opinion leadership in a system.

Late majority

Individuals in this category will adopt an innovation after the average member of the society. These individuals approach an innovation with a high degree of scepticism and after the majority of society has adopted the innovation. **Late majority** people are typically sceptical about an innovation, have below average social status, very little financial lucidity, are in contact with others in late majority and early majority, very little opinion leadership.

Laggards

Individuals in this category are the last to adopt an innovation. Unlike some of the previous categories, individuals in this category show little to no opinion leadership. These individuals typically have an aversion to change-agents and tend to be advanced in age. **Laggards** typically tend to be focused on 'traditions', likely to have lowest social status, lowest financial fluidity, be the oldest of all other adopters, are in contact with only family and close friends, and have very little to no opinion leadership.

While it is to be expected that all categories are probably represented in most schools, imagine what the ramifications are for learners. If a class had a teacher who was a laggard, what would their learning experiences be like? Are we all supposed to aim to be innovators? Probably not; it would be nice to think that we aim for either early adopter or early majority—users of technology who have seen the effects and value its use and have thought about ways to include them meaningfully in their teaching and learning.

CASE STUDY 1: SUSAN—LATE MAJORITY

Susan has been a primary school teacher for six years. Currently she is teaching a grade 5 class, but she has had experience in grades 4, 6 and 7. Her natural preference is for the upper primary grades, as she enjoys the complex project work she can achieve with this age group. She has been in the same school since graduation, and is a keen committed teacher. She describes herself as a self-taught technology user, not having experienced any ICT training in her pre-service teaching degree. Her classroom has an IWB, a PC at the front of the room hooked up the IWB and she has a laptop that she generally takes home with her at the end of each week so that she can do her preparation. The class has access to computer-on-wheels (COW), which is a movable trolley with thirty laptops set up on it for classes to use. She books this, on average, once per term. The school has its own internet server and there is a good strong Wi-Fi network for the staff and students to connect to. She has undergone several training sessions for the IWB and does try to use it once or twice a week. She has noticed that the students enjoy these lessons and are eager to come up to the front of the class to use it—but feels it is just a novelty and distraction. She realises that the students want to use more technology in their learning, and does try to meet these needs, but not at the cost of learning, so it is hard for her to feel that it is appropriate to use.

CASE STUDY 2: JOHN—EARLY ADOPTER

John has been a primary school teacher for 15 years. He has been an early years specialist for most of that time, but in the last two years he has moved up to the mid-primary grades and is currently teaching a grade 4 class. He has worked in several schools, and is a passionate educator. He is currently engaged in studying for his Master's degree, as he wanted to re-fresh his pedagogical knowledge. His classroom has a data projector, roll-down screen, teachers' laptop, and four PCs along the back wall of the classroom for the students to use. He has no formal training in ICT. The school also has another ten PCs set up in the library, which, he uses regularly, and he was instrumental in organising the school to purchase gaming consoles for teachers to use in their lessons (two PlayStations, two Wii's and two Xboxes). He will often help other teachers with their use of technology, mentoring them until they feel confident in using it. At year-level meetings he often suggests new websites, resources or digital technologies that could be used to enrich the learning experiences of the students. His students are generally engaged in their lessons and enthusiastic users of technology. He no longer uses paper-based letters or newsletters to inform parents what is happening in the class but has a regular class electronic newsletter that he emails to parents.

CASE STUDY 3: GORDON—INNOVATOR

Gordon is a newly qualified teacher and this is his second year teaching. He has a grade 7 class which he is enjoying teaching and previously he taught a grade 4 class. His classroom is equipped with an IWB connected to a PC at the front of the room, plus there are four PCs along one wall for the students to use. There are Wi-Fi connections throughout the school. He has also collected together some other equipment, donated by family and friends: four digital cameras, one digital video camera, five old laptops that can connect to the internet wirelessly and he sometimes brings in his iPad. He has tried different types of technologies with his students, often listening to what they like to use at home or have seen on TV. He feels that this engagement and enthusiasm are important to build upon. Sometimes he is unfamiliar with different websites or technologies and lets the students 'teach him' how to use them. He has often made changes to his lessons or planned activities based on student interests. Some of these lessons have worked well, some have not, but he has not been put off from trying. The Principal is quite interested in what Gordon does in his classroom and often pops in to see; other teachers also drop by to see what he is doing. He has scheduled two or three technology-based lessons per week into the class timetable, and has found that it is hard to restrict it at times. He is currently thinking up ways to use mobile phones in a lesson.

Critical Reflection

Diffusion of innovation: Which is the best type of teacher profile?

Each of the case studies above has been based on real examples of teachers and they would represent the typical range of teachers you would expect to encounter in a school. If we consider the diffusion of innovation as a continuum, it might look like this:

Innovator → Early Adopter → Early Majority → Late Majority → Laggard

If you think about the average school, we could place each member of the teaching staff somewhere on this continuum.

Task 1:

Think about one of the schools you have been on practicum at or perhaps a workplace you are familiar with. Think about each member of that workplace and allocate them to one of these categories along the continuum.

- Where do the majority sit? What might be the cause of this?
- Which category had the least number? Why?
- Was there any category you couldn't allocate people to? Why do you think so?
- Roughly, what were the percentages for each? Does your allocation match a bell curve, like the one in the diagram above? How does it differ?

It has been suggested above that ideally, most teachers should be sitting around the early adopter or early majority position on this continuum. You have three case studies above that illustrate different attitudes towards technology.

Task 2:

Have a close look at the three case studies above and answer the following questions:

1. Susan is an example of a late majority teacher—describe the learning experiences of her students with regards to technology. What would be their technology learning outcomes? Would you expect them to have progressed in their digital fluency?

2. John is an example of an early adopter teacher—describe the learning experiences of his students with regards to technology. What would be their technology learning outcomes? Would you expect them to have progressed in their digital fluency?

3. Gordon is an example of an innovator teacher—describe the learning experiences of his students with regards to technology. What would be their technology learning outcomes? Would you expect them to have progressed in their digital fluency? Do you anticipate that there would be any problems with having an Innovator as a teacher?

Developing your digital pedagogy: Creating digital content creators

In order to provide opportunities for students to develop into digital content creators, the focus should be moved away from teacher-led learning to student-led learning. Strategies that illustrate this shift are:

- problem-solving
- inquiry learning
- collaborative learning
- peer-led learning
- application of knowledge to new contexts
- higher-order thinking.

The teacher would initially set up the learning activity by scaffolding the content, skills and processes, but then stepping back and allowing the students to lead the learning; thereby taking on a role of resource, co-collaborator or guide. But where is the technology in all of this? These are merely teaching strategies that encourage independent learning, cooperative learning and higher-order thinking. Technology here is not as explicit as you might assume. Imagine that the technology skills and experiences of the class have been developing throughout the term; they have experienced different ways to seek information, construct presentations, use different digital technology tools and are equipped with a set of skills that they may call on to complete their learning tasks. Your scaffolding of a task may require a digital outcome, such as the production of an animation based on the novel that the class has been studying, so you might provide them with a list of outcomes they must produce. For example:

- a script based on Chapter 2 of the novel *My Place* by Sally Morgan—produced using Word
- a five-minute animated movie based on your script.

The key here is to provide the scaffold, but not the details. To encourage digital content creation, the students must be allowed the freedom to be creative, to think up ways of achieving the task and not be too constrained by limits. What might be produced here?

- A script presented using a Word template—or one that includes illustration, or perhaps a storyboard setting with the text underneath. Perhaps the front cover has hand-drawn illustrations; perhaps it is presented digitally? The options are endless.
- The animation may have been done using clay figures, dolls, drawings, computer images, finger puppets—it might have a narration, a soundtrack, it might be compiled from still shots or filmed as a continuous video. These are limited ideas compared to some of the ideas your students may come up with.

Critical Reflection
Lessons that encourage digital content creation

Lessons that encourage digital content creation are not limited to a particular subject—these types of rich learning experiences can occur across the curriculum. Look at the list below and think of lesson ideas that might result in creative uses of technology by a class. One has been done for you as an example.

Subject area	Idea
Science	
English—poetry	
Mathematics	
History—early explorers of Australia	
Art—painting	You are going to hold a class exhibition. The students have been exploring the use of colour wheels and have produced one painting each that demonstrates opposites of colours. They have been based on Cubist painters—so the students have selected two colours on a colour wheel and their opposite two colours, and created a cubist painting. Their task is to develop a poster and brochure advertising their upcoming exhibition. They must use examples of the art they have produced in the posters and brochures. (They have been taught how to use the scanner and digital camera.)

Now critically examine your ideas—what possible technologies might the students use to complete the task? How would this be an extension of their pre-existing knowledge or skills?

So the expertise you need to acquire within your suite of skills that comprise your digital pedagogy is quite broad. The aim of developing a class of digital content creators really relies upon the skills and experiences a class has throughout the year. You cannot expect them to use technologies if you have not taught them or used them before. There is a certain amount of technology fearlessness in younger learners, but for them to be able to produce what you expect them to, then they need a basis of skills. Thus it's important for you to consider:

- What have they learnt to date?
- What are they able to use, with regard to digital technologies?
- What would they be able to apply those skills and knowledge to?
- What is the spread of ability in your class? Would all learners be able to engage with the task?

When you have a clear understanding of the present technological abilities of your class you will be able to design learning activities that provide opportunities for creativity. When deciding on these activities, some suggestions include:

- Make sure that the artefacts, or the items they are producing are 'real'—something that is tangible, something they might be able to find or see in the 'real' world outside school. For example, asking a class to prepare a class newspaper, with pairs of students contributing a story.

Encourage them to set it out like a real newspaper—don't ask them to submit it as a typed single A4 page. Imagine the engagement if they were using a newspaper template in Word, that will set their text in columns, provide them with an eye-catching headline and spaces for images.

- Set up some requirements—but keep these to a minimum. You want to direct them in what the outcome should be but the details can be relaxed. Try to keep the requirements to 4–5, as this will provide enough structure but not stifle creativity.

- Be prepared to make changes based on the suggestions of the students. Often when you are explaining or setting up an activity, voices will pop up and ask if they could do this or that—listen to the voices! Those ideas might be worth trying. As long as the learning outcomes can be achieved, go with variations.

- Think about the types of activities you would like the class to be engaged with and start up-skilling the students. Planning for a rich learning task at the end of the term requires skills and experience to be built prior to then. A good idea is to make a list of the types of skills you hope they will acquire by the end of the term. Work your way through the list and it will also give you an idea of the skills you need to brush up on to be able to teach your class!

Developing your digital pedagogy: Encouraging technological innovations

In order to provide opportunities for students to develop into technology innovators, the focus should be moved to understanding processes; for example how something works, what happens when you change or make a modification. Strategies that illustrate this shift are:

- discovery learning
- inquiry learning.

The emphasis is not only on how something works, but also on how to make something work. Think about some of the design and construction elements within syllabus documents. Students might be trying to work out how an arch can be built out of stone or how gears work, in order to construct one themselves. It's important to briefly define these two approaches.

Discovery learning

Discovery learning is a method of inquiry-based instruction and is considered a constructivist approach to education. It is supported by the work of learning theorists and psychologists such as Jean Piaget and Seymour Papert (see Chapter 4). Discovery learning takes place in problem-solving situations where the learner draws on his or her own experience and prior knowledge, and is a method of instruction through which students interact with their environment by exploring and manipulating objects, wrestling with questions and controversies, or performing experiments.

Inquiry learning

Inquiry-based learning is a form of active learning where progress is assessed by how well students develop experimental and analytical skills rather than how much knowledge they possess.

- Inquiry learning emphasises constructivist ideas of learning. Knowledge is built in a step-wise fashion. Learning proceeds best in group situations.
- The teacher does not begin with a statement, but with a question. Posing questions for students to solve then allows the students to search for information and learn on their own with the teacher's guidance.
- The topic or problem to be studied and the methods used to answer the problem are determined by the student and not the teacher.

Discovery learning and inquiry learning provide many opportunities for students to innovate with technology. To encourage technology innovation, there is a four-step process that you should adopt in your pedagogical approach.

The four steps to innovation

1. Value experimentation—innovation does not always happen quickly or the first time you try something. It is a process of experimenting and trying different solutions. With regard to technology, imagine when students are trying to edit movies, change graphical images or program a robot to follow a particular path—all of these outcomes might require many attempts. Your role here is to support, offer some guidance or feedback, and encourage your students to keep trying.

2. Setting goals—innovation needs an end point that it is working towards. This might be a problem to be solved, something to be built, or an answer to a question. There needs to be an outcome that you are working towards.

3. Understanding failures—failure is not an end point, and students need to understand this. When we are innovating, there is no failure; we are engaging in different ideas or actions that might solve the problem or that might provide us with further information to help us reach a conclusion. It can be very disheartening for students if, after all of their efforts, their product doesn't work or fails to do what was hoped. Your role here is to set up a climate of understanding what failure means, provide positive constructive feedback, and help learners to re-group and try again.

4. Achieving success—success that is built upon hard work and perhaps multiple failures is all the more powerful. It is also a lesson that remains with the students. Success should be framed within the objectives of the lesson—if the goal was to program a robot that moved forward two paces and then turned right, achieving that is the success, not achieving it faster than everyone else, or any other variation!

A good example of group of technology innovators who illustrate these four points is provided as the next case study.

CASE STUDY

Land Yachts is an annual project, conducted by the OzTeacherNet, which involves primary schools around Australia. Classes who sign up to participate are involved in a technology design project conducted over a period of three or four weeks. The classes divided students up into teams of four, each team chooses a name (students choose), and the teams are tasked with building a land yacht made out of recycled materials such as toilet rolls or tissue boxes). The classes practise over a period of weeks to see how far the land yachts can travel, what modifications need to be made, and all of the processes, trials and stages of development are charted in blog entries. Each team has its own blog and uploads digital images of its yacht, its drawings and videos of the yacht trials, and records all of these events with online blog entries. All of the schools involved in the project can access each other's blogs and, often, teams from different schools leave advice and supportive comments for each other. This is a clear example of the effectiveness of the four points described above.

Developing your digital pedagogy: Developing digital fluency

Developing digital fluency in your students is essentially the acquisition of skills and understandings associated with digital technologies. Where will this 'list' of skills and understandings come from?

- Syllabus and curriculum documents: These skills are quite explicitly stated for each phase of learning. Make sure you are familiar with the documents pertaining to your class. An organisational tool would be to compile a list of the technology objectives you need to achieve and consider this to be your *minimum*.
- School expectations: Different schools have different expectations. If you are working in the private school sector, you might be teaching a class of pupils that each have a laptop with them every day at school. Or you might be working in a school that has a particular quota or expectation regarding technology. If you don't have any of these to consider, set yourself some! Think about your students—put yourself in their shoes. How often would you like to use technology if you were in their place? Examine unit plans and make sure there are enough opportunities for technology to be included.
- Student and parental expectations: As discussed in Chapter 4, there is a growing sense of digital expectation from students and their parents. Students expect to learn using digital technologies and parents expect their children to exit the school with higher levels of digital experience and abilities than when they entered.
- Your expectations: What are you hoping to achieve this year with your class? Have a clear map of where you are going with regards to technology. Have some milestones; for example, by the end of term, students can create a Word document, by the end of March students can edit digital images. Think about technology learning outcomes—formalise them into a list achievable attributes.

Therefore, as listed above, you have four contributors to developing your list of skills and experiences you plan to include within your classroom teaching and learning for the school year. What next?

1. Construct your list of technology skills and experiences.
2. Consider the most suitable way to cover this list. Where can it support or contribute to the other content that needs to be covered?

3. Map the list into your units of work.
4. Highlight the technology aspects so that you can see at a glance where they are and how often they occur. Do you need to move anything around? Is it balanced?
5. Consider your own skill set. Is there anything you need to seek help with or training?
6. Is there any equipment you need to purchase or borrow?
7. At the end of each term, do a short audit:
    - What have the students learnt with regard to technology?
    - What are they able to do better?
    - What are have they learnt that was new?
    - How have they demonstrated their fluency?
    - Are there any gaps that need filling? Is there anything you need to go back to and cover again?
    - What would you do differently next time?

A digital pedagogy for the primary classroom

This chapter has endeavoured to demonstrate the elements that contribute to a digital pedagogy for teachers in the primary phase of learning. It is essentially comprised of three competencies: encouraging students to become digital content creators, providing opportunities for students to engage in technology innovations and developing digital fluency in students (see Figure 10.2).

Figure 10.2: Components of a digital pedagogy for primary teachers

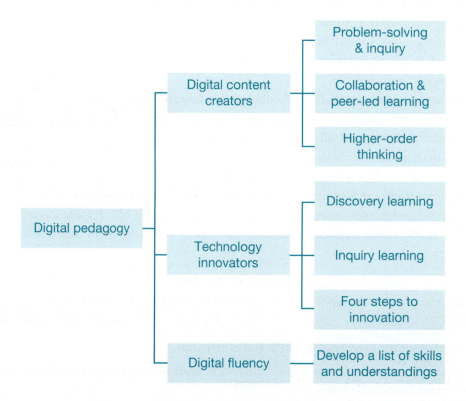

As shown in Chapter 9, there are a wide range of technologies suitable for this phase of learning. Careful planning is needed if teachers are to build on the skills the students have acquired in the early phase of learning, and if those skills are to contribute to meaningful learning. It is not enough that digital technologies are 'taught'; teachers in this phase of learning need to view technologies as tools.

Personal Reflection

How would you rate your digital pedagogical skills?

This section of the book has presented much information and discussion about the use of technology in the primary phase of learning and the types of learning activities teachers need to incorporate if they are to develop the skills of their students. It's time to consider your digital pedagogy and, more specifically, your developing set of skills. You might be at the start of your pre-service teacher training or you might be nearing completion; where you are is not important.

Digital content creators

Self-rate your digital content creation skills.

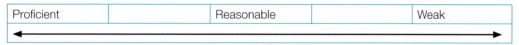

Proficient		Reasonable		Weak

Do you have a clear understanding of the following terms?

1. Problem-based learning
2. Inquiry learning
3. Peer-led learning
4. Higher-order thinking collaborative learning.

Could you construct a lesson based on each of the above?

Technology innovator

Self-rate your skills in technology innovation.

Proficient		Reasonable		Weak

How confident are you that you could develop lessons that provide students with opportunities to innovate?

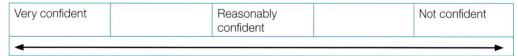

Very confident		Reasonably confident		Not confident

Digital fluency

Self-rate your own digital fluency.

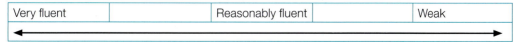

Very fluent		Reasonably fluent		Weak

After answering these questions you should have a rough idea of your abilities. Now answer the following questions:

1. What are your areas of weakness?
2. What can you do to improve these areas?
3. What *will* you do to improve?

Summary

This chapter is the final in the section pertaining to Primary schooling and technology. It ties together all of the ideas presented in Chapter 8, such as the focus on creating digital content, technology innovators and digitally fluent learners, and combines those understandings with the examples of technology presented in Chapter 9. In this chapter we have brought these ideas together so that they form the basis upon which a digital pedagogy, specifically geared towards the primary phase of schooling, can be based.

Encouraging students to be digital content creators requires a basis of skills and abilities, and the opportunity to experience creative technologies and, in turn, create digital artefacts. Technology innovation needs a focus on processes in order to create the abilities and understanding in learners that can be applied to new situations, while digital fluency requires a constant engagement with and exposure to technology. These three aspects form the basis of the digital pedagogy required in this phase of learning.

A digital pedagogy for the primary phase of schooling is a complex and rich set of skills. There is the development and refining of pre-existing skills, and providing opportunities to apply that knowledge in new ways, but it is also the exposure to rich technology experiences. The breadth of examples presented in Chapter 9 illustrate this potential. This is a phase of schooling that can really delve into more creative technologies. In the next phase, the emphasis is upon building a set of skills that can be used beyond formal schooling.

FURTHER READING

Casey, L. (2009). *Digital Literacy: New Approaches to Participation and Inquiry Learning to Foster Literacy Skills among Primary School Children.* [Online] From https://www.ideals.illinois.edu/handle/2142/9765.

Howitt, C., Upson, E. & Lewis, S. (2011). *It's a Mystery! A Case Study of Implementing Forensic Science in Preschool as Scientific Inquiry.* [Online] From http://search.informit.com.au/documentSummary;dn=342469307149602;res=IELHSS.

Jeffrey, B. & Woods, P. (2009). *Creative Learning in the Primary School.* [Online] From http://books.google.com.au/books?hl=en&lr=&id=Zn-vvyDMiLkC&oi=fnd&pg=PP1&dq=discovery+learning+%2B+primary+school&ots=7FsLhfAtyi&sig=INrs4zvZdhc9cw93PIlIgepL7wE#v=onepage&q=discovery%20learning%20%2B%20primary%20school&f=false.

Looi, C-K., Zhang, B., Chen, W., Seow, P., Chia, G., Norris, C. & Soloway, E. (2010). *1:1 Mobile Inquiry Learning Experience for Primary Science Students: A Study of Learning Effectiveness*. [Online] From http://onlinelibrary.wiley.com/doi/10.1111/j.1365-2729.2010.00390.x/full.

Novak, J.D. (2010). *Learning, Creating and Using Knowledge*. [Online] From http://books.google.com.au/books?hl=en&lr=&id=kzx7l6MMy-8C&oi=fnd&pg=PP1&dq=discovery+learning+%2B+primary&ots=p9YCGZvAll&sig=eA0ocL0-I5tdVIyXDDT7un56nV4#v=onepage&q=discovery%20learning%20%2B%20primary&f=false.

WEBSITES

Edutech Wiki—Discovery learning
http://edutechwiki.unige.ch/en/Discovery_learning
More information about discovery learning, models, advantages and disadvantages. The site also has some lesson ideas and examples.

Lesson Planet—Inquiry learning lesson ideas
http://beta.lessonplanet.com/search?keywords=inquiry-based&media=lesson&gclid=CKLNhuPKpqwCFQwY4godCTZy1
This is an interesting resource site for teachers as it has a number of lesson ideas and actual lesson plans uploaded by other teachers. There is also a worksheet repository, so you can find a lot of resources on this site.

eThemes—Inquiry-based learning
http://ethemes.missouri.edu/themes/1496?locale=en
This is an online resource for teachers and students designed and maintained by the University of Missouri. The resources are all linked to technology-based lessons, and you can send requests to the online community for help or ideas on particular topics.

QuEST
http://ictnz.com/Activityideas.htm
This is a resource site based in New Zealand that has lesson ideas and resources. Some particularly good ideas for inquiry-based lessons.

Educational Origami
http://edorigami.wikispaces.com/
A great wiki space that you can join, share ideas, download resources and improve your understanding of particular topics. It does have a particular focus on educational technology, which is helpful for ideas.

PART 4

Digital Technologies for All Subject Areas

CHAPTER 11

The role of
technology across
all subject areas

Learner Outcomes

After reading this chapter, you should be able to:

- understand how digital fluency is developed in this phase of learning
- understand clearly the different stages of development secondary students pass through in engaging in with technologies
- understand the important of developing digital fluency in secondary school learners
- know the role discipline-specific technologies play in the secondary phase of learning.

Key Terms

- digital fluency
- digital proficiency
- discipline-specific technology
- consolidation of skills

The secondary classroom

Part 3 explored the use of technology in the primary and early secondary phases of learning, defined as the last four years of primary schooling (for example, grades 4 to 7) and the first three years of secondary schooling (for example, grades 8 to 10). The focus for technology in these phases is three key areas:

1. the inclusion of technology-rich *creative activities* in order to develop students into digital content creators
2. the inclusion of *experimental activity*, rich learning tasks that potentially use technology in order to encourage our students to become technology innovators
3. the use of *purposeful activity* in order to develop **digital fluency** in our students.

A digital pedagogy for those phases of learning is designed to support these three areas. So, how will the use of technology in the senior phase of schooling differ? It's important that we first clarify the context of secondary schooling. As you would know, secondary school is divided into subject areas; for example, English, History and PE. It would be easy to dismiss technology as being the domain of the ICT or technology subject teachers. However, we know that with the development of new revised learning outcomes for each phase of learning, the implementation of the Australian Curriculum and the revision of syllabus documents across the country, the intention now is that every teacher, regardless of discipline area, is a technology-based teacher. The teaching and learning strategies we use should be rich in technology-based opportunities for our students. Therefore, all teachers working in the secondary phase of schooling need a digital pedagogy.

First, let's define what we mean by 'secondary'. To put it simply, secondary refers to grades 8–12. How this manifests might vary. There is an increasing movement towards P–12 schools; however, some states have followed a middle school and senior school framework. So the grades and mix that might be present on a secondary school campus can vary. It might also include schools with particular focus areas, such as vocational education streams, aviation streams or a focus on languages. The traditional concept of what makes up a secondary school, the subjects offered and how schooling is organised has undergone some changes. Regardless of how it is physically set up, the secondary phase of schooling refers to post grade-7 learning.

The secondary and *some* primary classes, are quite different from other phases of schooling, in that students do not remain in the same homogenous grouping for the entire school day. Students may split into different groups when they are doing different subjects; they may be allocated to different classes for the same subject; and they have between five and seven teachers in one school year. There is also the physical moving between classrooms to take into consideration. Many of these aspects have in the past been used as reasons why teachers couldn't or wouldn't use technology in their teaching—it was too hard to book the computer lab, you set it all up and then they move off to another class and you have to quickly put everything away before the next class and teacher come into the room. The list of reasons not to use technology can be endless. However, with advances in technology, such as mobile devices like iPads, laptops, wireless networks and WiFi, all of these hurdles are slowly being nullified. Schools are now equipping classrooms with more technology—data projectors, computer points and interactive whiteboards are increasingly present in secondary classrooms, hence the technology is there waiting for the teacher to use it. Old excuses are becoming redundant.

Critical Reflection

Technology in the secondary classroom: past and present*

This is a time for you to reflect upon the technology you experienced as a student in secondary school. Remember, technology is not limited to digital technologies or computers; it could be something as basic as a tape-recorder, overhead projector or camera. Your task:

1. Write down a list of all the technologies you can remember experiencing when you were in secondary school.

2. Write down how they were used—was it in a lesson, how was the class organised (for example, individually, in pairs, whole class), who used it (the class teacher or a specialist teacher), what impact did it have you as a learner (on your learning and your subjective responses)?

Hopefully you have a list of at least five or six items, perhaps more. It's important to write down how they were used, as the way we use technology has changed dramatically.

Now we are going to repeat this experience based on the schools you have visited as a prac student. Your task this time is:

1. Write down a list of all the technologies you have either seen, seen your supervising teacher use or you have used while on prac.

2. Write down how they were used—was it in a lesson, how was the class organised (i.e. individually, in pairs, whole class), who used it (the students, class teacher, teacher aide or yourself), what impact did it have you as a teacher and what observed impact did it have on the students?

*Compare these two reflections—what are the key differences? Are there any similarities?

Starting grade 8: The digitally experienced learner

Let's now examine what skills a student entering grade 8 might have. As we have seen in the previous chapters of this book, the primary phase of learning was building on the basic skills acquired in the early years but, more importantly, focused on three main areas; fostering digital content creators, technology innovation and digital fluency. The list of technologies that could be used in the primary and early secondary classroom (Chapter 9) was extensive, so we could expect that students will start grade 8 with a suite of skills. However, every school is different and every school has a different set of resources and staff—so the range of abilities could be quite wide. Let's adopt an optimistic stance and hope that the students have been able to experience some of the suggestions made in Chapters 8 through 10.

What are we hoping the students are able to do by this stage?

- They will be able to turn on and turn off a computer, start commonly used programs (for example, Word or Internet Explorer) and perform basic tasks.
- They should be able to save files, know how to save in different formats (for example, doc, pdf, txt).
- They should be experienced in sending a document to be printed and know how to change preferences for printing.
- They should be reasonably proficient in word processing, spreadsheets and presentation software.
- They are able to search for information on the internet efficiently and are familiar with Boolean operators and truncation.
- They able to critically evaluate sources of information.
- They will be able to create animations using a variety of different media.
- They have experience in producing digital videos and editing.
- They have made a podcast.
- They have experience in blogging, using a wiki and Web 2.0 applications.
- They are experienced in using publishing software and have produced a variety of different items, such as flyers and brochures.
- They should be able to use a digital camera, frame photographs, use the zoom button, transfer images to a computer and perhaps do some basic editing.
- They might have experience in web design; know how to use html coding, and software programs such as Dreamweaver.
- They might have experience in more creative and complex technologies such as robotics (for example LEGO Robotics, Bee-Bot).
- They should have an enthusiastic attitude towards technology.

These would be the basic expectations we might have of students starting grade 8—these are the digital skills pertaining to learning; their skills in recreational technologies such as online gaming and console games contribute to a techno-savvy attitude and an enthusiasm for technology but are not quantifiable skills that we can assume or build on during school. If we examine this list of attributes, it is a sound collection of skills, but as we have suggested, it's not an assumption that we can make about everyone in our class at that grade. Hence, as suggested for primary grade 4, perhaps grade 8 needs to be a year of consolidation and 'catch-up'. We need to ensure that everyone in the class has the same opportunities to engage with technology; hence, we need to ensure that every learner has a similar set of basic skills. For the five years of secondary schooling the focus should be as set out in Table 11.1.

Table 11.1: Digital fluency goals, grades 8–12

Developing digital fluency in the secondary phase of schooling				
Grade 8	Grade 9	Grade 10	Grade 11	Grade 12
Consolidation of skills—ensuring a similar level of digital fluency for all learners	Building on digital skills—developing new skills and experience in new technologies	Individual development of digital fluency—based on skills, interests and needs	Extending digital fluency—building on what has been learnt and applying to new contexts	Digital proficiency

Let's examine this in further detail.

Grade 8

This year should focus on consolidating the skills of the students. The unevenness of prior experiences with regard to digital technologies is difficult to determine, so there is a need for at least part of the year to be spent consolidating skills and ensuring that all learners are at a similar level of digital fluency.

Grade 9

This is the start of developing new skills and exposing students to new experiences with digital technologies. This might also be the time to introduce students to the digital technologies specific to each of the subject disciplines.

Grade 10

It would be assumed that by this stage in their schooling learners have a sound level of skills. Digital fluency should be evident, and the types of learning activities and assessment that students engage in at this level allow for more independent pursuit of technologies based on interest and appropriateness for the task. There is a sense that there is less teacher-led use of technology and more independent selection of the types of technologies that the learner would like to use.

Grade 11

At this stage there is a sense that students are consolidating skills; however, with the start of their senior subjects they may come into contact new technologies or devices in their different subject disciplines. Hence, there might be a need to develop new skills or understandings. At this stage, more complex programs are used and students are engaging in more technical learning. So this is perhaps a stage of new learning and new experiences with regard to digital technology.

Grade 12

This is a consolidation stage of new leanings from the previous year, and a refining of skills and abilities. At this stage it would be hoped that the students are **digitally proficient**, that they also have an aptitude that will help them when they encounter new and emerging technologies in the future.

Thus the five years of secondary schooling have clear, distinct stages in the development of digital fluency and the move towards being digitally proficient. There is the necessary stage of consolidating skills and ensuring that there are a basic set of abilities to build upon but, importantly, there is the growing influence of technology specific to different subject disciplines. These specific learnings are important aspects in the ability of students to be life-long learners; they also meet the expectations of future employers and professions. There is also a sense that the types of technologies students use take a more professional and challenging step in the senior years—with the type of programs, tasks and technology devices students may engage in. This would vary depending on the school and its access to resources. The secondary phase of schooling is unique due to the influence of the subject discipline areas, but it does build upon the learnings of previous phases and there is a sense of 'finishing off' the development of the learners' digital fluency, resulting in digitally proficient learners.

Technology in the secondary classroom: Across discipline areas

So we now have a clearer understanding of the types of skills we expect the students will be starting secondary school with, and the types of skills we should be aiming on developing across their five years of studies. The development of digital fluency during this time has three key stages:

1. Stage 1: Grade 8—**consolidation of skills** across all subject disciplines

2. Stage 2: Grades 9 and 10—extending skills and building new competencies specific to subject disciplines (that is, in **discipline-specific technologies**)

3. Stage 3: Grades 11 and 12—refining proficiency in discipline-specific technologies.

As we can see, in stages 2 and 3 the emphasis is upon discipline-specific technologies, while in stage 1 the focus is on consolidating skills across the discipline areas.

Stage 1—consolidating skills

The consolidation of skills is an important stage if the fluency and proficiency that we aim to develop in the senior years is to be achieved. In the previous phases of schooling there may have been more of an emphasis upon creativity. While that is still present in secondary school, there is a shift towards authentic real-life skills. Secondary schools up-skill the future workforce and prepare students for further study before they enter a specific profession, either via an apprenticeship, vocational study or study in a higher education institution. The minimum levels of proficiency we would be expecting at the end of grade 8 are:

- basic computer skills—saving, printing, installing and deleting programs, transferring files and performing basic tasks
- proficient use of word processing, spreadsheets and presentation software
- efficient internet search techniques, including use of Boolean operators and truncation
- the ability to critically evaluate sources of information
- the ability to create animations using a variety of different mediums
- experience in producing digital videos and editing software
- experience in taking digital images and basic editing of images
- the ability to record and upload a podcast
- experience in using blogs, wikis, online communities and common Web 2.0 applications such as Twitter, Facebook and Tumblr
- proficient in the use of publishing software
- understanding of and basic skills in web design, html coding and software programs such as Dreamweaver
- expert use of digital communication (for example, eBooks)
- experience in creative technologies such as robotics and gaming
- an enthusiastic attitude towards technology.

Significantly, these are to be developed across the different subjects that students are studying during this year.

Personal Reflection
Technology experiences across the secondary subjects

Let's examine your technology experiences during secondary school. For this exercise we are going to focus on four core subjects:

1. Try to list all of the different types of technology you experienced as a student.
2. What types of technologies did your teachers use to *teach* you this subject?
3. What types of learning activities did you engage in?
4. What types of technology did you *use* to complete your studies in this subject?

Subject	Experiences
English	
English	
Mathematics	
History (junior or senior)	
Science (junior science, biology, chemistry, physics)	

Now re-evaluate this list against the skills listed above that are suggested to be attained by the end of grade 8. How much of the list can you tick off as being achieved? What were the gaps in your digital fluency?

So we are suggesting that stage 1 in secondary school should be about consolidation. How then does the framework that has been embedded in the early and primary years fit in the secondary context?

Figure 11.1: Aspects of learning in the primary and early secondary phase of schooling

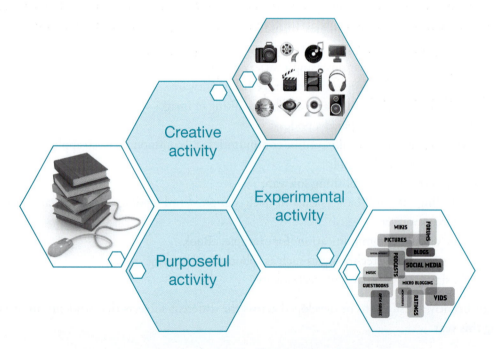

Quite effectively—it can be applied to all subject disciplines equally and can be tailored to each of these areas specific needs. For example, see how it fits into English and Mathematics in Table 11.2.

Table 11.2: Technology in particular subject disciplines

	English	Mathematics
Creative activity	Produce a script and movie of a scene from a play.	Devise a programming sequence that will turn a cog wheel forward 4 rotations and then reverse for 2 rotations. Repeat this sequence 5 times then stop.
Experimental activity	Create a blog for a character from a novel that is being examined—create a series of entries that explain the thoughts, feelings and actions of that character, it must demonstrate the 'stream of consciousness' device.	Create a digital 3-D model that illustrates the concept of XX using the software program of your choice.
Purposeful activity	Develop a multimedia presentation of a biographical narrative—there is a list of particular technologies that have to be used.	Create a pivot table using Microsoft Excel.

These are quite basic examples, but they illustrate how this framework can be used across the phases of learning. A frame work also provides a useful model for teachers working in the different subject disciplines to embed technology in their teaching and learning activities.

Stage 2—extending skills

This stage is largely concerned with moving learners' digital fluency forward now that a level of consolidation has been achieved. It is also the stage when the subject-specific digital technologies begin to be used. The amount of digital technologies appropriate or required for each subject area varies—but what is important is that there is the understanding that *all* subjects can and should make use of digital technologies and all teachers of the different subjects should realise that their learning outcomes need to include some that specifically focus on this area. There should be a sense that the different subject areas are building on the skills developed in the primary phase:

1. Students become skilled learners who are digital content creators.
2. Students become learners who are technology innovators.
3. Students become learners who are digitally fluent.

Figure 11.2: Technology skills for learners

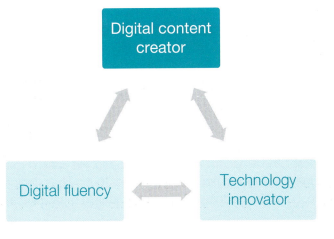

We can now add to this list of skills:

1. Students become learners who are acquiring digital skills in specific subject areas.
2. Students become learners who can see new applications of technologies in different disciplinary domains.

This last point is quite important. Imagine skills that may have been acquired in a particular subject being transferred to a new context. There is a sense that skills are being acquired, used in particular contexts, being applied to new contexts, being modified and built on—students are working their way towards being digitally proficient.

CASE STUDY

Julie, applying old skills to new contexts

Julie is a student in grade 9 in an urban secondary school in Sydney. She has a written assignment to complete for English. It is a creative writing task and it has the following requirements:

Length: 800 words

You are to produce an example of narrative writing. This can be based on a real or imagined event.

She has decided to produce a newspaper story describing the recent events off the coast of New Zealand when a shipping container ran aground. She has decided to write it as a first-hand series of observations: from a local who has watched it happen from the beach, a member of the ship's crew and an official from the emergency disaster team. Last year in English her class teacher created a class newspaper using a template in Publisher. Each student's story was added to the newspaper and it resulted in a class 'edition'. She has decided to use some of these skills. She is going to create an electronic newspaper—this time using Publisher but submitting her assignment electronically saved in an html format, so that it appears to be an online newspaper. She is going to find some images of the disaster online and add them to the finished product.

CASE STUDY

Mick, capitalising on students' pre-existing skills and learning from them

Mick has a grade 10 physical education class. The students have been struggling with learning the skills of long jump. He has shown them some videos of top athletes performing, and also some instructional videos but still students are having a hard time understanding what to do and how to improve their technique. He heard from their English teacher that last year in a media studies unit, the students had written a script and filmed their own short movies. He doesn't really have that much knowledge about filming and making movies, but he has decided that as his students do, he might use these skills. He decides to organise the students into groups and gets them to film themselves doing the long jump. There is a lot of discussion about camera position, zoom, the difficulty of filming outside and controlling the light. He realises that the students really do know quite a lot about filming. They successfully manage to film themselves and they spend a lesson examining the finished products. The students can see what each of them is doing well or what they need to do to improve their long jump skills. He noticed an immediate improvement in their skills. He had planned to finish the use of technology there, but the students asked to make another film demonstrating their abilities at long jump. He agrees and they spend a session after school filming their efforts. Some of the students then took on the task of editing the movie, adding a soundtrack and finishing off the movie. They staged a movie screening and many of the students wanted copies of their efforts. Also, Mick now had a useful resource to show at parent information nights. He learnt a lot from the students and now the PE department has purchased three video cameras of its own and has set up editing software on two computers in its resource room.

There is another aspect that should be noted here—the differing skills and abilities of teachers. While it is the obligation of every teacher to up-skill and be able to use technology, there are always differences in actual ability. We have explored the *Diffusion of Innovation* idea in previous chapters, and we know that we can categorise teachers as being somewhere along the continuum of early adopter to laggard. Let's view these differences in a more positive light. Within the secondary school setting, we have different teachers for each subject, which could mean that a student will have five to seven teachers in one school year. The variety of abilities and the variety of technologies that those teachers might engage with are a broad range—even if some teachers fall in the late majority or laggard category, their contribution to the development of digital fluency in their students might be the reinforcing of useful programs (for example, word processing) and skills (for example, searching the internet), while at the other end of the continuum there might be more creative or challenging technologies being used. All teachers have a role to play and all make a contribution. This stage of development should be concerned with extending skills; however, realistically not all teachers will be 'extending' their students; some teachers may be more suited or able to remain at the consolidating stage. This is not of serious importance if most teachers a student has are focused upon the development and extension of digital skills.

Stage 3—digital proficiency

This stage is concerned with refining proficiency in discipline-specific technologies. If each of the different subject areas has been steadily using digital technologies in its teaching and learning activities, then we are approaching twelve years of technology-rich learning. Students should be digitally proficient in a number of different software programs, technology devices and also subject-specific applications of those learnings. What types of learning experiences or skills development would we anticipate students to be engaged with in this stage? Some examples are:

- using Flash—being able to design and created artefacts using Flash
- using scientific technologies: for example, analysis equipment, centrifuge, digital microscopes
- using mathematical programs

- creating digital games, using apps for iPhones and iPads
- using server technology, setting up networks
- using programming languages
- using more sophisticated web design.

Personal Reflection
Mapping your digital fluency

As we have seen above, the development of digital fluency during secondary schooling has three key stages:

1. Stage 1: Grade 8—consolidation of skills across all subject disciplines
2. Stage 2: Grades 9 and 10—extending skills and building new competencies specific to subject disciplines (discipline-specific technologies)
3. Stage 3: Grades 11 and 12—refining proficiency in discipline-specific technologies.

Let's examine these three stages through two different lenses, as a student and as a teacher.

Part (a) Student

When you were studying in secondary school, technology might have been understood quite differently from what we understand technology to mean now. For example, overhead projectors (OHPs) rather than data projectors may have been used. Technology may also have been limited to something the teacher used to teach, rather than a tool that was taught to students, and used by them. So, we can see there have been some significant changes in how technology is used. In the table below, list the types of technology regularly used by the teachers in these stages and also those used by the learner. *Remember to base these ideas on your experiences of school and if possible the different grades.*

	Used by the teacher	Used by the student
Stage 1 **Grade 8**		
Stage 2 **Grades 9 and 10**		
Stage 3 **Grades 11 and 12**		

- What did you discover?
- Where there more entries for technologies used by the teacher?
- Or is there an even balance between the two?
- Did different stages emphasis the teacher more? Or the student?

Part (b) Teacher

Now we are going to project a little into the future and see what types of technologies you can list for your subject areas across the three stages. Look at the table below and fill in the information. You have to do this for both of your teaching areas and, while you might be limited by your knowledge of technology, try to be creative, think about the possibilities and how you could incorporate technology in teach of the stages.

	Subject area 1:	Subject area 2:
Stage 1 Grade 8		
Stage 2 Grades 9 and 10		
Stage 3 Grades 11 and 12		

- What did you discover?
- Was one of your subject areas more easily to do than the other? Why?
- Did you find that your use of technology was balanced between the three stages? Or was there one particular stage that was technology-rich?
- Have you been able to include more creative or different technologies?
- Do you think there is a sense of building on the present across the stages or is there a sense that you are using more complex technologies as you progress through the stage?

An aptitude for emerging technologies

The technologies we teach at any given moment are specific to their time—versions of particular software programs, new technology devices, even the popularity of particular programs or the expectations of students vary dramatically. If you consider the types of technologies you might have experienced during your schooling compared with those available and being used now, it would be quite different. How then are we to realistically prepare students to be digitally fluent or users of digital technologies of the future? New emerging technologies are booming; each year we see new versions, upgrades and new devices enter the market. It would be impossible to prepare our students with detailed knowledge and experiences of all of these developments. Yet, in policy, syllabus and curriculum documents we are asked to prepare students to use emerging technologies and prepare them to be life-long users of digital technologies. How do we achieve this? By developing a positive aptitude towards the use of technology. This can be achieved via a number of different strategies:

- teachers demonstrating the use of technology in their lesson preparation, how they interact with students (types of formats for feedback), their setting of technology-based tasks and assessment, and their positive comments regarding its use
- teachers working with students regarding the types of technologies to use in the classroom—building upon the interests and current habits of the class
- teachers adopting an inquisitive mindset—exploring new developments, going to professional development workshops and learning, asking colleagues and students to show them how particular programs work or what particular devices work
- students experiencing a variety of different digital technologies that have a variety of different uses or applications; that is, not being limited to using word-processing programs, but creating clay animation movies, building robots and creating their own movie

- students playing a role in selecting and choosing different technologies to use in their learning, engaging in conversations with their teachers about how the technology could be used in their learning, being innovators and guides, mentoring their teachers in the use of those technologies.

There should be a balance between educational technology and popular technology being used for educational purposes. This will result in students not only developing skills but also developing a positive inquiring mind regarding the use of technology. What we are trying to produce are learners who are not fearful but who fearlessly engage with new and emerging technologies, and look for a way to incorporate them in their lives.

Critical Reflection
Emerging technologies in the classroom

The most currently discussed recent innovations are often associated with Web 2.0; social networking applications like Facebook, Tumblr and Twitter. There have been many stories reported in the media of the dangers of some these programs, so much so that many teachers are loath to consider them as learning tools and many departments of education and individual schools have blocked these sites from being accessible on school premises. However, their popularity with students remains high. Some schools have embraced these programs and developed some interesting uses for them. Read the following real example.

Blue Haven State High School

The students in grade 9 art are being taken on a field trip to the art gallery in the city as a culminating activity at the end of the school year. The point of the trip is to provide the students with more examples of the different styles and schools of painting that have been covered this semester, and to experience real-life examples rather than digital images. All of the students have been asked to bring along their mobile phones, and they have been paired to ensure that everyone has access to one mobile phone.

The three teachers supervising the field trip have designed an electronic scavenger hunt—they have a series of questions based on the displays. They have set up Twitter accounts, for example ArtTeacher1, and each of the three classes has subscribed to one of the teachers. Once they arrive at the gallery, the teachers will tweet a question, the students then have to discover the answer, send it back to the teacher, and if it is correct, receive the next question. The teachers will keep a record of who answers first, and there is a prize for the pair with the most points. Examples of the type of questions are:

- Find an example of French Impressionism.
- What year was the Tom Roberts painting completed?
- Who was the subject in Sydney Nolan's *First-class Marksman*?

As there are three teachers, with three sets of questions, the students will swap after lunch and have a second set of questions to complete.

It is an engaging way to get a class to examine different examples of work. The last tweet was not a question, but a task—students have to select one painting that illustrates a particular style or school of art, take a digital image of it, then draw the painting themselves and write a short explanation of why they think it illustrates the style.

These types of learning activities are becoming increasingly popular and more organised, with museums and galleries offering mobile learning software or applications to schools.

Summary

This has been the first chapter in the section pertaining to secondary schooling and technology. Clearly, we can see that this phase of schooling and the technology expectations are quite different. While in the early and primary phases there was a focus on developing a set of basic skills, exploring more creative types of technology and then widening the breadth of technology experiences, this phase of schooling starts to see the shift towards discipline-specific technologies being used and the transition towards becoming digitally proficient.

Due to the nature of secondary schooling and the impact of learning within different subject areas, development in the use of technology is in stages. Stage 1 is concerned with the consolidation of skills due to the anticipated differences in technology experiences that students may begin secondary schooling with. Stage 2 has two areas of focus: initially the development of new digital skills and experience in new technologies, then a focus on individual development based upon interests and needs. This is an important aspect, as students are finishing grade 10 at the end of stage 2 and would be specialising in particular subjects and preparing for the transition into senior secondary school. Finally, in stage 3, the aim is for digital proficiency to emerge. While this might appear to be quite a high expectation, as each of the different subject areas has been steadily using digital technologies in its teaching and learning activities, students have been refining their proficiency in discipline-specific technologies.

This is not the end of the journey for secondary teachers, as we also need to prepare our students to engage with emerging technologies in the future as part of our educating learners to be life-long learners. It is hard to guess at the emerging technologies of the future; hence, what is needed is a positive attitude and aptitude in learners that will help them engage with new developments. We are hoping to establish a mindset of techno-fearlessness and positive inquiry. If this is to be achieved, we need to model these traits ourselves. The following chapters explore some examples of technology that can be used in this phase of schooling and then examine what a digital pedagogy for secondary school teachers comprises.

FURTHER READING

Garofalo, J., Drier, H., Harper, S., Timmerman, M.A., & Shockey, T. (2000). Promoting appropriate uses of technology in mathematics teacher preparation. *Contemporary Issues in Technology and Teacher Education* [Online serial] From http://www.citejournal.org/vol1/iss1/currentissues/mathematics/article1.htm

Gibbone, A., Rukavina, P., & Silverman, S. (2010). Technology integration in secondary physical education: teachers' attitudes and practice. *Journal of Educational Technology Development and Exchange*, 3(1), 27–42.

Goos, M., & Cretchley, P. (2004). Teaching and learning mathematics with computers, the internet, and multimedia. In B. Perry, G. Anthony, & C. Diezmann (Eds), *Research in Mathematics Education in Australasia 2000–2003* (pp. 151–74). Flaxton, Qld: Post Pressed.

Marzano, R. J. (2009). Teaching with interactive whiteboards. *Educational Leadership*, 67(3), 80–2.

Samarawickrema, G., Benson, R. & Brack, C. (2010). Different spaces: Staff development for Web 2.0. *Australasian Journal of Educational Technology*, 26(1), 44–9. [Online] From http://www.ascilite.org.au/ajet/ajet26/samarawickrema.html

Sorgo, A., Verckovnik, T. & Kocijancic, S. (2010). Information and communication technologies (ICT) in biology teaching in Slovenian secondary schools. *Eurasia Journal of Mathematics, Science & Technology Education*, 2010, 6(1), 37–46.

Wood, R. & Ashfield, J. (2008). The use of the interactive whiteboard for creative teaching and learning in literacy and mathematics: A case study. *British Journal of Educational Technology*, 39(1), 84–96.

WEBSITES

MobiLearn

http://www.mobilearn.org/

MOBIlearn is a worldwide European-led research and development project exploring context-sensitive approaches to informal, problem-based and workplace learning by using key advances in mobile technologies. It is a useful website to collect ideas for using mobile technologies and to see what is emerging in this fast changing area.

EduBlog

http://edublogs.org/

This is an education-only blog site. You can use it with your students and be sure that other users are all in education, either primary, secondary or tertiary and that the audience and also connections you make with other people through this site are safe and secure.

BBC Kids 11-16
http://www.bbc.co.uk/schools/websites/11_16/
Don't be put off by the word 'kids' in the title—this is a particularly useful website with resources organised into separate subject areas. It has multimedia resources, so is rich with podcasts, videos and text-based resources.

NASA Educators
http://www.nasa.gov/audience/foreducators/index.html
A wonderful site for teachers with interesting articles, teaching materials and grade-specific worksheets. Not a site for science-only teachers, as it has a lot of relevance to SOSE, Geography, History and English.

National Geographic for Teachers
http://education.nationalgeographic.com/education/
This is a useful site with a lot of different teaching resources arranged around themes, such as population or big cats. There are a number of education projects you can get involved in and a particularly useful tool is MapMaker.

CHAPTER 12

Scaffolding digital fluency in learners

Learner Outcomes

After reading this chapter, you should be able to:

- understand the stages of technology development in secondary learners
- understand some of the ways discipline-specific technologies can be used
- list some of the examples of technology most suited to the secondary phase of learning and some of their uses in the classroom.

Key Terms

- online communities
- digital portfolios
- multimedia
- virtual worlds
- Flash
- mashups
- cloud computing
- gaming consoles
- Photoshop
- Jing

Technology for upper primary and secondary schools

The development of digital fluency in the upper primary and secondary phases of learning is a different process from that of the early and primary phases. The context of having the learning divided into subject areas adds a complexity to the digital skills that need to be acquired. As suggested in Chapter 11, there are three distinct stages and these influence the types of technology used in a lesson.

Stage 1: Grades 7 and 8—consolidation of skills across all subject disciplines

The consolidation of digital skills is the main concern for grades 7 and 8; consequently, learners should have:

- basic computer skills—saving, printing, installing and deleting programs, transferring files and performing basic tasks
- proficient use of word processing, spreadsheets and presentation software
- efficient internet search techniques, including use of Boolean operators and truncation
- the ability to critically evaluate sources of information
- the ability to create animations using a variety of different mediums
- experience in producing digital videos and editing software
- experience in taking digital images and basic editing of images
- the ability to record and upload a podcast
- experience in using blogs, wikis, **online communities** and common Web 2.0 applications such as Twitter, Facebook and Tumblr
- proficient use of publishing software
- have an understanding of and basic skills in web design, html coding and software programs such as Dreamweaver
- expert use of digital communication (such as eBooks)
- experience in creative technologies such as robotics and gaming
- an enthusiastic attitude towards technology.

All of these technologies are presented in greater detail in Chapter 9. While it is a list of ideal abilities, it would be a reasonable expectation that students would have achieved the majority of these after completing primary school.

Stage 2: Grades 9 and 10—extending skills and building new competencies in discipline-specific technologies

This is an important stage in the development of digital fluency. While there is a sound set of skills and experiences by this stage, the separation into discipline-specific subjects and the use of technologies in potentially new contexts is an important stage for students. Seeing how technologies can be used across disciplines and applying prior experiences to new contexts is illustrative of high-order thinking and process skills. It would be interesting to consider which is emphasised more in this stage—extending existing skills or the building of new competencies. It largely depends on the discipline area—some subjects are more technology and device-rich, such as the sciences, while other subjects might use more 'traditional' technologies but in new ways, such as history. What is important is that as teachers we do not become complacent, we must ensure that technology is embedded in both teaching and learning. The aim is to maintain, extend and build new competencies in technology.

Personal Reflection

Extending skills and building new competencies in your discipline areas

As pre-service teachers you will be developing your knowledge and expertise in your chosen discipline areas. At present you should have a reasonable idea of what would be typically used with regards to technology and what could be used in these areas. Spend some time reflecting and writing down some ideas in the table below.

Subject/Discipline area	Ways to extend pre-existing technology skills	Ways to build new competencies
1.		
2.		

Now answer the following questions:

- Was one of your discipline areas easier to do? Why?
- Are there any discipline-specific technologies in your area?
- Do you feel able to use all of the technologies listed above?

Stage 3: Grades 11 and 12—refining proficiency in discipline-specific technologies

The use of discipline-specific technologies requires specialised knowledge in your subject area. It would be difficult and perhaps unnecessary to list all of the different discipline-specific technologies, as there are many different subjects and variations in secondary schools. However, there are some technologies that can be used across subject areas and these are described in greater detail below. It should be noted that there is also an expectation that technology is embedded in all teaching and learning activities at this stage. Learners in grades 11 and 12 are often more digitally expectant than other age groups, as there is an increased amount of technologies being used in their personal lives than in other grades. Therefore, while discipline-specific technologies should be a focus, there should also be a general 'technologising' of all aspects of their learning.

Digital portfolios (ePortfolios)

Digital portfolios are useful tools commonly used outside education. They have been used as portfolios for job applications, records of achievement during a career and have also been used to present results from projects, surveys or other data. Increasingly, they are gaining in popularity in educational settings.

An electronic portfolio, also known as an ePortfolio or digital portfolio, is a collection of electronic evidence assembled and managed by a user, usually on the web. Such electronic evidence may include text, electronic files, images, **multimedia**, blog entries, and hyperlinks. Digital portfolios are both a demonstration of the user's abilities and platforms for self-expression and, if they are online, they can be maintained over time. Some ePortfolio applications permit varying degrees of audience access, so the same portfolio might be used for multiple purposes.

An ePortfolio can be seen as a type of learning record that provides actual evidence of achievement. Students have, in the past, been taught to create digital portfolios using presentation software. There are three main types of ePortfolios, although they may be referred to using different terms:

- developmental (for example, working),
- reflective (for example, learning), and
- representational (for example, showcase).

Digital portfolios take a variety of formats; they can be part of a school Learning Management System (LMS) and such as Blackboard, which has an ePortfolio built in as a tool; they can be purchased as separate software programs such as Pebble Pad and Desire2Learn; or they can be built using a number of different software programs, such as PowerPoint, Adobe Publisher and Word.

A developmental ePortfolio is a record of things that the owner has done over a period of time, and may be directly tied to learner outcomes or rubrics. A reflective ePortfolio includes personal reflection on the content and what it means for the owner's development. A representational ePortfolio shows the owner's achievements in relation to particular work or developmental goals and is, therefore, selective. When it is used for a job application it is sometimes called a career portfolio. The three main types may be mixed to achieve different learning, personal or work-related outcomes, with the ePortfolio owner usually being the person who determines access levels.

Digital portfolios, like traditional portfolios, can facilitate students' reflection on their own learning, leading to more awareness of learning strategies and needs. There are several aspects associated with their use that should be noted:

- For teachers
  - They provide evidence of student learning that focuses on both content and process.
  - They showcase learning, reflections and engagement with learning over longer periods of time.
  - If used as a whole-school approach, then this record of learning covers the five years of secondary schooling, providing teachers with background information about the learning outcomes, preferred learning styles, strengths and weaknesses of all their students.
  - They can be used in conversations with parents or caregivers, resulting in evidence-rich discussions.
  - The can be a combination of school work plus administration data.

- For students
  - They facilitate personalised learning.
  - They enable a clearer understanding of their own abilities and accomplishments.
  - Provide opportunities to engage with a digital technology commonly in the professional world.

Lesson Ideas
Some ideas for using digital portfolios in the classroom

- Subject-specific portfolios of work completed over a particular time period (for example, a school year, or senior school)
- A mock-job application
- Group presentation tool—group outputs and work can be stored in the ePortfolio and all group members can access, modify or leave messages for other members
- Character-study—create an ePortfolio for a character, famous person or historical figure
- Experiment logs—collect together electronic files of experiments or lab work conducted over a semester.

Digital portfolios are interesting tools that initially collected a lot of positive responses. The usefulness of the tool lies in how it is tied to the content or learning objectives. They are simple online templates that can be used as repositories for information that is then presented in a standardised format. Some of the ePortfolios are quite restrictive and limit the amount of creativity or innovation you can attempt, so careful selection is needed. As a tool for collecting evidence of learning, they are powerful.

A quick overview of digital portfolios

How do students develop as digital content creators?	How do students develop as technological innovators?	How do digital portfolios aid digital fluency?
The students are creating a digital artefact, the ePortfolio itself.	Some ePortfolios do not allow for much innovation so careful choice is needed.	Students gain familiarity with another digital tool. Students gain further experience in uploading files, and modifying and preparing electronic documents.

Virtual worlds

Some background to virtual worlds

A **virtual world** is an online community that often takes the form of a computer-based simulated environment through which users can interact with one another and use and create objects. The term has become largely synonymous with interactive 3-D virtual environments, where the users take the form of avatars visible to others. These avatars usually appear as textual, two-dimensional, or three-dimensional representations, although other forms are possible (auditory and touch sensations for example). Some, but not all, virtual worlds allow for multiple users.

The computer accesses a computer-simulated world and presents perceptual stimuli to the user, who in turn can manipulate elements of the modelled world and thus experience a degree of telepresence. Such modelled worlds and their rules may draw from reality or fantasy worlds; example rules are gravity, topography, locomotion, real-time actions and communication. Communication between users can range from text, graphical icons, visual gesture, sound and, rarely, forms using touch, voice command and balance senses.

The first virtual worlds presented on the internet were communities and chat rooms, some of which evolved into MUDs and MUSHes. The first MUD, known as MUD1, was released in 1978. The acronym originally stood for 'Multi-User Dungeon', but later also came to mean 'Multi-User Dimension' and 'Multi-User Domain'. A MUD is a virtual world with many players interacting in real time. The early versions were text-based, offering only limited graphical representation and often using a command line interface. Users interact in role-playing or competitive games by typing commands and can read or view descriptions of the world and other players. Such early worlds began the MUD heritage that eventually led to massively multiplayer online role-playing games, more commonly known as MMORPGs, a genre of role-playing games in which a large number of players interact within a virtual world.

Educational use of virtual worlds

Virtual worlds represent a powerful new media for instruction and education that presents many opportunities but also some challenges. Persistence allows for continuing and growing social interactions, which themselves can serve as a basis for collaborative education. The use of virtual worlds can give teachers the opportunity to have a greater level of student participation. It allows users to be able to carry out tasks that could be difficult in the real world due to constraints and restrictions such as cost, scheduling or location. Virtual worlds have the capability to adapt and grow to different user needs; for example, classroom teachers are able to use virtual worlds in their classroom leveraging their interactive whiteboard with the open-source project Edusim. They can be a good source of user feedback; typical paper-based resources have limitations that virtual worlds can overcome. Virtual worlds can also be used with virtual learning environments, as in the case of what is done in the Sloodle project, which aims to merge Second Life with Moodle.

Virtual worlds allow users with specific needs and requirements to be able to access and use the same learning materials from home as they would be receiving if they were in the presentation. This can help users to keep up to date with the relevant information and needs, while also feeling involved. Having the option to be able to attend a presentation via a virtual world from home or from their workplace can help users to be more at ease and comfortable. The flexibility of virtual worlds has greatly improved the options for student study and business collaboration. Although virtual worlds are a good way of communicating and interacting between students and teachers, this is not a substitute for actual face-to-face meetings. When using virtual worlds, the downside is that you lose the body language and other more personal aspects.

Lesson Ideas

Some ideas for using virtual worlds in the classroom

- Create your own environment in a virtual world site. Some ideas are: digital classroom, science lab, an archaeology dig site, a different country (with a different language, good for LOTE), a sports arena, swimming pool, dive pool, horse racing (for mathematics), a mountainous region with particular geographical anomalies—the subject-specific alternatives are endless. Once you have created this digital space, you can plan a lesson inside the virtual world. Interacting inside this virtual world requires some technology skills, which will be built upon while the students engage in the space.
- Plan the creation of a virtual world with your students and build it together.
- Visit virtual spaces that are already created—critique them, turn this into a critical literacy lesson.

Virtual worlds are a wonderful subject-specific space for learning. They can be tailored to suit your needs, your content area and your learners' needs, and do not require high levels of digital fluency. The current commercial interfaces have been designed to be easy to use. There are many examples of schools working in virtual spaces, and much of the research conducted in this area reports high levels of engagement with the learners.

A quick overview of virtual worlds

How do students develop as digital content creators?	How do students develop as technological innovators?	How do virtual worlds aid digital fluency?
If they are involved in the building of or modifying of the virtual world there are opportunities for creating digital artefacts.	The skills learnt in creating virtual objects and modifying their virtual world provide opportunities for creativity and innovation.	Participating in a virtual world is a demonstrably high-level digital skill and indicative of digital fluency.

Flash

Adobe **Flash** (formerly Macromedia Flash) is a multimedia platform used to add animation, video and interactivity to webpages. Flash is frequently used for advertisements, games and flash animations for broadcast. Flash manipulates vector and raster graphics to provide animation of text, drawings and still images. It supports bi-directional streaming of audio and video, and it can capture user input via mouse, keyboard, microphone and camera. Flash contains an object-oriented language called ActionScript and supports automation via the Javascript Flash language (JSFL). Flash content may be displayed on various computer systems and devices using Adobe Flash Player, which is available free of charge for common web browsers, some mobile phones and a few other electronic devices (using Flash Lite).

Flash files are in the SWF format, traditionally called 'ShockWave Flash' movies, 'Flash movies' or 'Flash applications', usually have a '.swf' file extension, and may be used in the form of a webpage plug-in, strictly 'played' in a stand-alone Flash Player, or incorporated into a self-executing Projector movie (with the '.exe' extension in Microsoft Windows). Flash video files have a '.flv' file extension and are either used from within '.swf' files or played through a flv-aware player, such as VLC, or QuickTime.

Lesson Ideas

Some ideas for using Flash in the classroom

- Animate digital images produced by students
- Design a banner for the school moving Flash animation
- 'Bring to life' historical figures
- Produce advertising campaigns and use Flash to animate the product
- Plan an updated version of existing electronic content

Flash is undoubtedly one of the more challenging technologies, and requires a level of familiarity and proficiency in the teacher before it is used with students. It is perhaps not for everyone to try, but it is something you should be aware of and understand, as students may ask questions about this commonly used tool.

A quick overview of Flash

How do students develop as digital content creators?	How do students develop as technological innovators?	How does Flash aid digital fluency?
The flash animations are evidence of digital creations.	As it is a high-level technology, Flash offers many opportunities to innovate as animations are constructed.	The ability to use Flash and produce animations is evidence of digital proficiency.

Multimedia and mashups

Multimedia is media and content that uses a combination of different forms. The term is used in contrast to media that use only rudimentary computer display such as text-only, or traditional forms of printed or hand-produced material. Multimedia includes a combination of text, audio, still images, animation, video or interactivity content forms.

Multimedia is usually recorded and played, displayed or accessed by computerised and electronic devices, but can also be part of a live performance. Multimedia also describes electronic media devices used to store and experience multimedia content. Multimedia is distinguished from mixed media in fine art, by including audio. Multimedia presentations may be viewed by a person on stage, projected, transmitted, or played locally with a media player. Digital online multimedia may be downloaded or streamed. Streaming multimedia may be live or on-demand.

Mashup may refer to:

- mashup (digital), a digital media file containing any or all of text, graphics, audio, video and animation, which recombines and modifies existing digital works to create a derivative work
- mashup (music), the musical genre encompassing songs that consist entirely of parts of other songs
- mashup (video), a video that is edited from more than one source to appear as one
- mashup (book), a book that combines a pre-existing text, often a classic work of fiction, with a certain popular genre such as vampire or zombie narratives.

Lesson Ideas

Some ideas for using multimedia and mashups in the classroom

- Research projects for which results are presented as digital mashups rather than written essays
- Modifications to existing forms of media—such as a song or video—to re-develop them to carry a different message
- Blending music genres to illustrate similarities or differences
- Video mashups of different works of art to show the characteristics of a particular school or movement
- Re-writing endings or chapters in novels
- Blending two short stories together into a mashup

Multimedia mashups are essentially digital artefacts that use more than one form of media, such as a video combined with audio. These can be complex and creative, or quite simple yet still be highly effective. The format can vary; for example, a PowerPoint presentation can be a rich multimedia experience with a variety of different forms embedded in the presentation. Alternatively, it might be a movie that has text, sound files and animations mixed in with the traditional 'film'. They present as very creative technology experiences for teachers and learners.

A quick overview of multimedia and mashups

How do students develop as digital content creators?	How do students develop as technological innovators?	How do multimedia and mashups aid digital fluency?
Mashups are creative artefacts. Multimedia artefacts demonstrate creative skills in several different types of media.	Mashups are innovative and original. Multimedia presentations are also original works.	The ability to manipulate different digital formats, files and create new artefacts would aid the development of digital proficiency. Familiarity with new file formats.

Cloud computing

Cloud computing is most simply a storage facility located in cyberspace, or the internet. Storage space is provided by companies, who have servers that provide connections to networks in order to access the data being stored (see Figure 12.1, which presents these ideas visually). Cloud computing providers deliver applications via the internet, which are accessed from web browsers and desktop and mobile apps, while the business software and data are stored on servers at a remote location. There are four types of 'cloud' models:

1. public cloud—most commonly used type of cloud, which is accessible by the general public via the internet and is provided by a third-party providers

2. community cloud—a cloud shared by several organisations with a common concern (for example, government departments) and can be hosted internally or by a third-party provider

3. hybrid cloud—a combination of two or more clouds (for example, public, community or personal), which allows more movement of data between multiple clouds

4. private cloud—a cloud operated solely for one organisation and is managed either internally or through a third-party organisation.

Figure 12.1: Overview of cloud computing

Lesson Ideas

Some ideas for using cloud computing in the classroom

- A repository for groups to share resources, working documents and files
- A class site so that all members can access files
- A site for parents to access information

Cloud computing is essentially a data storage facility, but it can be accessed by multiple individuals, so that sharing of files, resources and other digital materials is much easier. It removes the need to send attached files via email or to copy files on to sticks. A class could share a space for working documents or to access files from the teacher. It is a facility that will increase in popularity and use, therefore warrants being included in educational settings.

A quick overview of cloud computing

How do students develop as digital content creators?	How do students develop as technological innovators?	How does cloud computing aid digital fluency?
The ability to use, upload and download files is a key skill.	Opportunities for innovation are a bit limited, but the knowledge of cloud computing and its different uses might be applied in the future.	Students gain experience in using an increasingly common digital tool.

A different look at online communities

It's important to re-examine online communities, beyond their Web 2.0 manifestation and examples such as Facebook. They are useful learning tools for both teachers and students. An online community is a virtual community that exists online and whose members enable its existence through taking part in membership rituals. An online community can take the form of an information system where anyone can post content, such as a bulletin board system or one where only a restricted number of people can initiate posts, such as weblogs. Online communities have also become a supplemental form of communication between people who know each other primarily in real life. Typical characteristics of online communities are:

- *content:* articles, information and news about a topic of interest to a group of people
- *forums or newsgroups and email:* so that your community members can communicate in delayed fashion
- *chat and instant messaging:* so that the community members can communicate more immediately.

Lave and Wenger (2001) suggested that there is a cycle of becoming a member of an online community that all individuals transition through. They suggest five types of trajectories in a learning community:

1. peripheral (lurker)—an outsider, unstructured participation
2. inbound (novice)—a newcomer is invested in the community and heading towards full participation
3. insider (regular)—a fully committed community participant
4. boundary (leader)—a leader, sustains membership participation and brokers interactions
5. outbound (elder)—a member in the process of leaving the community due to new relationships, new positions, new outlooks.

Lesson Ideas

Some ideas for using online communities in the classroom

- Create a class online community
- Join existing online communities that are concerned with a particular subject or topic

- Use the online activities of students as assessment items—posting to the online community, respond to others
- Use an online community to build positive community within your class
- Join school online communities—those set up specifically for school students, which are closely monitored and supervised

Online communities are interesting spaces for students to engage in a different form of communication. There are a number of pre-existing communities that you could access, but the safest and easiest option is to create your own. This can be achieved easily if your school uses an online learning program or has its own webpage; alternatively, you can set up your own site via different commercial sites, some of which are free for schools to join. Various departments of education also have space for online communities on their eLearning sites, so it is worth investigating these as an option.

A quick overview of online communities

How do students develop as digital content creators?	How do students develop as technological innovators?	How do online communities aid digital fluency?
They are participating in online communication that is text-based and digital.	The innovation is in the mode of communication and how fluent students become.	Students gain experience in online communities. Students develop digital communication skills. Students learn online group dynamics.

Gaming consoles

Gaming consoles are interactive entertainment computers or customised computer systems that produces a video display signal that can be used with a display device (a television or monitor, for example) to display a video game. The term 'gaming console' is used to distinguish a machine designed for consumers to buy and use solely for playing games from a personal computer, which has many other functions.

Below are some examples of popular gaming consoles.

Xbox 360

The Xbox 360 is the second video game console produced by Microsoft. The main features of the Xbox 360 are its integrated Xbox Live service that allows players to compete online, download arcade games, game demos, trailers, TV shows, music and movies, and its Windows Media Centre multimedia capabilities.

PlayStation 3

The PlayStation 3, officially abbreviated as PS3, is the third home video game console produced by Sony Computer Entertainment. Major features of the console include its online gaming service, the PlayStation Network, its multimedia capabilities, connectivity with the PlayStation Portable and its use of the Blu-ray disc as its primary storage medium.

Nintendo Wii

The Wii is a home video game console released by Nintendo. A distinguishing feature of the console is its wireless controller, the Wii Remote, which can be used as a handheld pointing device and detects movement in three dimensions. Another distinctive feature of the console is WiiConnect24, which enables it to receive messages and updates over the internet while in standby mode.

Lesson Ideas
Some ideas for using gaming consoles in the classroom

- Wii is has a wide variety of sporting games, which can teach skills and techniques; Wii Fit is also a useful tool in this subject area.
- There are different games—some designed for educational settings that can be used.
- Racing games are good for teaching probability, distance, speed and velocity.

The usefulness of gaming consoles is probably only limited by the knowledge of the teacher of what is available. It would be wise to keep current with new developments in this area and increasingly, companies are producing educational games for the home-learning market, which is gaining in popularity. Selecting games needs careful consideration, and teachers need to be sure that they will achieve the desired learning outcomes! But apart from this warning, games are an engaging and motivating tool that students are often highly proficient in already.

A quick overview of gaming consoles

How do students develop as digital content creators?	How do students develop as technological innovators?	How do gaming consoles aid digital fluency?
Some games allow for choice and creativity.	Students learn new applications of existing technologies, such as games, to learning.	Students gain skills in playing the games, saving games. Students gain understanding of the educational applications.

Photoshop

Photoshop is a graphics editing program designed by Adobe. It can edit a variety of different graphics formats (for example bmp, gif, jpeg) and has over the years evolved in an easier to use program. It has a wide range of basic operations, but a feature of the program is that you can add to it with plug-ins (extra capabilities) such as colour correction plugins, special effects and 3-D plugins. In the early and primary phases we suggested that student be taught how to make simple edits to digital images. This program is at a professional level and can produce more sophisticated graphics editing. The ability to create 2-D or 3-D images from 1-D images is a technique that can be used in a number of different contexts and subject areas.

Lesson Ideas

Some ideas for using Photoshop in the classroom

- Manipulation of any digital image that the students have created themselves or found on the internet
- Creating polished, professional-looking publications such as flyers and magazines
- Can be used in mashups—combining a number of different media

Photoshop is a professional graphics editor, but it is commonly found in schools for subjects such as technology and design. This does not preclude it from other subject areas. It does require a set of skills or experience that perhaps not all students have, but the end result is often motivation for students to improve their techniques with this program.

A quick overview of Photoshop

How do students develop as digital content creators?	How do students develop as technological innovators?	How does Photoshop aid digital fluency?
They are creating edited digital images which can be used in a variety of ways.	The editing of the image is innovative; the different tools in the program students use and plugins that they might seek out to use offer opportunities for technological innovation.	It enables a higher level of digital editing and allows students to demonstrate a highly competent level of skills and abilities.

Jing

Jing is a useful tool that allows you to create videos with narrations of what you see on your computer screen. It is an excellent alternative to filming and then adding a sound track, as you can record what you are doing on your computer with narration. The video is produced in a swf format, so it is easily played on most systems, and with the free version you have up to 5 minutes of recording time. There are also online communities associated with this tool, where you can share and view other Jing videos.

Lesson Ideas

Some ideas for using Jing in the classroom

- Use Jing instead of oral presentations—students show the video rather than stand in front of the class. This allows for more multimedia to be used.
- Create Jing videos on topics for the students to use—set up independent learning tasks.
- Set homework via a Jing video—email it to the class.
- Record demonstrations, so that students can see step by step what they need to do, with the added narration to explain everything.

This is a tool that can be used by both the teacher and student. It has many different applications, as either an alternative to presentations or as a demonstration of how to do something. The program is very easy to use, but the finished product is very effective. A suggestion is that you invest in a quality microphone, to ensure the audio recording is clear.

A quick overview of Jing

How do students develop as digital content creators?	How do students develop as technological innovators?	How does Jing aid digital fluency?
The students produce swf videos that have audio files embedded in them.	How they film, what they film what they say all provide room for innovation.	The ability to produce short films with audio recordings will be a useful skill.
	How they use the films and where they upload them can also be quite creative and innovative.	Students learn to upload the film, convert into another format and do some simple editing.

Summary

The use of digital technologies is quite different in the secondary phase of learning, as school is divided into discipline areas and students experience a number of different teachers with different abilities in technology in any given year. This is not a negative observation, but is an opportunity for variety and demonstrations of the multiple uses we can have for the same technologies, in different contexts, subject areas or levels of expertise. This is a strength of secondary schools, the potential variety a range of teachers can offer learners.

As we have seen in Chapter 11, secondary learners pass through three stages of development with technology. Stage 1 is the important consolidation stage in grade 8. The variety of schooling backgrounds and experiences students have prior to beginning secondary school means that we cannot really assume that their level of digital fluency is the same or even comparable. Hence this year is a time for 'catching up', filling in gaps in knowledge and skills. Excitingly, it is also a time when students experience schooling broken up into their different subject areas, hence the development of digital fluency will occur in multiple disciplinary contexts—offering opportunities to see skills applied to new contexts, used in different ways, enhanced or maintained. In stage 2 there is the introduction of discipline-specific technologies and their use in teaching and learning. The types of digital technologies that learners will experience will vary according to each school, but with the internet there is also the opportunity to be aware of these technologies, even if they are not physically able to access them. This stage also sees the transition towards a more personal, individual development, as students start to focus on particular discipline areas and personal fluency. These are important stages in the transition into senior years. The final stage hopefully sees the learner make the transition towards digital proficiency. There is a strong emphasis upon discipline-specific technologies, but also the application of skills, building upon areas of expertise and a general higher-level engagement with digital technologies present that you would expect from senior learners.

The secondary phase is also concerned with preparing students to engage with emerging technologies. This can be developed via a positive attitude, aptitude and wider experiences of a variety of different technologies throughout their schooling. It will prepare them for the technologies to come in the future. Some of the technologies described above, such as cloud computing, could be described as emerging technologies. We are experiencing the initial form of these technologies; it is likely they will transform into something quite different in the future as technology improves and new uses are envisaged.

This chapter has presented a number of different technologies that are suitable for the secondary learner. But it should also be remembered that the technologies presented in Chapter 9 for primary learners are also suitable and, more importantly, should be used in secondary schools. This list is not definitive; it is merely an example of the types of technologies we should use. In Chapter 13 these ideas are brought together as we examine the characteristics of a digital pedagogy for secondary teachers.

FURTHER READING

Charlier, N. & De Fraine, B. (2008). *Games-based Learning in Teacher Education: A Strategy to Integrate Digital Games into Secondary Schools*. [Online] From http://books.google.com.au/books?hl=en&lr=&id=r6mPyaObITEC&oi=fnd&pg=PA77&dq=teacher+journal+%2B+technology+%2B+secondary&ots=IRgz82PbFt&sig=4WWjB_sK_6JTYntkq8ceqb0n8T8#v=onepage&q=teacher%20journal%20%2B%20technology%20%2B%20secondary&f=false.

Kim, A.J. (2000). *Community Building on the Web: Secret Strategies for Successful Online Communities*. [Online]. From http://www.citeulike.org/group/1188/article/347188.

Lave, J. & Wenger, E. (1991). *Situated Learning: Legitimate Peripheral Participation*. [Online] From http://books.google.com.au/books?hl=en&lr=&id=CAVIOrW3vYAC&oi=fnd&pg=PA9&dq=lave+and+wenger+1991&ots=OAmyxp-DHj&sig=n7s_rn2eqxtWBEcMJwpOb2E2A8Y#v=onepage&q&f=false.

Li, Q. (2007). Student and teacher views about technology: A tale of two cities?, *Journal of Research on Technology in Education*, 39(4), 377–97.

Miller, D. & Robertson, D. (2009). *Using a Games Console in the Primary Classroom*. [Online] From http://onlinelibrary.wiley.com/doi/10.1111/j.1467-8535.2008.00918.x/full.

WEBSITES

Desire2Learn ePortfolio

http://www.desire2learn.com/eportfolio/k12/

This is an example of a commercially produced ePortfolio that is quite popular with schools and higher education. This site has some videos demonstrating the characteristics of the portfolio that will give you a good idea of what it looks like and how it can be used.

Pebble Pad

http://www.pebblepad.co.uk/user.prospect.asp

This is another commercially produced ePortfolio, but it is much more than that. It is also an online learning program that can be used with groups or classes. It has communication tools such as blogs and chat spaces built in. Explore some of the examples on this site.

Second Life

http://secondlife.com/

Perhaps the most famous virtual world. Explore some of its examples and see what the creators of this world say about its use.

Croquet

http://www.opencroquet.org/

A free open-source virtual world that you can download and create yourself. It is relatively easy to use, though some aspects are a bit technical. However, it has been designed solely for educational use so it is quite appealing for teachers to use.

OzTeacherNet

http://www.oz-teachernet.edu.au/

An online community for teachers in Australia. It host a number of online activities that you can participate in with your class, has email lists and these are very useful for help, suggestions and support when you are attempting to try new technologies in your classroom. It is free to join.

CHAPTER 13

Developing a digital pedagogy for digitally fluent learners

Learner Outcomes

After reading this chapter, you should be able to:

- understand the technology requirements of the secondary phase of learning
- understand what a digital pedagogy for digitally fluent learners requires
- understand the importance of developing digital fluency in secondary-aged learners
- list the ways that the digital pedagogies for the three phases of schooling are interconnected.

Key Terms

- digital proficiency
- digital fluency
- discipline-specific technologies
- digital content creators
- technology innovators
- creative activity
- experimental activity
- purposeful activity
- wordle

The secondary classroom

In Chapters 11 and 12 we explored the types of technologies that might be used in upper primary and secondary classrooms, and also the types of skills we are trying to develop in learners at these stages of schooling. We need to briefly re-cap these points as they will form the cornerstones to the digital pedagogy we need to develop as secondary school teachers. As we are building on the skills developed during the early and primary phases of learning, our students are at the stage described as digitally fluent and, hopefully, digitally proficient by the end of grade 12. Across the five years of secondary schooling, learners are engaged in specific types of learning concerned with technology—ranging from consolidation to **digital proficiency** (see below). A key difference in this phase is of course the separation of the school day into specific subjects. But, as we have suggested, this does not mean that **digital fluency** is left to the technology teachers, but is the responsibility of all teachers, across all subjects, across the five years.

Table 13.1: Digital fluency goals, grades 8–12

Developing digital fluency in the secondary phase of schooling				
Grade 8	Grade 9	Grade 10	Grade 11	Grade 12
Consolidation of skills—ensuring a similar level of digital fluency for all learners	Building on digital skills—developing new skills and experience in new technologies	Individual development of digital fluency— based on skills, interests and needs	Extending digital fluency—building on what has been learnt and applying to new contexts	Digital proficiency

A digital pedagogy for digitally fluent learners

We are getting a clearer sense of what a digital pedagogy for secondary teachers or those who wish to develop digitally fluency regardless of phase of learning comprises. There are different sets of skills required at different stages during the five years of secondary schooling, but these are not limited to these grades and could easily be applied to primary grades. As detailed in Chapter 11, these are:

1. Stage 1: Grade 8—consolidation of skills across all subject disciplines
2. Stage 2: Grades 9 and 10—extending skills and building new competencies specific to subject disciplines (**discipline-specific technologies**)
3. Stage 3: Grades 11 and 12—refining proficiency in discipline-specific technologies

This in turn means that there are three key stages with complementary pedagogical skills required by secondary teachers.

Stage 1—consolidating skills

When learners begin grade 8 it cannot be assumed that they have had similar learning experiences or opportunities with technology. Schools vary considerably in the types of technology they have available for use. Nor can we assume that all students have access to technology at home; the digital divide is present in modern Australia. There are vast differences in the types of technologies we have in our homes. Thus, regardless of subject discipline, grade 8 should be concerned with consolidating pre-existing technology skills and building new ones where there are gaps in learning or experience. It is hoped that upon completion of grade 8, all learners are at a similar level of digital fluency. So what sets of skills do we need to develop within our digital pedagogy? They are skills in using a mixture of commonly used software programs, internet search techniques, critical evaluation skills and skills in using some more creative digital technologies. They should be digital technologies that you commonly use and can confidently instruct students in. In Chapter 11 we listed a suggested set of skills and experiences that students should acquire by the end of grade 8; these are presented in Table 13.2. They might be a consolidation of pre-existing skills for some students, but for others this might be the acquisition of a new set of skills. Let's now conduct an audit of your pre-existing skills and experience. Examine Table 13.2. You have the suggested skills and experiences for students set out. Now examine this list and think of examples that might be used in either of your teaching areas. Which programs do you commonly use? Which truncation terms are most helpful? What types of digital literacy and critical analysis skills do you develop in your students? Then go over these two lists and self-audit your skills. Can you use these digital technologies? Yes or no? Be honest.

Table 13.2: Self-audit of skills

Digital technology or skills to be acquired by the end of grade 8	Examples that are used in your subject area	Audit of existing skills	
		Yes	No
Basic computer skills—saving, printing, installing and deleting programs, transferring files and performing basic tasks			
Proficient use of word processing, spreadsheets and presentation software			
Efficient internet search techniques, including use of Boolean operators and truncation			
The ability to critically evaluate sources of information			
The ability to create animations using a variety of different mediums			
Experience in producing digital videos and using editing software			
Experience in taking digital images and basic editing of images			
The ability to record and upload a podcast			
Experience in using blogs, wikis, online communities and common Web 2.0 applications such as Twitter, Facebook and Tumblr			
Proficient use of publishing software			
Understanding of and basic skills in web design, html coding and software programs such as Dreamweaver.			
Expert use of digital communication such as eBooks			

Digital technology or skills to be acquired by the end of grade 8	Examples that are used in your subject area	Audit of existing skills	
		Yes	No
Experience in creative technologies such as Robotics and Gaming			
An enthusiastic attitude towards technology			

You should now have a clear idea of where your strengths and weaknesses are. The above list of digital technologies and skills forms the basis of your digital pedagogy in the secondary phase of schooling; if you are weak in a particular area you need to strengthen your proficiency, as the second stage of schooling (Grade 9 and 10) will build on these abilities.

CASE STUDY
Creative technology in ancient history

John is a teacher in a secondary school, teaching grade 11 ancient history. Part of the program of work for this subject is a unit of work entitled *Studies of Archaeology*. This unit focuses upon the techniques and practices of archaeologists. Having taught this unit for several years, he has thought that a more practical hands-on way of learning would be more engaging for the students. He decides that in order to learn the techniques and practices, the students would participate in a dig. At the end of the previous school year John, with the help of the groundsmen, dug up an area of the school grounds and buried a number of artefacts. This area was then filled in and allowed to settle so that no visible differences between the plot with artefacts and the surrounding area was noticeable.

After learning about the different techniques and how to set up trenches, grid systems, recording finds and progress, the students were timetabled into groups to work on the site. They used digital cameras and video to visually record their progress, then transferred these images and files to a graphics editing program. Here they added a grid over the top of the image, recorded where finds were located and created digital records of progress which they could annotate. The combination of hands-on practice and the use of technology in a real and authentic way resulted in high levels of engagement and motivation.

While the technology used was not complex, it did present to the students practical applications of the skills they already possessed. This activity did require forward planning, but the learning outcomes were, in John's opinion, worth the effort. He has now run this program for three years. Each time, he has made some modifications. For example, the science department in the school purchased four new electronic microscopes, which he had access to; so this year he buried a mixture of seeds within one of the pots, which students were then able to analyse and match with seed samples.

The message from this case study is simple—the use of technology does not need to be complicated, but it is powerful when used in real and authentic ways.

Task

List three examples, like the one above, that you could try in both of your teaching areas. Be creative; try to think of authentic activities that make use of technology in realistic ways.

Stage 2—extending skills

We can now make an assumption about the level of digital fluency that students starting grade 9 may possess. There would be a set of skills and experiences that can be built upon throughout their studies in grades 9 and 10. What does this mean for a teacher's digital pedagogy? This is the time when subject discipline specialisations start to impact on the technology choices you make for teaching and learning. There is an increase in the digital expectations you may have of your students, such as the ability to produce assessment items using digital technology (for example, word-processed and printed assignment submissions). Within the different subject disciplines there is also the expectation that the students become:

1.   skilled learners who are **digital content creators**
2.   learners who are **technology innovators**
3.   learners who are digitally fluent
4.   learners who are acquiring digital skills in specific subject areas
5.   learners who can see new applications of technologies in different disciplinary domains.

Personal Reflection
Extending technology skills

Let's examine your technology experiences during your teaching practicum. Think back to the different supervising teachers you have had during these placements. Select one who you think has tried to incorporate digital technology in their teaching and learning.

1.   Try to think of an example of the teacher's practice that illustrates each of the five skills we hope to develop during this stage of secondary schooling.

Students to become during grades 9 and 10	Example that illustrates this skill
Skilled learners who are digital content creators	
Learners who are technology innovators	
Learners who are digitally fluent	
Learners who are acquiring digital skills in specific subject areas	
Learners who can see new applications of technologies in different disciplinary domains	

Now answer the following questions:
- Was there any skill that was not developed? Why not?
- Was there any skill that was emphasised more than others? What do you think are the reasons for that?

So how do we prepare our digital pedagogy to meet these needs? There are a number of different strategies you could use:

- Start with the basic skills listed for grade 8 in Chapter 11; ensure you are able to do all that is listed. If not, up-skill.
- Commit to regular professional development in the area of digital technology—particularly technologies used specifically in your subject area.
- Use digital technologies in your lesson preparation, teaching and communication with colleagues and parents. Keep your own levels of digital proficiency high.
- Investigate the types of technologies used in your subject area; read professional journals in your subject area, join professional associations, put yourself in a position where you will hear about new developments and have opportunities to talk with colleagues teaching in the same area, so that you can learn new skills and collect ideas for lessons.
- Talk to other colleagues and find out what they are doing with regards to technology use. If they are from another subject area, think about how you can apply that idea to your subject.
- Force yourself to be technological! Set yourself some quotas to achieve—number of lessons per week based on digital technology, electronic homework assignments and assessment.
- Remember, skills are not only physical. You also need to explore ways to teach your students critical literacy skills, how to evaluate sources of information and how to search for information effectively. How will you incorporate that into your lesson? Find out what other teachers do and see if it is something you can adopt.

In a sense, you could achieve the skills required in this part of your digital pedagogy by engaging in a cycle of evaluation—examining the content you plan to teach, your teaching strategies and intended digital technologies, and determining if you are constantly building on these five skills. Look at Figure 13.1. It has five questions that you could ask yourself that would help you to direct your teaching and learning strategies towards developing the five skills you should be focusing upon in grades 9 and 10.

Figure 13.1: How to direct your technological skills development

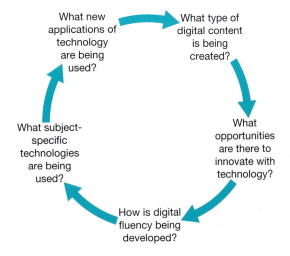

These five questions will guide you towards developing an effective digital pedagogy for this stage within secondary schooling.

Critical Reflection
Technology use in a grade 10 English lesson

A grade 10 class in an urban secondary school is coming towards the end of a unit on the poetry of World War 1. Their final assessment piece for this unit is focused on making links between the historical context or setting and the poem. Students have been asked to:

- Select a poem that has been studied in class.
- Produce an electronic diary for the poet of the selected poem, describing the historical events they experienced leading up to when the poem was written (historical context). The format of this electronic diary is open to interpretation.
- Include some biographical and personal information about the poet in the diary entries.
- The diary it is to be written in first person, in the style and manner of the poet.
- The diary it may include some visual images.

This is a very brief description of the task, but it does provide you with a basic idea of the requirements. Your aim is to evaluate the task using the five questions presented in the cycle above—then offer ideas to improve the task, to ensure that it meets the skill requirements that we are aiming to achieve in this stage of secondary school.

Part (a) Evaluation questions

1. What type of digital content is being created?
2. What opportunities are there to innovate with technology?
3. How is digital fluency being developed?
4. What subject-specific technologies are being used?
5. What new applications of technology are being used?

Part (b)

Suggested improvements:

1.
2.
3.
4.

Stage 3—refining skills

This final stage requires a specific set of skills within your digital pedagogy and these are subject related. Within any subject discipline there exists content knowledge and practical skills specific to that area of study. Some subjects would appear to have more technology devices associated with them than others and, consequently, require greater breadth of technological experience. However, digital proficiency itself is a concept that is best suited to being a continuum of skills. Different subjects have different areas of expertise; for example, it could be assumed that history teachers might be highly proficient in searching for information on the internet, whereas science teachers must have more skills with particular technology devices (for example, microscopes or filtration systems). It would be incorrect to state that one discipline area is more technological than the other; they merely have a different set of technology skills and requirements. Simply put, there is no disciplinary hierarchy of 'technology-ness'; we must all aim to be digitally proficient, regardless of our subject area. Hence digital proficiency for teachers is a combination of two types of skills:

1. Teachers need digital fluency in a breadth of technologies and experiences.

2. There needs to exist a wide range of skills across technologies, some of which might not be used in your teaching and learning activities, but they add to a general sense of understanding and experience with technology. As secondary teachers, we teach across a range of grades, so in any one year we may be teaching classes in each of the three stages; hence, we need a breadth of skill ourselves.

3. Teachers need proficiency in subject-specific technologies. Within each of our discipline areas there are commonly used technologies. We should be confident in their use. Also, there are technologies that perhaps might not usually be used in our discipline area, but that we innovate or use because of student interest, experience or currency.

The combination of expertise in these two types of technologies results in the necessary digital proficiency needed for stage 3.

Figure 13.2: Components of digital proficiency for teachers

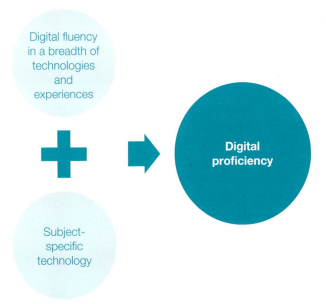

This conceptualisation of digital proficiency is very teacher-centred; our understanding of this term outside this context would be quite different but the intention is the same. We are aiming for a digital pedagogy that has some element of disciplinary expertise and digital fluency that is at a professional level.

A digital pedagogy for the secondary classroom

This chapter has endeavoured to demonstrate the elements that contribute to a digital pedagogy for teachers in the secondary phase of learning. It is essentially comprised of three stages: consolidating digital skills, extending digital fluency and refining digital proficiency (see Figure 13.3).

Figure 13.3: Elements that comprise a digital pedagogy for secondary teachers

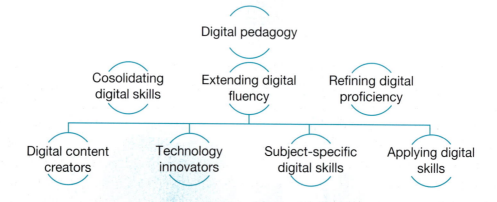

The digital pedagogy needed for the secondary phase of schooling is quite different from those ones needed for the other phases. There is more of a sense of expertise and technological proficiency within our discipline area rather than lists of prescribed skills that we need to acquire.

A significant difference

If you have worked your way through the previous two sections concerned with the early and primary phases of learning, you will have realised that the digital pedagogy proposed for secondary teachers is significantly different from those suggested for the other phases of learning. Both the early and primary phases were based upon three kinds of activities:

1. **creative activities**
2. **experimental activities**
3. **purposeful activities**.

Why is the digital pedagogy for secondary teachers different? In a sense, it is not. The skills we are suggesting here are described differently, but they still fit this framework. As secondary school is arranged based on subject disciplines, then this framework becomes a structure for each of these subjects. The digital pedagogy required by teachers is still concerned with creative, experimental and purposeful activities, but with the added difference of subject-specific technologies to be included. The diagram below shows how this subject-centeredness applies to each of the three types of activities.

Figure 13.4: Applying discipline areas to creative, experimental and purposeful activities

Creative activities in discipine areas that provide…	*Experimental activities* in discipine areas that provide…	*Purposeful activities* in discipine areas that provide…
• opportunities to consolidate, extend and refine skills • develop subject-specific technology skills	• opportunities to consolidate, extend and refine skills • develop subject-specific technology skills	• opportunities to consolidate, extend and refine skills • develop subject-specific technology skills

Putting it all together

While this is a chapter concerned with the development of a digital pedagogy for secondary teachers, as it's the last phase of formal schooling, it would be a good opportunity to put it all together and see the connections and comprehensiveness of the different skills needed by teachers at the different stages of schooling. One set of skills is not limited to the teachers who work in that particular phase. A digitally engaged pedagogue would be one who is interested in the digital technologies and associated pedagogical skills for each phase of learning, and who develops those skills themselves. Education is in a contestant state of flux; as new structures and organisations are trialled, teachers increasingly find themselves working in a phase of schooling they might not have originally planned to teach in. So a state of preparedness is a smart idea.

The early phase of learning

A digital pedagogy for the early years of schooling is a complex blend of skills and aptitude. There are three elements that are central to the development of digital pedagogical skills in teachers who specialise in the early years of learning (prep to grade 3). Figure 13.5 demonstrates how each of these types of activity is associated with an aspect of technology that is particular to this phase of learning.

To be pedagogically prepared, teachers need to acquire skills and experience in the types of technologies most likely to be found or that create learning opportunities that suit that particular type of activity. It is assumed that an effective digital pedagogy starts with a positive aptitude towards technology, which could be either nervous acceptance of its place in the classroom to enthusiastic embracing of different kinds of technology. We all start somewhere along this continuum. However, to develop a set of pedagogical skills that will allow you to use technology effectively in your teaching and learning activities in the early years classroom, you need to develop a set of skills that are quite specific. To be pedagogically prepared, teachers need to acquire skills and experience in the types of technologies most likely to be found or that create learning opportunities that suit a particular type of activity. From this point we are aiming to develop students' skills in three main ways:

1. The inclusion of technology-rich *creative activities* in order to develop students into digital content creators

2. The inclusion of *experimental activity*, rich learning tasks that potentially use technology in order to encourage our students to become technology innovators

3. The use of *purposeful activity* in order to develop digital fluency in our students.

Figure 13.5: A digital pedagogy for the early years

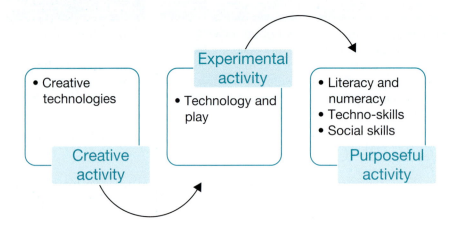

Digital fluency in the early years is a combination of skills to be learnt and experiences. The experiences are as important as the skills as they will facilitate a positive aptitude towards technology and enable learners to continue to use digital technologies in their learning. It is important that a basic grounding in technology skills is developed in this phase of schooling as these skills form the basis for later technology-based learning. The early years are an important phase, as learners enter the schooling system with differing levels of technology experience and skills but, hopefully, by the end of their first four years of schooling, they have a sound set of skills and a wide range of technology experiences. In Chapters 5 and 7, the Technology and Play Framework was presented as an effective tool for learning in the early years. It can be used to scaffold the different ways that technology can be used and the different types of learning activities that can be developed.

The primary phase of learning

The digital pedagogy required for the primary phase builds closely on the early years phase. It is comprised of three competencies: encouraging students to become digital content creators, providing opportunities for students to engage in technology innovations and developing digital fluency in students (see Figure 13.6), but these are now expanded to include particular teaching strategies and approaches to learning that create opportunities for digital technologies to contribute in a meaningful way. The intent of the creative, experimental and purposeful activities remains but has been altered slightly to fit the phase of learning and its focus.

1. Creative activity → Digital content creators
2. Experimental activity → Technology innovators
3. Purposeful activity → Digital fluency

Figure 13.6: A digital pedagogy for the primary phase of learning

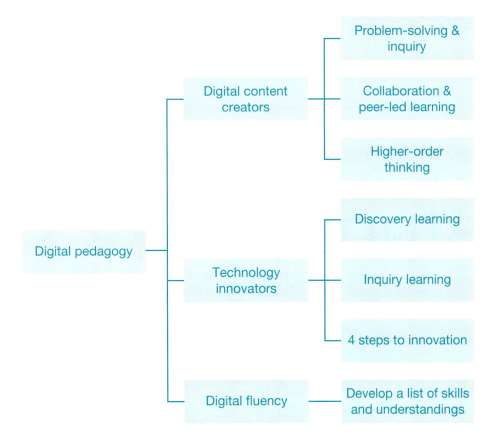

As can be seen in Figure 13.6, the digital pedagogy for the primary phase has several teaching strategies attached to it. These approaches to teaching provide contexts within which it is more likely that students will engage in digital content creation, innovate with technology and develop their digital fluency.

The secondary phase of learning

The final phase of schooling and the accompanying digital pedagogy is firmly grounded on the previous phases. Similarly, it is comprised of three stages but, rather than describing a type of activity (creative, experimental or purposeful), they describe the types of learning that students are engaged in: consolidating, extending and refining digital fluency. A common feature of the digital pedagogy in this phase is the focus on particular goals, common to the early and primary phases, which are:

- helping students to be digital content creators
- helping students to be technology innovators.

In the secondary phase there are also the secondary-specific additions of:

- subject-specific digital skills
- the application of digital skills to new contexts.

Critical Reflection
The evolution of a digital pedagogy

A digital pedagogy, simply defined, is the process of teaching using digital technologies. Look at the **wordle** in Figure 13.7:

Figure 13.7: Wordle on defining digital pedagogy

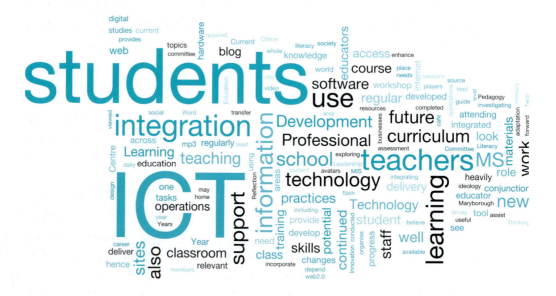

A wordle is a map of the frequency with which a particular word appears in a body of text. The more often it appears the larger it will be in the wordle; it is designed to show value via size of font, which is based on frequency. Is it accurate? Perhaps not, but wordles can be representative of a particular topic and they can be used to stimulate debate or discussion.

The wordle in Figure 13.7 is based on a text describing a teacher's reflection of how they define a digital pedagogy. Closely examine this wordle and then answer the following questions:

1. Do you agree with the different aspects presented in this wordle?
2. Is there anything missing from the wordle?

3. Write your definition of digital pedagogy—try to include as many aspects as you can; make it a rich, complex definition. Alternatively, search on the internet for a definition that you agree with.

4. Create your own wordle at http://www.wordle.net/.

Teaching note: How could you use wordle in your teaching and learning? List three ideas.

Summary

This chapter is the conclusion to the section concerning the secondary phase of learning. It builds on the ideas presented in Chapter 11, where it was suggested that digital fluency in the secondary phase should be a combination of consolidating, extending and refining existing digital skills and the development of skills in discipline-specific technologies. These understandings were then illustrated in Chapter 12 with examples of different types of technologies suited to this phase of learning. In this chapter we have attempted to draw these ideas together to illustrate the skills and understandings needed for a digital pedagogy suited to this phase of learning.

Secondary teachers are disciplinary practitioners; they have a specialised knowledge of two disciplines and, with that expertise, their associated technologies. These are important areas of knowledge that are imparted to students in this phase. Combined with this are the general technology skills we would expect to be present in digitally proficient educators. Secondary teachers require a breadth of skills—general digital skills and experience with a wide range of technologies, plus disciplinary technologies. As this is the final stage of formal schooling, there is an expectation that students will complete their studies as digitally proficient learners with a set of skills and dispositions that will enable them to engage with emerging technologies and be life-long learners.

This chapter also took the opportunity to review the interconnectedness of the digital pedagogies required for the three phases of learning: early year, primary and secondary. It is clear that there is an interconnectedness and sense of building on each phase's requirements and this is purposeful. Schooling is undergoing constant change and the current move towards P–12 schools, often means that we end up teaching in a grade or area we might not have initially thought we would be. Also, as effective pedagogues, we need to be aware of what happens in each phase, the skills required to teach in each phase and the anticipated technology outcomes for the learners.

As we can see from Figure 13.8, the digital pedagogies for the three phases of schooling are interconnected. The early and primary digital pedagogies have an emphasis on creativity and breadth of technology experiences, while the secondary pedagogy requires a balance between discipline-specific technologies and building on existing digital skills.

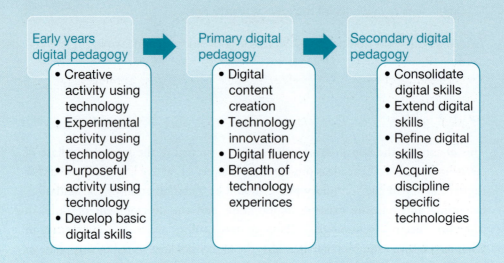

Figure 13.8: Digital pedagogies for early, primary and secondary schooling

As we stated in Chapter 1, teachers face the constant challenge of refining teaching and learning techniques to keep up with the increasing demands and expectations of students, whom we have described as *digitally expectant*. They expect that the teaching and learning they experience will be rich in digital technologies. They use digital technologies outside of school and enthusiastically take up new technologies as they appear on the market.

Parents, employers, and the wider community also expect the education system to produce technologically fluent students. Often the reality is far from that. For example, many universities have found school leavers entering university to be quite weak in technological skills.

Therefore we can see there is a clear need for us to develop a digital pedagogy suited to the phase of learning we aim to work in. As we have seen, each has its particular areas of focus and requires a specific set of skills from teachers. What is common to all though is an enthusiasm and desire to be a technology-rich pedagogue. Engage with technology, use it in your teaching and learning; become techno-savvy. The rewards will be motivating—your students will be more engaged, you have the satisfaction of knowing their learning will be current, authentic learning and becoming techno-savvy provides you with opportunities for rich, complex learning tasks.

FURTHER READING

Bennison, A., & Goos, M. (2010). Learning to teach mathematics with technology: A survey of professional development needs, experiences and impacts. *Mathematics Education Research Journal,* 22(1), 31–56.

Brown, W., Klein, H., & Lapadat, J. (2009). Scaffolding student research in a digital age: An invitation to inquiry. *Networks,* 11(1), 1–11.

Cuban, L. (2001). *Oversold and Underused: Computers in the Classroom*. Cambridge, MA: Harvard University Press.

Davies, J., & Merchant, G. (2009). *Web 2.0 for Schools: Learning and Social Participation*. New York: Peter Lang.

Ferdig, R. E. (2006). Assessing technologies for teaching and learning: Understanding the importance of technological pedagogical content knowledge. *British Journal of Educational Technology*, 37(5), 749–60.

Ferrer, F., Belvis, E., & Pamies, J. (2010). Tablet PCs, academic results and educational inequalities. *Computers & Education*.

Haydn, T., & Barton, R. (2008). 'First do no harm': Factors influencing teachers' ability and willingness to use ICT in their subject teaching. *Computers & Education*, 51(1), 439–47.

Hayes, D. (2006). Making all the flashy stuff work: The role of the principal in ICT integration. *Cambridge Journal of Education*, 36(4), 565–78.

Ilomäki, L., & Rantanen, P. (2007). Intensive use of ICT in school: Developing differences in students' ICT expertise. *Computers & Education*, 48(1), 119–36.

Loveless, A. (2007). Preparing to teach with ICT: subject knowledge, Didaktik and improvisation. *The Curriculum Journal,* 18(4), 509–22.

Sutherland, R., Armstrong, V., Barnes, S., Brawn, R., Breeze, N., Gall, M., Matthewman, S., Olivero, F., Taylor, A., Triggs, P., Wishart., J., & John, P. (2004). Transforming teaching and learning: embedding ICT into everyday classroom practices. *Journal of Computer Assisted Learning*, 20, 413–25.

Ward, L., & Parr, J. M. (2010). Revisiting and reframing use: Implications for the integration of ICT. *Computers & Education*. 54(1), 113–22.

Warschauer, M., & Matuchniak, T. (2010). New technology and digital worlds: Analyzing evidence of equity in access, use, and outcomes. *Review of Research in Education*, 34(1), 179–225.

Williams, P. (2008). Leading schools in the digital age: a clash of cultures. *School Leadership and Management*, 28(3), 213–28.

WEBSITES

Tumblr

https://www.tumblr.com/

A free-to-join photo-blog. As it is open to all, some caution is needed. But as a visual display tool it can be quite interesting to use for presentations or for folios of work.

Creative Commons

http://creativecommons.org/

Creative Commons is a site for sharing material with the world and avoiding copyright issues. A CC attached to an image or document means that it is able to be downloaded and used, free from copyright restrictions. It is an interesting idea and the website has some useful documents for you to share with students about this idea.

Google Earth
http://www.google.com/earth/index.html
A fun and interesting program that is free to download. It can be used to look at current images of anywhere in the world, historical images from the past, 3-D images and topography.

Smashing Magazine
http://www.smashingmagazine.com/
An online magazine with an emphasis on emerging technology and Web 2.0. Good to read just to keep up-to-date, but also useful when you need something explained! Some interesting blogs are linked to it.

Podcast Alley
http://www.podcastalley.com/
A search engine for podcasts—much easier way to find podcasts on particular topics or by specific people.

Technorati
http://technorati.com/
A search engine for blogs and other user-created digital content on the internet.

NewsGator
http://www.newsgator.com/
Web-based news aggregator, which acts as a deep data mining tool. You can type in a particular topic and it will search for information on that topic across a range of digital sources and formats.

Glossary

Ageism
Ageism is a form of discrimination of people according to age rather than ability and personal characteristics. It is particularly applied to the negative stereotyping of the elderly. There is a growing conflict between the generations in OECD countries with aging population profiles, whereby the elderly are depicted by ageists as unproductive, non-working, welfare dependents.

Chapter 1

digital pedagogy
The ability to teach using digital technologies.

digital native
Individuals who are digitally fluent across all aspects of their life.

digital immigrant
Based on Prensky (2001), someone who was not born into the digital age but who has adopted the skills and behaviours to be digitally fluent or proficient.

digital fluency
The ability to use digital technologies in a confident manner.

Chapter 2

constructivism
A theory of knowledge that states that individuals generate knowledge and meaning from the interaction between their experiences and their ideas. Based on the work of Jean Piaget.

social constructivism
A theory of knowledge that positions social interactions as the most important experience in the development of knowledge and understanding. Based on the work of Lev Vygotsky.

distributed cognition
A theory of learning that views knowledge and cognition as an inter-connected network of representations, connecting the individual with their environment.

constructionism

An approach to learning that states learning happens most effectively when individuals are actively making tangible objects in the real world. Based on the work of Idit Harel and Seymour Papert.

distributed constructionism

Electronic networks that can enable the shared construction of knowledge.

social constructionism

An approach to learning that seeks to uncover the ways in which individuals and groups participate in the construction of knowledge.

connectivism

A view of learning that perceives knowledge as something that exists within systems (i.e. nodes on a network) which are accessed through people participating in activities.

computer-supported collaborative learning (CSCL)

A pedagogical approach wherein learning takes place via social interaction using a computer or through the internet.

technological pedagogical and content knowledge (TPACK)

A framework to understand and describe the kinds of knowledge needed by a teacher for effective pedagogical practice in a technology enhanced learning environment.

community of practice (CoP)

A process of social learning that occurs when people who have a common interest in a subject or area collaborate over an extended period of time, sharing ideas and strategies.

online community of practice (OCoP)

Also known as a 'virtual community of practice', it is a community of practice that is developed and maintained using the internet.

Chapter 3

British Educational Communications and Technology Agency (BECTA)

The British Educational Communications and Technology Agency) was a non-departmental public body funded by the UK Department of Children, Schools and Families. Its main role was to investigate the use of ICTs in education. It ceased to exist in March 2011 due to funding cuts.

Joint Information Systems Committee (JISC)

The Joint Information Systems Committee (JISC) conducts research into the use of ICTs in higher education (universities).

Education Services Australia (ESA)

Education Services Australia is a national, not-for-profit company owned by all Australian education ministers. The company was established to support delivery of national priorities and initiatives in the schools, training and higher education sectors.

Melbourne Declaration

The *Melbourne Declaration* is a national document that explicitly sets out the educational goals for Australian education systems. It is supported by a series of actions plans.

Digital Education Revolution

The *Digital Education Revolution* (DER) has the explicit aim of contributing sustainable and meaningful change to teaching and learning in Australian schools that will prepare students for further education and training, and to live and work in a digital world. It is a national initiative, begun in 2008, and is ongoing.

Australian Curriculum

The Australian Curriculum is being introduced into schools (K–12)in phases, with particular subjects allocated to each phase:

Phase 1: English, Mathematics, Science and History

Phase 2: Geography, Languages and the Arts

Phase 3: Design and Technology, Health and PE, Economics, ICT, Business, Civics and Citizenship.

The body responsible for this is the Australian Curriculum, Assessment and Reporting Authority (ACARA).

Chapter 4

digital divide

The gap between what can be afforded or cannot be afforded regarding ICTs and digital technologies.

digital expectancy

The digital technology expectations of learners.

knowledge-based society

This refers to the type of society that is needed to compete and succeed in the changing economic and political dynamics of the modern world.

electronic era

This refers to the increasing amount of electronic devices that surround us, more than previous generations have experienced, including household, communication, recreational and work devices.

Chapter 5

emerging literacy

The skills that are just emerging or breaking through in children's development of formal language.

emerging numeracy

The skills that are just emerging or breaking through in children's development of formal mathematics and numeracy.

innumeracy

The lack of numeracy.

mathematical literacy

To be able to use mathematics effectively to meet the general demands of life.

educational technology

Technology tools that assist in learning.

instructional technology

Technology tools that assist in teaching.

technology of education

Tools that might prove helpful in advancing student learning and may be measured in how and why individuals behave.

Chapter 6

digital camera

A camera that takes video or still photographs, or both, digitally, by recording images via an electronic image sensor. These images are stored on a memory card or hard drive within the device and can be uploaded to a computer.

digital image

An image taken by a digital camera. It can be manipulated and edited using a software editing program and is generally saved as a jpeg or gif.

creative technology

Technologies that can be used with or to facilitate learning activities that are creative and play-based.

play

Play is the *act* of putting in action or motion. However, play in a learning context has a learning outcome associated with these types of actions.

iPad

A tablet computer designed by Apple Inc.

interactive whiteboard (IWB)

This is a large interactive display that connects to a computer and projector. A projector projects the computer's desktop onto the board's surface, where users control the computer using a pen, finger, stylus or other device. The board is typically mounted on to a wall or floor stand.

tablet PC

A mobile computer with a flat touch screen. It is operated via the touch screen rather than a keyboard.

LEGO Robotics

Robotic kits based on LEGO bricks and designs which contain software and hardware to create small, customisable and programmable robots.

touch tables

A table with a large touch screen as its surface that can be operated in a similar way as a tablet PC. They are designed to be multi-touch devices.

web-based learning

Learning that is based on the resources and materials that can be found on the internet.

Bee-Bot (Robotics)

Programmable floor robots that are suited to early years learners.

Chapter 7

digital fluency

The ability to use digital technologies in a confident manner.

purposeful activities

Activities concerned with the hard learning associated with the curriculum and specific content knowledge.

digital pedagogy for the early years

The ability to teach using digital technologies most suited to the early years of schooling.

creative activities

Creative, rich learning activities that engage learners and involve some level of participation and activity.

experimental activities

Activities that is concerned with creativity but also processes. Learners engage in a process of trying to understand how something works or with problem-solving.

Chapter 8

technology neophyte

Technology beginners who have a solid grounding in the basics and are ready for more complex learning experiences with technology.

digital fluency

The ability to use digital technologies in a confident manner.

digital content creator
Learners concerned with the creation of a digital artefact.

technology innovator
Individuals who independently engage with the technology and start innovating as they try to work out how something works, what it can do and what it cannot.

wiki
A wiki is a website that allows for the creation and editing of any number of interlinked web pages via a web browser by multiple users (e.g. Wikipedia).

html
Hyper Text Markup Language (html) is the main language used for building web pages.

metacrawler
Metasearch engines that blend the web search results from other popular search engines.

data mining
The process of discovering new patterns from large data sets.

truncation
A searching technique used in databases in which a word ending is replaced by a symbol. For example, red + ginger.

blogging
The ability to contribute to or create a blog. A blog (a blend of the term 'web log') is a type of website that can be regularly updated with new content.

mLearning
Learning that occurs using a mobile device (e.g. iPad or smartphone).

diffusion of innovation
A theory that seeks to explain how, why, and at what rate new ideas and technology spread through cultures.

Chapter 9

word processing
The ability to use a word-processing program to produce documents.

publishing
Software programs that have templates and formats that assist in producing professional 'published' outputs, such as newsletters.

spreadsheets
Useful tools for presenting data, particularly columns of numbers that need to be sorted or added together.

advanced web-searching skills
High-level skills in searching for information on the internet that combine practical skills that assist in searching efficiently for information with critical skills in analysing the information found.

WebQuests
An inquiry-oriented lesson format in which most or all the information comes from the web. These can be created using various programs, including a simple word-processing document that includes links to websites.

animation
The rapid display of a sequence of images of 2-D or 3-D artwork or model positions in order to create an illusion of movement.

presentation software
Software programs designed to assist in the presentation of information (for example, Power Point).

podcasting
A podcast is a series of digital media files (either audio or video) that are released episodically.

blogging
The ability to contribute to or create a blog. A blog (a blend of the term 'web log') is a type of website that can be regularly updated with new content.

Web 2.0
Web applications that facilitate participatory information sharing (social networking) and collaboration on the World Wide Web e.g. Facebook.

making a video or movie
The act of filming and editing a digital movie.

web design
The process of planning and creating a website.

Chapter 10

technology neophyte
Technology beginners who have a solid grounding in the basics and are ready for more complex learning experiences with technology.

digital content creator
Learners concerned with the creation of a digital artefact.

technology innovator
Individuals who independently engage with the technology and start innovating as they try to work out how something works, what it can do and what it cannot.

digital fluency

The ability to use digital technologies in a confident manner.

diffusion of innovation

A theory that seeks to explain how, why, and at what rate new ideas and technology spread through cultures.

innovator

A term from the theory of diffusion of innovation proposed by Everett Rogers (1962). Innovators are the first individuals to adopt an innovation.

early adopter

A term from the theory of diffusion of innovation proposed by Everett Rogers (1962). This is the second fastest category of individuals who adopt an innovation.

early majority

A term from the theory of diffusion of innovation proposed by Everett Rogers (1962). Individuals in this category adopt an innovation after a varying degree of time.

late majority

A term from the theory of diffusion of innovation proposed by Everett Rogers (1962). Individuals in this category will adopt an innovation after the average member of the society.

laggard

A term from the theory of diffusion of innovation proposed by Everett Rogers (1962). Individuals in this category are the last to adopt an innovation.

Chapter 11

digital fluency

The ability to use digital technologies in a confident manner.

digital proficiency

The ability to be a proficient user of a wide range of digital technologies.

discipline-specific technology

Technologies that are used in specific disciplines or subjects (e.g. Accounting, English).

consolidation of skills

The reinforcement of a pre-existing set of skills.

Chapter 12

online communities

An online space, such as a web page, which has a membership of users who share content, and can communicate synchronously or asynchronously (i.e. chat or forums).

digital portfolios

A collection of electronic evidence assembled and managed on the internet. Such electronic evidence may include input text, electronic files, images, multimedia, blog entries and hyperlinks. There are a number of commercially prepared tools (e.g. Pebble pad) or they can be created using presentation software (e.g. Power Point) or word-processing software.

multimedia

Media and content that uses a combination of different forms such as; text, audio, still images, animation or video.

virtual worlds

An online community that takes the form of a computer-based simulated environment through which users can interact with one another and use and create objects (e.g. Second Life).

Flash

A multimedia platform used to add animation, video, and interactivity to web pages.

mashups

A combination of different forms of multimedia, e.g. a music mashup is a combination of two or more songs.

cloud computing

A storage facility located in cyberspace, or the internet.

gaming consoles

Interactive entertainment computers that produce a video display signal which can be used with a display device (a television, monitor, for example) to display a video game (e.g X-box).

Photoshop

A graphics editing program designed by Adobe.

Jing

A software program that enables you to capture your screen and produce short videos.

Chapter 13

digital proficiency

The ability to be a proficient user of a wide range of digital technologies.

digital fluency

The ability to use digital technologies in a confident manner.

discipline-specific technologies

Technologies that are used in specific disciplines or subjects (e.g. Accounting, English).

digital content creators

Learners concerned with the creation of a digital artefact.

technology innovators

Individuals who independently engage with the technology and start innovating as they try to work out how something works, what it can do and what it cannot.

creative activity

Creative, rich learning activities that engage learners and involve some level of participation and activity.

experimental activity

Activity that is concerned with creativity but also processes. Learners engage in a process of trying to understand how something works or with problem-solving.

purposeful activity

Activities concerned with the hard learning associated with the curriculum and specific content knowledge.

wordle

The digital image or output of a word cloud based on a text. The size of font depends of the frequency of the word appearing in the text, i.e. the more frequently a word appears, the larger the font. It creates a visual summary of the key points of a text.

Bibliography

AAMT (1997). *Numeracy = Everyone's Business*. Report of the Numeracy Education Strategy Development Conference. Adelaide: AAMT.

ACARA (2009). *The Australian Curriculum. Phases 1, 2 and 3*. [Online] From http://www.acara.edu.au/curriculum.html.

Archambault, L., & Crippen, K. (2009). Examining TPACK among K–12 online distance educators in the United States. *Contemporary Issues in Technology and Teacher Education*, 9(1), 71–88.

Arthur, L., Beecher, B. & Downes, T. (2001). Effective learning environments for young children using digital resources: An australian perspective. *Information Technology in Childhood Education Annual*, 2001(1), 139–53. Norfolk, VA: AACE. Retrieved from http://www.editlib.org/p/8493.

Association for Educational Communications and Technology (AECT). (2001). *What is the Knowledge Base?* [Online] From http://www.aect.org/standards/knowledgebase.html.

BECTA (2009). *Harnessing Technology: Transforming Learning and Children's Services*. [Online] From http://webarchive.nationalarchives.gov.uk/20110130111510/http:/www.becta.org.uk.

BECTA (2010). *Narrowing the Gap*. [Online] From http://webarchive.nationalarchives.gov.uk/20110130111510/http:/www.becta.org.uk.

BECTA (2010). *The Impact of Technology: Value-added Classroom Practice*. [Online] From http://webarchive.nationalarchives.gov.uk/20110130111510/http:/www.becta.org.uk.

Bennison, A., & Goos, M. (2010). Learning to teach mathematics with technology: A survey of professional development needs, experiences and impacts. *Mathematics Education Research Journal,* 22(1), 31–56.

Bers, M. (2008). *Blocks to Robots: Learning with Technology in the Early Childhood Classroom*. New York: Teachers College Press.

Brooker, L. (2003). *Integrating New Technologies in UK Classrooms: Lessons for Teachers from Early Years Practitioners*. [Online] From http://www.freepatentsonline.com/article/Childhood-Education/104520645.html.

Brown, W., Klein, H., & Lapadat, J. (2009). Scaffolding student research in a digital age: An invitation to inquiry. *Networks*, 11(1), 1–11.

Bruns, A. & Jacobs, R. (Eds) (2006). *Uses of Blogs*. New York: Peter Lang Publishing.

Burnett, C., Dickinson, P., Myers, J. & Merchant, G. (2006). *Digital Connections: Transforming Literacy in the Primary School*. [Online] From http://extra.shu.ac.uk/bvw/Cambridge%20Journal%20piece.pdf.

Carrington, V. & Robinson, M. (2009). *Digital Literacies: Social Learning and Classroom Practices*. [Online] From http://books.google.com.au/books?hl=en&lr=&id=AAe7vnChUsoC&oi=fnd&pg=PR5&dq=early+years+%2B+digital+pedagogy&ots=oGDhUTnI1X&sig=xIRdSn-GH7m-uZZP8OJ4jPZzxjU#v=onepage&q=early%20years%20%2B%20digital%20pedagogy&f=false.

Casey, L. (2009). *Digital Literacy: New Approaches to Participation and Inquiry Learning to Foster Literacy Skills among Primary School Children*. [Online] From https://www.ideals.illinois.edu/handle/2142/9765.

Chantel, R. (2005). Computers use in preschool: Trixie gets a screen name. *New England Reading Association Journal*, 41(2), 49–52.

Charlier, N. & De Fraine, B. (2008). *Games-based Learning in Teacher Education: A Strategy to Integrate Digital Games into Secondary Schools*. [Online] From http://books.google.com.au/books?hl=en&lr=&id=r6mPyaObITEC&oi=fnd&pg=PA77&dq=teacher+journal+%2B+technology+%2B+secondary&ots=IRgz82PbFt&sig=4WWjB_sK_6JTYntkq8ceqb0n8T8#v=onepage&q=teacher%20journal%20%2B%20technology%20%2B%20secondary&f=false.

Clements, D. H., Sarama, J. & DiBiase, A. (2004). *Engaging Young Children in Mathematics*. New York: Routledge.

COAG (2009). *The National Early Childhood Development Strategy*. [Online] From http://www.coag.gov.au/coag_meeting_outcomes/2009-07-02/docs/national_ECD_strategy.pdf.

Cuban, L. (2001). *Oversold and Underused: Computers in the Classroom*. Cambridge, MA: Harvard University Press.

Davies, J. & Merchant, G. (2009). *Web 2.0 for Schools: Learning and Social Participation*. New York: Peter Lang Publishing.

DEEWR (2007). *Digital Education Revolution (DER)*. [Online] From http://www.deewr.gov.au/Schooling/DigitalEducationRevolution/Pages/default.aspx.

DEEWR (2008). *Review of Australian Higher Education. Final Report*. [Online] From http://www.deewr.gov.au/HigherEducation/Review/Pages/ReviewofAustralianHigherEducationReport.aspx.

DEEWR (2009). *Belong, Being and Becoming. The Early Years Learning Framework for Australian*. [Online] From http://www.deewr.gov.au/Earlychildhood/Policy_Agenda/Quality/Documents/Final%20EYLF%20Framework%20Report%20-%20WEB.pdf.

Department of Education (2010). *The Importance of Teaching*. [Online] From http://www.education.gov.uk/.

DEST (2000). *Numeracy, a Priority for All: Challenges for Australian Schools*. [Online] From http://www.dest.gov.au/NR/rdonlyres/AA01AA6A-4EF5-4D1B-93BA-B1ED1392BC6C/3991/numeracy.pdf.

Dwyer, J. (2007). *Computer-based Learning in a Primary School: Differences between the Early and Later Years of Primary Schooling.* [Online] From http://www.tandfonline.com/doi/abs/10.1080/13598660601111307.

Dye, J. (2007). *Meet Generation C: Creatively Connecting through Content.* [Online] From http://www.econtentmag.com.

Exley, B. (2008). *Communities of Learners: Early Years Students, New Learning Pedagogy and Transformations.* [Online] From http://eprints.qut.edu.au/17360/.

Ferdig, R. E. (2006). Assessing technologies for teaching and learning: Understanding the importance of technological pedagogical content knowledge. *British Journal of Educational Technology*, 37(5), 749–60.

Ferrer, F., Belvis, E. & Pamies, J. (2010). Tablet PCs, academic results and educational inequalities. *Computers & Education*, available online 3 August 2010.

Garofalo, J., Drier, H., Harper, S., Timmerman, M. A. & Shockey, T. (2000). Promoting appropriate uses of technology in mathematics teacher preparation. *Contemporary Issues in Technology and Teacher Education.* [Online serial] From http://www.citejournal.org/vol1/iss1/currentissues/mathematics/article1.htm.

Gibbone, A., Rukavina, P. & Silverman, S. (2010). Technology integration in secondary physical education: Teachers' attitudes and practice. *Journal of Educational Technology Development and Exchange,* 3(1), 27–42.

Goldberger, P. (2003). *Disconnected Urbanism.* [Online] From http://www.metropolismag.com/html/content_1103/obj/index.html.

Goos, M. & Cretchley, P. (2004). Teaching and learning mathematics with computers, the internet, and multimedia. In B. Perry, G. Anthony, & C. Diezmann (Eds), *Research in Mathematics Education in Australasia 2000–2003* (pp. 151–74). Flaxton, QLD: Post Pressed.

Graham, L. (2008). *Teachers are Digikids Too: The Digital Histories and Digital Lives of Young Teachers in English Primary Schools.* [Online] From http://onlinelibrary.wiley.com/doi/10.1111/j.1467-9345.2008.00476.x/full.

Harris, J., Mishra, P. & Koehler, M. (2009). Teachers' technological pedagogical content knowledge and learning activity types: Curriculum-based technology integration reframed. *Journal of Research on Technology in Education*, 41(4), 393–416.

Haydn, T. & Barton, R. (2008). 'First do no harm': Factors influencing teachers' ability and willingness to use ICT in their subject teaching. *Computers & Education*, 51(1), 439–47.

Hayes, D. (2006). Making all the flashy stuff work: The role of the principal in ICT integration. *Cambridge Journal of Education*, 36(4), 565–78.

Hlyna, D. & Jacobsen, M. (2009). What is educational technology anyway? *Canadian Journal of Educational Technology.* [Online] From http://www.cjlt.ca/index.php/cjlt/article/view/527/260.

Howard, S. (1998). *Wired-up: Young People and the Electronic Media*. [Online] From http://books. google.com.au/books?hl=en&lr=&id=oYfcY3On8fwC&oi=fnd&pg=PP1&dq=primary+school+ %2B+digital+pedagogy&ots=twqL-_5Eo7&sig=-hWWH76XOY5VFrlPRrkQdoYPz18#v= onepage&q&f=false.

Howitt, C., Upson, E. & Lewis, S. (2011). *It's a Mystery! A Case Study of Implementing Forensic Science in Preschool as Scientific Inquiry*. [Online] From http://search.informit.com.au/documentSummary; dn=342469307149602;res=IELHSS.

Ilomäki, L. & Rantanen, P. (2007). Intensive use of ICT in school: Developing differences in students' ICT expertise. *Computers & Education*, 48(1), 119–36.

Jeffrey, B. & Woods, P. (2009). *Creative Learning in the Primary School*. [Online] From http://books. google.com.au/books?hl=en&lr=&id=Zn-vvyDMiLkC&oi=fnd&pg=PP1&dq=discovery+learning+ %2B+primary+school&ots=7FsLhfAtyi&sig=INrs4zvZdhc9cw93PIlIgepL7wE#v=onepage& q=discovery%20learning%20%2B%20primary%20school&f=false.

JISC (2009). *Getting Started with Second Life*. [Online] From http://www.jisc.ac.uk/publications/ generalpublications/2009/gettingstartedsecondlife.aspx.

JISC (2010). *Effective Assessment in the Digital Age*. [Online] From http://www.jisc.ac.uk/whatwedo/ programmes/elearning/assessment/digiassess.aspx.

Judge, S., Puckett, K. & Bell, S. M. (2006). Closing the digital divide: Update from the early childhood longitudinal study. *Journal of Educational Research*, 100(1), 52–60.

Kim, A. J. (2000). *Community Building on the Web: Secret Strategies for Successful Online Communities*. [Online]. From http://www.citeulike.org/group/1188/article/347188.

Koehler, M. J. & Mishra, P. (2008). Introducing TPCK. In J. A. Colbert, K. E. Boyd, K. A. Clark, S. Guan, J. B. Harris, M. A. Kelly & A. D. Thompson (Eds), *Handbook of Technological Pedagogical Content Knowledge for Educators* (pp. 1–29). New York: Routledge.

Lave, J. & Wenger, E. (1991). *Situated Learning: Legitimate Peripheral Participation*. Cambridge: Cambridge University Press.

Leask, M. & Meadows, J. (2000). *Teaching and Learning with ICT in the Primary School*. [Online] From http://books.google.com.au/books?hl=en&lr=&id=Cz08wZ4duigC&oi=fnd&pg=PR10&dq= primary+school+%2B+digital+pedagogy&ots=6qzTqJrFPZ&sig=SvlEp1-25PHWOanL09mXBRqd7as# v=onepage&q&f=false.

Lenhart, A., Madden, M., Ranking Macgill, A. & Smith, A. (2007). *Teens and Social Media. Pew Internet and American Life Project*. [Online] From http://www.pewinternet.org/pdfs/PIP_Teens_Social_Media_ Final.pdf.

Lessig, L. (2002). *The Future of Ideas*. New York: Vintage Books.

Levy, R. (2009). *You Have to Understand Words ... but Not Read Them: Young Children Becoming Readers in a Digital Age*. [Online] From http://onlinelibrary.wiley.com/doi/10.1111/j.1467-9817. 2008.01382.x/full.

Li, Q. (2007). Student and teacher views about technology: A tale of two cities? *Journal of Research on Technology in Education,* 39(4), 377–97.

Looi, C-K., Zhang, B., Chen, W., Seow, P., Chia, G., Norris, C. & Soloway, E. (2010). *1:1 Mobile Inquiry Learning Experience for Primary Science Students: A Study of Learning Effectiveness.* [Online] From http://onlinelibrary.wiley.com/doi/10.1111/j.1365-2729.2010.00390.x/full.

Lorenzo, G., Oblinger, D. & Dziuban, C. (2006). *How Choice, Co-creation, and Culture are Changing What it Means to be Net Savvy.* [Online] From http://connect.educause.edu/Library/EDUCAUSE+Quarterly/HowChoiceCoCreationandCul/40008.

Loveless, A. (2007). Preparing to teach with ICT: Subject knowledge, Didaktik and improvisation. *The Curriculum Journal,* 18(4), 509–22.

Marzano, R. J. (2009). Teaching with interactive whiteboards. *Educational Leadership,* 67(3), 80–2.

MCEETYA (2008). *The Melbourne Declaration on Educational Goals for Young Australians* [Online] From http://www.mceetya.edu.au/mceecdya/melbourne_declaration,25979.html.

McNeely, B. (2005). *Using Technology as a Learning Tool, Not Just the Cool New Thing. Educating the Net Generation.* EDUCAUSE E-book. [Online] From http://www.educause.edu/UsingTechnologyasaLearningTool,NotJusttheCoolNewThing/6060.

Miller, D. & Robertson, D. (2009). *Using a Games Console in the Primary Classroom.* [Online] From http://onlinelibrary.wiley.com/doi/10.1111/j.1467-8535.2008.00918.x/full.

Ministry of Economic Development (2008). *The Digital Strategy 2.0.* [Online] From http://www.med.govt.nz/templates/StandardSummary____43904.aspx.

Ministry of Education (2008). *Masterplan for ICT in Education (Singapore).* [Online] From http://www.moe.gov.sg/media/press/2008/08/moe-launches-third-masterplan.php.

Mishra, P. & Koehler, M. J. (2006). Technological pedagogical content knowledge: A framework for teacher knowledge. *Teachers College Record,* 108(6), 1017–54.

Novak, J. D. (2010). *Learning, Creating and Using Knowledge.* [Online] From http://books.google.com.au/books?hl=en&lr=&id=kzx7l6MMy-8C&oi=fnd&pg=PP1&dq=discovery+learning+%2B+primary&ots=p9YCGZvAll&sig=eA0ocL0-I5tdVIyXDDT7un56nV4#v=onepage&q=discovery%20learning%20%2B%20primary&f=false.

Oblinger, D. G. & Oblinger, J. L. (2005). *Educating the Net Generation.* [Online] From http://www.educause.edu/educatingthenetgen.

OECD (1999). *Measuring Student Knowledge and Skills: A New Framework for Assessment.* Paris: OECD.

Papert, S. (1991a). Constructionism: *A New Opportunity for Elementary Science Education.* Award Abstract #8751190. [Online] From http://nsf.gov/awardsearch/showAward.do?AwardNumber=8751190.

Papert, S. (1991b). Situating constructionism. In I. Harel, & S. Papert (Eds), *Constructionism* (pp. 1–12). Norwood, NJ: Ablex Publishing.

Papert, S. (1993). *The Children's Machine: Rethinking School in the Age of the Computer*. New York: BasicBooks.

Piaget, J. (1977). *The Essential Piaget*. Ed. by Howard E. Gruber and J. Jacques Vonèche. New York: Basic Books.

Pillay, H., Boulton-Lewis, G. & Wilss, L. (2004). Changing workplace environments: Implications for higher education. *Educational Research Journal*, 19(1), 17–42.

Prensky, M. (2001). Digital natives, digital immigrants. *On the Horizon*. Vol. 9, No. 5: NCB University Press. [Online] From http://www.marcprensky.com/writing/.

Resnick, M. (1996a). *Distributed Constructionism*. [Online] From http://llk.media.mit.edu/papers/Distrib-Construc.html.

Resnick, M. (1996b). Toward a practice of 'constructional design'. In L. Schauble & R. Glaser (Eds), *Innovations in Learning: New Environments for Education* (pp. 161–74). Mahwah, NJ: Lawrence Erlbaum Associates.

Resnick, M. (2007). *All I Really Need to Know (About Creative Thinking) I Learned (By Studying How Children Learn) in Kindergarten*. ACM Creativity & Cognition Conference, Washington DC, June 2007. [Online] From http://web.media.mit.edu/~mres/papers/CC2007-handout.pdf.

Rheingold, H. (2002). *Smart Mobs*. Cambridge: Basic Books.

Sabelli, N. (2008). Constructionism: A new opportunity for elementary science education. *DRL Division of Research on Learning in Formal and Informal Settings* (pp. 193–206). [Online] From http://nsf.gov/awardsearch/showAward.do?AwardNumber=8751190.

Samarawickrema, G., Benson, R. & Brack, C. (2010). Different spaces: Staff development for Web 2.0. *Australasian Journal of Educational Technology*, 26(1), 44–9. http://www.ascilite.org.au/ajet/ajet26/samarawickrema.html.

Selwyn, N., Potter, J. & Cranmer, S. (2008). *Primary Pupils' Use of Information and Communication Technologies at School and Home*. [Online] From http://onlinelibrary.wiley.com/doi/10.1111/j.1467-8535.2008.00876.x/full.

Shipley, D. (2008) *Empowering Children. Play Based Curriculum for Lifelong Learning* (4th edition). USA: Nelson Education.

Shulman, L. (1986). Those who understand: Knowledge growth in teaching. *Educational Researcher*, 15(1), 4–14.

Shulman, L. (1987). Knowledge and teaching: Foundations of the new reform. *Harvard Educational Review*, 57(1), 1–22.

Sorgo, A., Verckovnik, T. & Kocijancic, S. (2010). Information and communication technologies (ICT) in biology teaching in Slovenian secondary schools. *Eurasia Journal of Mathematics, Science & Technology Education*, 6(1), 37–46.

Sutherland, R., Armstrong, V., Barnes, S., Brawn, R., Breeze, N., Gall, M., Matthewman, S., Olivero, F., Taylor, A., Triggs, P., Wishart, J. & John, P. (2004). Transforming teaching and learning: Embedding ICT into everyday classroom practices. *Journal of Computer Assisted Learning*, 20, 413–25.

Tapscott, D. (2009). *Grown Up Digital*. New York: McGraw Hill.

Taylor, M. (2006). 'Generation NeXt Comes to College: Today's postmodern student.' [Online] Accessed May 9 2008. http://globalcscc.edu/tirc/blog/files/Gen%20NeXt%20handout%2006%20oln.pdf.

Trendwatching (2004). *Generation C*. [Online] From http://www.trendwatching.com/trends/ GENERATION_C.htm.

UNESCO (2006). *Education for All: Global Monitoring Report*. [Online] From http://www.unesco.org/ new/en/education/themes/leading-the-international-agenda/efareport/reports/2006-literacy/.

United Nations Human Development Report 2007/2008. [Online] From http://hdr.undp.org/en/ data/map/.

US Department of Education (2001). *No Child Left Behind (NCLB)*. [Online] From http://www.ed. gov/esea.

US Department of Education (2009). *National Education Technology Plan*. [Online] From http://www. ed.gov/technology/netp-2010.

US Department of Education (2011). *Educate to Innovate*. [Online] From http://www.whitehouse.gov/ issues/education/educate-innovate.

Van Scoter, J. & Ellis, D. (2001). *Technology in Early Childhood Education*. [Online] From http://www. netc.org/earlyconnections/byrequest.pdf.

Vygotsky, L. S. (1971). *The Psychology of Art*. Cambridge, MA: MIT Press.

Vygotsky, L. S. (1978). *Mind in Society. The Development of Higher Psychological Processes*. Cambridge, MA: Harvard University Press.

Vygotsky, L. S. (1989). *Thought and Language*. Cambridge, MA: MIT Press.

Ward, L. & Parr, J. M. (2010). Revisiting and reframing use: Implications for the integration of ICT. *Computers & Education*, 54(1), 113–22.

Warschauer, M. & Matuchniak, T. (2010). New technology and digital worlds: Analyzing evidence of equity in access, use, and outcomes. *Review of Research in Education*, 34(1), 179–225.

Wells, G. (2002). Inquiry as an orientation for learning, teaching and teacher education. In G. Wells & G. Claxton (Eds), *Learning for Life in the 21st Century* (pp. 197–210). Oxford, UK: Blackwell.

Wenger, E. (2006). *Communities of Practice: A Brief Introduction*. [Online] From http://www.ewenger. com/theory/communities_of_practice_intro.htm.

Willet, R. (2007). *Technology, Pedagogy and Digital Production: A Case Study of Children Learning New Media Skills*. [Online] From http://www.tandfonline.com/doi/abs/10.1080/17439880701343352.

Williams, P. (2008). Leading schools in the digital age: A clash of cultures. *School Leadership and Management*, 28(3), 213–28.

Windham, C. (2007). *Father Google and Mother IM: Confessions of a Net Gen Learner*. Presented at ELI Annual Meeting, January 23, 2007. [Online] From http://connect.educause.edu/library/abstract/FatherGoogleandMothe/39228.

Wood, R. & Ashfield, J. (2008). The use of the interactive whiteboard for creative teaching and learning in literacy and mathematics: A case study. *British Journal of Educational Technology,* 39(1), 84–96.

Zevenbergen, R. (2007). *Digital Natives Come to Preschool: Implications for Early Childhood Practice.* [Online] From http://www.wwwords.co.uk/pdf/freetoview.asp?j=ciec&vol=8&issue=1&year=2007&article=3_Zevenbergen_CIEC_8_1_web.

Websites

ABC for kids http://www.abc.net.au/abcforkids/
Activities for children of all ages, including kids' TV guide, chat rooms and games.

ACARA http://www.acara.edu.au/curriculum.html
The Australian Curriculum, Assessment and Reporting Authority is the body responsible for the Australian Curriculum. This site has all of the new curriculum documents, plus the drafts open for public feedback. There are links to assessment and reporting programs, such as The National Assessment Program, NAPLAN and MySchool. The material is updated regularly, and with all the changes in this area within Australia it is a site that should be bookmarked on your computer.

KidsHQ http://www.awm.gov.au/kidshq/
Kids HQ is a website designed by the Australian War Memorial education team mainly for upper primary students, however, the site also offers an introduction to the study of Australia's military history for secondary students. Site includes stories, animals in wartime, military technology, and wartime military and home front occupations.

ACEC http://acce.edu.au/
ACEC is the Australian Council for Computers in Education. A useful organisation that has a professional journal, bi-annual conference and holds other professional learning programs throughout the year. Its membership is comprised of teachers and educational researchers.

BBC KS1 Bitesize http://www.bbc.co.uk/schools/ks1bitesize/literacy/
An activity-rich website designed by the BBC in the United Kingdom. Great resources that you can rely on for being correct, safe to use and engaging. They have been designed in collaboration with teachers working in this phase of learning.

BBC Kids 11-16 http://www.bbc.co.uk/schools/websites/11_16/
Don't be put off by the word 'kids' in the title—this is a particularly useful website with resources organised into separate subject areas. It has multimedia resources, so is rich with podcasts, videos and text-based resources.

Lesson Planet—Inquiry learning lesson ideas http://beta.lessonplanet.com/search?keywords= inquiry-based&media=lesson&gclid=CKLNhuPKpqwCFQwY4godCTZy1
This is an interesting resource site for teachers as it has a number of lesson ideas and actual lesson plans uploaded by other teachers. There is also a worksheet repository, so you can find a lot of resources on this site.

Creative Commons http://creativecommons.org/

Creative Commons is a site for sharing material with the world and avoiding copyright issues. A CC attached to an image or document means that it is able to be downloaded and used, free from copyright restrictions. An interesting idea and the website has some useful documents for you to share with students about this idea.

Desire2Learn ePortfolio http://www.desire2learn.com/eportfolio/k12/

This is an example of a commercially produced ePortfolio that is quite popular with schools and higher education. This site has some videos demonstrating the characteristics of the portfolio that will give you a good idea of what it looks like and how it can be used.

DEEWR http://www.deewr.gov.au/Schooling/DigitalEducationRevolution/Pages/default.aspx

The Department of Education, Employment and Workplace Relations, is the national education authority in Australia. Of particular note on this site is the Digital Education Revolution.

The Digital Divide Network http://www.digitaldivide.net/

The Digital Divide Network is the Internet's largest community for educators, activists, policy makers and concerned citizens working to bridge the digital divide.

http://dontapscott.com/

An interesting website of yet another social commentator. Provides some nice reviews of his books, which give you a better idea of the types of speculative offerings he makes. His work should be noted, and interestingly his books are based upon his own children and what he has observed as they have grown up (a little like Piaget and his work observing his daughter!).

EmergingEdTech http://www.emergingedtech.com/

A semi-professional blog site with multiple contributors.

ESA http://www.esa.edu.au/

Education Services Australia is an interesting organisation who primarily enact the reforms and policy of MCEECDYA. Along with this, there are several projects currently being conducted concerning technology and it is a body that will probably undergo some changes in the future.

http://www.earlychildhoodaustralia.org.au/eylfplp/play_based_learning_and_the_eylf.php

This website is actually a presentation by Lennie Barblett on play-based learning and the Early Years Learning Framework. It has a video embedded of the presentation, the PowerPoint file and links to an online discussion. All useful if you are keen to explore this teaching strategy further.

eLearn Magazine http://elearnmag.acm.org/index.cfm

A useful online magazine to keep bookmarked on your computer. All of the article are written by practising teachers, so the tips and tricks are very practical.

Digital Pedagogies http://education.qld.gov.au/smartclassrooms/dp.html

This is the portal for the Queensland Depart of Education and the various professional learning programs, initiatives, classroom activities and other technology-based projects conducted by the department. Rich with ideas and resources.

Edutech Wiki—Discovery learning http://edutechwiki.unige.ch/en/Discovery_learning
More information about discovery learning, models, advantages and disadvantages. The site also has some lesson ideas and examples.

eThemes—Inquiry-based learning http://ethemes.missouri.edu/themes/1496?locale=en
This is an online resource for teachers and students designed and maintained by the University of Missouri. The resources are all linked to technology-based lessons, and you can send requests to the online community for help or ideas on particular topics.

Educational Origami http://edorigami.wikispaces.com/
A great wiki space that you can join, share ideas, download resources and improve your understanding of particular topics. It does have a particular focus on educational technology, which is helpful for ideas.

EduBlog http://edublogs.org/
This is an education-only blog site. You can use it with your students and be sure that other users are all in education, either primary, secondary or tertiary and that the audience and also connections you make with other people through this site are safe and secure.

National Geographic for Teachers http://education.nationalgeographic.com/education/
This is a useful site with a lot of different teaching resources arranged around themes, such as population or big cats. There are a number of education projects you can get involved in and a particularly useful tool is MapMaker.

Funschool http://funschool.kaboose.com/
A commercially produced site for educational games, so there is a fair amount of advertising on this website. However, there are some nice activities for students to try, particularly the science games.

TeachingWithTechnology http://falconphysics.blogspot.com/
Steve Dickie is a secondary school teacher in America. Here he charts his thoughts, experiences and outcomes of trying to teach using different technologies.

Research for Teachers http://www.gtce.org.uk/tla/rft/pedagog0103/
This website contains some interesting and practical research reports. They emphasise making the link between what is happening in the education research world with teaching. It is a UK-based organisation with some interesting articles available.

Google Earth http://www.google.com/earth/index.html
A fun and interesting program that is free to download. It can be used to look at current images of anywhere in the world, historical images from the past, 3D images and topography.

QuEST http://ictnz.com/Activityideas.htm
This is a resource site based in New Zealand that has lesson ideas and resources. Some particularly good ideas for inquiry-based lessons.

JISC http://www.jisc.ac.uk/
The Joint Information Systems Committee is the government organisation concerned with the use of technology in higher education. It has a number of research reports freely available for downloading, plus useful 'tips and tricks' sheets for teachers.

Jumpstart http://www.jumpstart.com/free-online-game.aspx?pid=googpdau&cid=kindergar ten%20online%20games&gclid=CIKilLr6o6wCFYSI4godcSyO2A
An interesting portal for online learning games aimed at early years learners.

Kindersite http://www.kindersite.org/Directory/DirectoryFrame.htm
A useful site with songs, games and stories. They are clearly labelled to which age group they are suited for and do get updated regularly.

http://www.marcprensky.com/
While Prensky is not an educator, you could describe him as a social commentator. His articles are noteworthy, as he coined the phrases 'Digital Native' and 'Digital Immigrant', so it's worthwhile having a look at his ideas.

http://www.metropolismag.com/cda/
An online magazine that tends towards articles on worldwide trends, the impact of technology and how society is changing.

Metropolis Magazine—Disconnected Urbanism by Paul Goldberger http://www. metropolismag.com/story/20070222/disconnected-urbanism
This is a link to a specific article, *Disconnected Urbanism* by Paul Goldberger. It is an interesting social commentary on the impact telecommunications are having on society. Why it has been included is because of its links to connectivism.

MobiLearn http://www.mobilearn.org/
MobiLearn is a worldwide European-led research and development project exploring context-sensitive approaches to informal, problem-based and workplace learning by using key advances in mobile technologies. It is a useful website to collect ideas for using mobile technologies and to see what is emerging in this fast changing area.

Online Games for Early Years Learners http://www.miniclip.com/games/kindergarten/en/
Miniclip has some interesting games and video clips that can be used in the classroom. Explore all the different topics and games available.

MusicTechNet http://mustech.net/
An individual blog by Joseph Pisano—very interesting for music resources, commentaries and other links that might be useful for teachers.

http://www.nsn.net.au/digi_kids_snapshot_no_1
This is a digital snapshot of a program conducted by Lynda Page, a teacher at Coolum Beach State School. Lynda is a keen supporter of including digital technologies in early years programs and this website demonstrates some of the ways she has done this.

NASA Educators http://www.nasa.gov/audience/foreducators/index.html
A wonderful site for teachers with interesting articles, teaching materials and grade-specific worksheets. Not a site for science-only teachers, as it has a lot of relevance to SOSE, Geography, History and English.

NewsGator http://www.newsgator.com/

Web-based news aggregator, which acts as a deep data mining tool. You can type in a particular topic and it will search for information on that topic across a range of digital sources and formats.

One Laptop Per Child Organisation—Australia http://www.olpc.org.au/

The One Laptop per Child organisation was set up to oversee the creation of an affordable educational device for use in the developing world, in this case its focus is on Indigenous Australians. Its included here as a website of interest, as it is an interesting philanthropic organisation that seeks to address the digital divide on a global scale.

Croquet http://www.opencroquet.org/

A free open-source virtual world that you can download and create yourself. It is relatively easy to use, though some aspects are a bit technical. However, it has been designed solely for educational use so it is quite appealing for teachers to use.

OzTeacherNet http://www.oz-teachernet.edu.au/

An online community for teachers in Australia. It host a number of online activities that you can participate in with your class, has email lists and these are very useful for help, suggestions and support when you are attempting to try new technologies in your classroom. It is free to join.

http://www.papert.org/articles/const_inst/const_inst1.html

This is a transcript of a speech Seymour Papert delivered in Japan in the early 1980s, just at the start of his work with Logo programming and the development of constructionism. It's an interesting speech as it explores the differences between constructionism and instructionism.

Primary school http://www.primaryschool.com.au/learningtech.php

A useful website with links to other sites all sorted into categories and school grades. The list of resources is comprehensive, for example, web-based tools such as Google Sketch-up and resources for interactive whiteboards.

Kidsview: parliament in focus http://www.peo.gov.au/kidsview/menu.html

Explore parliamentary concepts and processes through fun and educational games and interactives. Learn about representation, law-making, democracy, Parliament House and parliamentary treasures. Includes teachers' notes for teachers and parents. Kidsview is designed for upper primary students and is a sub website of the Parliamentary Education Office.

Pebble Pad http://www.pebblepad.co.uk/user.prospect.asp

This is another commercially produced ePortfolio, but it is much more than that. It is also an online learning program that can be used with groups or classes. It has communication tools such as blogs and chat spaces built in. Explore some of the examples on this site.

http://playinginprep.wordpress.com/2011/07/30/technology-in-the-early-years-a-philosophical-discussion/

An interesting blog, hosted by WordPress that examines different topics associated with 'playing in prep'. This link will take you to the posting on technology in the early years, but there are other interesting postings to explores.

Blog site for Kathleen Morris, a Primary School Teacher in Victoria http://primarytech. global2.vic.edu.au/
This is a remarkable site as it inspires teachers to try new technologies. It is a blog of a primary school teacher in Australia, who explores the use of blogs, Web 2.0 tools and technology use in her classroom.

Podcast Alley http://www.podcastalley.com/
A search engine for podcasts—much easier way to find podcasts on particular topics or by specific people.

QSITE: Digital Pedagogy http://www.qsite.edu.au/keywords/digital-pedagogy
QSITE is the Queensland Society for Information Technology in Education. It is a useful association to join if you are located in Queensland, but it also has a number of reports, resources and links to professional development programs.

Newspaper article http://www.smh.com.au/lifestyle/back-to-school/technology-in-the-classroom-20100119-mhn3.html
An interesting article from *The Sydney Morning Herald* detailing some technology-based learning in primary classrooms.

SuperClubsPLUS Australia http://www.scplus.com/d/index.php
SuperClubsPLUS Australia is the only Australian age-verified and actively protected social learning network where young children can meet friends, make new ones, have fun and learn cool stuff. And they can do all these things knowing they are completely safe!

Smashing Magazine http://www.smashingmagazine.com/
An online magazine with an emphasis on emerging technology and Web 2.0. Good to read just to keep up-to-date, but also useful when you need something explained! Some interesting Blogs are linked to it.

Second Life http://secondlife.com/
Perhaps the most famous virtual world. Explore some of its examples and see what the creators of this world say about its use.

Tech & Learning http://www.techlearning.com
Another technology magazine, which is written by social commentators, journalists and researchers. It has few contributions by teachers, but still has some interesting observations.

Ted Talks http://www.ted.com/
TED is a non-profit organisation devoted to Ideas Worth Spreading. It started out (in 1984) as a conference bringing together people from three worlds: Technology, Entertainment and Design. This website hosts the videos of the presenters at their two annual conferences. They are free to download, you can subscribe to them as podcasts, and they are often inspiring and motivational presentations. They are on a broader range of topics in recent years, and could be useful in the primary and secondary phases of schooling.

Tumblr https://www.tumblr.com/

A free-to-join photo-blog. As it is open to all, some caution is needed. But as a visual display tool it can be quite interesting to use for presentation or for folios of work.

Technorati http://technorati.com/

A search engine for blogs and other user-created digital content on the internet.

http://trendwatching.com/

The name pretty much explains what this website is about. An interesting source of current trends and predictions about future trends.

http://teachingliteracy.global2.vic.edu.au/2011/07/12/using-technology-in-the-literacy-block/

This is a useful website concerned with teaching literacy in the early years, and the use of technology to achieve that. The content is updated fairly regularly so it's worth bookmarking and checking back to see what has been posted.

UNESCO—Education http://www.unesco.org/new/en/education/

The UNESCO Education site has a wealth of maps, tables, and other comparative data for the worlds developed and developing nations. Very useful materials that could be used in lessons and the site is updated regularly. There are also some interesting research reports available for downloading.

Woodvale Primary School http://www.woodvaleps.wa.edu.au/Information%20Technology/Information%20technology.html

A school website detailing the different information technology projects that students are engaged in. Shows the possibilities and range of projects that primary-aged students are capable of.

Index